Property Taxes and House Values
The Theory and Estimation of
Intrajurisdictional Property Tax Capitalization

This is a volume in
STUDIES IN URBAN ECONOMICS
Edited by Edwin S. Mills, *Princeton University*
A list of titles in this series appears at the end of this volume.

Property Taxes and House Values

The Theory and Estimation of Intrajurisdictional Property Tax Capitalization

JOHN YINGER

*The Maxwell School of
Citizenship and Public Affairs
Syracuse University
Syracuse, New York*

AXEL BÖRSCH-SUPAN

*Fachbereich Wirtschafts und
Socialwissenschaften
Universität Dortmund
Dortmund, Federal Republic of
Germany*

HOWARD S. BLOOM

*Graduate School of Public
Administration
New York University
New York, New York*

HELEN F. LADD

*Institute of Policy Sciences
and Public Affairs
Duke University
Durham, North Carolina*

ACADEMIC PRESS, INC.

Harcourt Brace Jovanovich, Publishers

Boston   San Diego   New York
Berkeley   London   Sydney
Tokyo   Toronto

HJ4227
.P75
1988

ACADEMIC PRESS, INC.
1250 Sixth Avenue, San Diego, CA 92101

United Kingdom Edition published by
ACADEMIC PRESS INC. (LONDON) LTD.
24–28 Oval Road, London NW1 7DX

Library of Congress Cataloging-in-Publication Data

Property taxes and house values: the theory and estimation of
  intrajurisdictional property tax capitalization / John Yinger . . .
  [et al.].
        p.   cm.—(Studies in urban economics)
    Bibliography: p.
    Includes index.
    ISBN 0-12-771060-4
    1. Real property tax—Massachusetts. 2. Real property and
taxation—Massachusetts. 3. Real property—Valuation-
-Massachusetts. I. Yinger, John, Date– . II. Title:
Intrajurisdictional property tax capitalization. III. Series.
HJ4227.P75 1988
333.33'8–dc 19   87-27965
                                                                   CIP

PRINTED IN THE UNITED STATES OF AMERICA

88 89 90 91   9 8 7 6 5 4 3 2 1

Contents

Preface

Property taxes and house values are subjects of seemingly constant public discussion. Most American families own a house, and most homeowners are concerned about the value of their houses and about the taxes they pay on them. Everyone knows that people with more expensive houses generally pay more property taxes, but many people do not realize that, all else equal, higher property tax payments can lead to lower house values. This book explains the link between property taxes and house values and in the process sheds some light on public policies that alter property taxes, such as assessment reform and state aid.

Our analysis and conclusions may be of interest to academics, public officials, and homeowners. Some of the material is highly technical and directed to professional economists. However, the first chapter, which introduces the concept of property tax capitalization, and the last chapter, which discusses the importance of tax capitalization for public policy, do not contain any technical material and are written for a wide audience.

This book has a long history. The basic research design was conceived by three of us (Bloom, Ladd, and Yinger) in 1977. With encouragement from David Puryear, who was the Director of the Urban Public Policy Unit at the Office of Policy Development and Research, U.S. Department of Housing and Urban Development (HUD), we submitted a formal proposal to HUD in June 1978. Our application was approved, and we began work in

July. After joint planning and design work that summer, Yinger conveniently left town for a year and Bloom and Ladd carried out the data collection and initial analysis. In the spring of 1979, we received supplemental funds from HUD to add another community, to carry out case studies in a few communities, and to extend the theory. Bloom, Ladd, and Yinger jointly carried out the analytical work and prepared the final report, which was sent to HUD in August 1980. We submitted this report to the Studies in Urban Economic Series at Academic Press, which accepted it for publication in November 1980.

The project might have ended there, but we discovered that the report was not yet ready for publication. In an attempt to deal with some of the technical problems inherent in estimating property tax capitalization, we had employed an *ad hoc* econometric procedure. After some reflection, we concluded that this procedure was not appropriate — and indeed probably yielded biased results. Thus, we began a second phase of the project in the spring of 1983 when the MIT–Harvard Joint Center for Urban Studies invited us to participate in a seminar series that was funded by the Lincoln Institute for Land Policy. During this phase, which was led by Yinger, we attempted to improve the conceptual foundations of our approach and develop a more appropriate econometric procedure. Although we made some progress in this phase, our time and money ran out before we could solve all the econometric difficulties.

The project was revived after a break of almost three years when Börsch-Supan joined the team in the spring of 1986. With financial assistance from the MIT–Harvard Joint Center for Urban Studies, Börsch-Supan developed a rigorous econometric procedure and carried out the estimation in this third phase of the project. Yinger refined the theory with help from Börsch-Supan. The final results were produced in February 1987, and the final draft was finished in July 1987 — 10 years after the project was originally conceived.

All of us played an important role in producing the final manuscript, although each of us took major responsibility for certain chapters. Yinger wrote Chapters 1, 3, and 7, with the help of extensive comments from the rest of us. Bloom wrote the first version of Chapter 2 in 1980. This version was subsequently published and was summarized and updated by Yinger for inclusion in this book. Ladd wrote Chapter 4. Börsch-Supan wrote Chapters 5 and 6. Yinger served as editor for the entire manuscript.

During the course of this project, we have accumulated debts to a large number of people: research assistants; federal, state, and local government officials; foundation officials; academic colleagues; secretaries and support staff. To each of these people we extend our thanks and appreciation.

Our greatest debt is to Stephen Erfle who, with incredible good humor and exceptional skill, carried out the computer work during the first and second phases of the project. Thanks to his carefully documented computer tapes, we easily transferred the data to personal computers for the third phase of the project, despite a time gap that covered the entire microcomputer revolution.

We also depended heavily on our other research assistants. Craig Albert, Karen Biow, Judith Danielson, Catherine Hetmansky, Laura Mac-Eachen, Peter Miller, Susan Morrison, Sharon Spaight, and H. Lawrence Webb helped us gather and check our data. Kerri Ratcliffe helped us update the literature, and Madeleine Henley and Mary Krans helped us prepare the index.

The cooperation of many state and local officials was essential to our project. Arthur Ecclestone of the Massachusetts Department of Revenue provided us with assessors' monthly sales reports. Harriet Taggert and her staff in the Research Department of the State Banking Commissioner's Office collaborated with us to collect data from the Metropolitan Mortgage Bureau. Assessors and other public officials in Arlington, Barnstable, Belmont, Brockton, Brookline, Waltham, and Wellesley gave generously of their time, experience, and official records.

Several other people also made valuable contributions to our data-gathering efforts. Katharine Bradbury first informed us about the Rothenberg data, and Jerome Rothenberg made it available to us. The people at the Metropolitan Mortgage Bureau kindly granted us access to their records.

We are grateful to David Puryear and Michael Schneider at the U.S. Department of Housing and Urban Development. David's initial interest in this project encouraged us to pursue it, while Michael's ongoing involvement assured the completion of the project's first phase. We are also grateful for financial support from HUD (Grant H2915RG) during the first phase of the project, from the Lincoln Institute for Land Policy during the second phase of the project, and from the MIT–Harvard Joint Center for Urban Studies during the third phase of the project.

John Avault of the Boston Redevelopment Authority provided advice and encouragement during the first phase of the project. Karl Case, Herman Leonard, Edwin Mills, Henry Pollakowski, and Andrew Reschovsky made valuable comments on early versions of our analysis. We benefitted from the comments of participants in seminars at the Lincoln Institute for Land Policy in 1983 and both the MIT–Harvard Joint Center for Urban Studies and the University of Dortmund in 1986.

The first phase of the project was greatly enhanced by the administrative assistance of Connie Mugnai and the secretarial help of Stephanie Falzone, Suzan Worland, and Carol Somer. The final manuscript was produced by the staff at the Metropolitan Studies Program in the Maxwell School at Syracuse University and would undoubtedly never have been assembled without the organizational skills of Esther Gray and the wordprocessing wizardry of Esther, Martha Bonney, and Deanna Phillips.

Finally, we are grateful to our families, who encouraged and supported us throughout this long, and sometimes arduous, project.

1

What Is Property Tax Capitalization?

Students of local public finance have long recognized that property taxes may be reflected in house values. This phenomenon, which is known as property tax capitalization, is the subject of this book.

1. WHAT IS PROPERTY TAX CAPITALIZATION?

Property taxes are said to be capitalized into house values if, all else equal, a higher property tax payment leads to a lower house value. If the value of a house is $1.00 lower whenever the present value of the stream of property tax payments on the house is $1.00 higher, then property taxes are said to be fully capitalized into house values; in other words, the degree of tax capitalization is 100%. Our objective is to estimate the degree of capitalization.

Because property taxes are paid every year, any comparison of the property taxes on two houses relies on the notions of present value and discounting. A household's discount rate, say i, is the return it could earn in an investment other than housing, such as bonds. The present value of a future flow is the amount someone would pay today in exchange for receiving that flow. The present value of $1.00 received (or a $1.00 payment avoided) next year is $1/(1 + i)$, the present value of a dollar received in two years is $1/(1 + i)^2$, and so on. Thus, the present value of avoiding $1.00 of property taxes every year from now until the expected lifetime of the house, N, is

$$\sum_{n=1}^{N} \frac{1}{(1 + i)^n}.$$

Housing lasts a long time, so it is reasonable to assume that N is large. If so, then this summation can be closely approximated by $1/i$.[1]

Consider, for example, Smith's house and Jones' house, which are in the same neighborhood and are identical except that the annual property tax payment on Smith's house is $300 higher. Suppose the relevant discount rate for households is 3%. Then the present value of the stream of future property taxes is $300/.03 = $10,000 higher for Smith's house than for Jones' house. (The choice of a discount rate obviously is important here. We will have more to say about this choice in Chapter 3.) Property taxes are fully capitalized if the market value of Smith's house, which is the amount Smith could sell it for, is $10,000 lower than the market value of Jones' house. If the market value of Smith's house is only $5000 lower than the market value of Jones' house, then the degree of capitalization is 50%.

Changes in property taxes can also be capitalized, that is, they can lead to changes in house values. In fact, we measure capitalization by examining the relationship between tax changes and value changes. Tax changes are fully capitalized into house values if a $1.00 increase, relative to other houses, in the present value of the stream of future tax payments leads to a $1.00 decrease in house value, relative to other houses.

Suppose that Smith's house and Jones' house begin with the same property tax payment. Now let Smith's annual tax payment increase by $300 while Jones' tax payment, and everything else that affects house values, stays the same. In this case, the present value of Smith's stream of tax payments increases by $300/.03 = $10,000 relative to the present value of Jones's tax payments. If this tax change leads to a $10,000 decrease in the market value of Smith's house relative to Jones' house, then the tax change is said to be fully capitalized into house values.

Property tax differences across jurisdictions and within a single jurisdiction can both be capitalized into house values. These two phenomena are generally known as interjurisdictional and intrajurisdictional property tax capitalization. The effective property tax rate for a house is defined to be the house's property tax payment divided by its market value. Interjurisdictional tax capitalization occurs when, all else equal, houses in towns with relatively high average effective property tax rates have relatively low market values. The tax payment for a house equals a nominal property tax rate, which is the same for all houses within a jurisdiction, multiplied by the assessed value of that house. Intrajurisdictional tax capitalization occurs when, all else equal, houses with relatively high assessed values have relatively low market values.

2. WHAT DOES THIS BOOK CONTRIBUTE?

This book studies intrajurisdictional property tax capitalization in seven Massachusetts cities and towns. We take advantage of a series of Massachusetts Supreme Court decisions that ordered cities and towns in Massachusetts to assess all houses at their full market value. As a result of these decisions, many communities revalued, that is, they calculated new assessed values for all their houses and other property. These revaluations caused large changes in assessed values and hence in tax payments. We collected data on houses that sold twice, once before and once after a revaluation, and use this double-sales data to investigate the extent to which changes in tax payments generated by revaluation are reflected in changes in house values.

Although property tax capitalization is a simple concept, it has proved to be difficult to estimate. As explained in Chapter 2, existing studies have encountered problems of simultaneity bias, left-out-variable bias, specification error, and inappropriate treatment of the discount rate. Consequently, the results of existing studies vary widely, and no consensus has emerged on the precise extent to which property taxes are capitalized into house values. We develop a methodology that solves these problems and provides more accurate and precise estimates of capitalization than those obtained from previous studies.

In the community with the best data, we estimate that the degree of property tax capitalization is 21%. This estimate of capitalization is highly significant statistically; that is, it is highly unlikely to have occurred by chance.

We also find that the degree of capitalization is not the same in every community. In two other communities with good data, we estimate capitalization rates of 16% and 33%. These estimates are also highly significant statistically. Because of data limitations, our estimates of capitalization in the four remaining communities are not as reliable. These estimates range from 9% to 79%.

Differences in our results across communities reveal the complexity of the capitalization phenomenon. As explained more fully in the next section, the degree of capitalization depends on the information available to and the expectations of house buyers, and on the sources of variation or change in property tax rates. Because these factors are not likely to be the same in all communities, the degree of capitalization is also not likely to be the same. Moreover, tax changes caused by revaluations may be capitalized at a different rate than tax rate differences across jurisdictions. One of the central conclusions of our study is that one cannot simply assume that property taxes are always capitalized at the same rate. We study the degree to which tax changes caused by revaluation are capitalized into house values; other studies must estimate the degree of capitalization under other circumstances.

3.   HOW DOES PROPERTY TAX CAPITALIZATION ARISE?

Property taxes are capitalized into house values because of simple economics: all else equal, the lower the property taxes on a house, the more a household is willing to pay for it. If the present value of the tax payments on Jones' house is $10,000 lower than the present value of the taxes on Smith's otherwise identical house, a rational household will bid $10,000 more for Jones' house than for Smith's. In other words, unless the market prices of houses fully reflect the associated property tax streams, some houses will be bargains and others will be overpriced.

Property tax capitalization expresses the link between an annual flow, property taxes, and the price of an asset, a house. The link between annual flows and asset prices is well known in other contexts. The price of a stock reflects the annual after-tax flow of dividends that accrues to the stockholder. The price of a bond reflects the annual interest payments received by the bondholder less the income tax paid on that interest. In all of these cases, buyers are willing to purchase the asset for a price equal to the present value of the expected stream of net benefits from holding it.

The existence of capitalization can also be explained by examining the calculations typically made by home buyers and real estate professionals. Suppose that a household has figured out the maximum portion of its annual income that it can spend on its annual mortgage payment plus its annual property tax payment. This portion often is formally imposed on the household by a lending institution. To keep the sum of mortgage and tax payments constant, therefore, a $1.00 higher tax payment must be offset by a $1.00 lower mortgage payment. The mortgage payment for a fully mortgaged house is approximately equal to the mortgage interest rate, m, multiplied by the value of the house, V.[2] Because a household has no influence on the mortgage rate, the only way it can reduce its mortgage payment is by reducing the amount it is willing to pay for its house, that is, by reducing V. To lower mV by $1.00, a household must reduce V by $1.00/m$. In other words, a $1.00 higher annual property tax payment leads to a $1.00/m$ lower house value, which is exactly the definition of complete capitalization presented earlier. Thus, property tax capitalization can be generated by simple household calculations, although its existence does not depend on the fixed-payment assumption.

Property taxes are not the only housing flow that can be capitalized. Indeed, anything that affects the flow of services to a homeowner, including the structural characteristics of the house itself, the amenities in the house's neighborhood, and the quality of local public services, can be capitalized into house values. The higher the public service quality in a community, for example, the more people are willing to pay for houses there, all else equal.

Local public services are financed by property taxes, so one might expect the capitalization of local public services and the capitalization of local property taxes to be connected. In particular, one might ask whether the capitalization of services offsets the capitalization of property taxes. The answer is, not necessarily. Within a single community, property tax differences caused by assessment errors are not related to variation in service levels. Similarly, changes in property taxes caused by revaluation, which are corrections of such assessment errors, are not linked to changes in service quality.

Even across communities, service and tax capitalization may work in opposite directions, but they are unlikely to offset each other completely. In fact, some communities with relatively high service quality also have relatively low property taxes because they have a large industrial tax base to share the tax burden. All else equal, the low taxes and high service quality both lead to relatively high property values in these communities. Other communities with relatively high property taxes may have relatively low service quality because their cost for providing services is relatively high; for example, they may have to pay higher wages than other communities to attract employees away from private business. The high taxes and low service quality both lead to relatively low property values in these communities. It is appropriate, therefore, to distinguish between the capitalization of property taxes and of public service quality and to estimate them separately.

A simple asset-pricing model indicates that property tax capitalization will be complete; a $1 difference in the present value of property taxes will lead to a $1 difference in house values. For three reasons, however, this simple model may not apply directly to intrajurisdictional property tax capitalization.

First, a household that is aware of the property taxes on a house it wants to purchase may not know how those taxes compare to the town average. In this book, we study the impact of a house's property tax relative to the average on its relative market value. With imperfect information about taxes on other houses, a household's bid on a house may not exactly reflect the present value of taxes on that house relative to the town average.

Second, even if a household is fully aware of the relative property taxes on a house, it may be willing to pay a price that does not fully reflect those relative taxes in order to avoid the costs of further housing search. People trying to sell houses with relatively high property taxes obviously would rather not lower their asking prices to reflect those taxes. The combination of sellers avoiding lower asking prices and buyers avoiding search costs could lead to less-than-complete property tax capitalization.

Third, even if households have perfect information and no search costs, they may not expect current property tax differences to persist indefinitely. In the context of this study, property tax differences arise because of assessment errors that occur before revaluation. Even before revaluation is announced, households may expect that these errors eventually will be corrected. The effect of this expectation can be dramatic; we show, for example, that if tax differences are expected to disappear in ten years, the capitalization of current tax differences could be as low as 26%. If errors that exist when a house is sold are expected to disappear over time, then house values will reflect only a fraction of the present value of current tax differences; that is, the capitalization of current tax differences will be incomplete.

We present several pieces of evidence to support the conclusion that the degree of capitalization is far below 100% primarily because households do not expect pre-revaluation property tax differences to persist. Revaluation was widely publicized and debated, for example, and in several communities housing prices in the period immediately preceding revaluation reflect anticipated property tax changes. We also find some evidence that capitalization varies across communities because of differences in information about relative property taxes and differences in housing search costs. The degree of capitalization appears to be lower, for example, in communities with more complex housing markets, where information is more difficult to obtain.

4. WHY DOES PROPERTY TAX CAPITALIZATION MATTER?

Property tax capitalization has an important influence on the evaluation of public policies that alter property tax payments, including assessment reforms, property tax classification, regional tax-base sharing, and state grants to local governments. These policies tend to raise the relative property tax payments of some property owners and lower the relative tax payments of others. Some policies, such as community-wide revaluation, have a direct effect on effective property tax rates within a community. Other policies, such as regional tax-base sharing and equalizing state aid, may lead to property-tax increases in some communities and property-tax decreases in others. The impact of these tax changes on property owners, which is central to an evaluation of the policies, depends on capitalization.

Consider a homeowner whose relative tax payment rises. Without capitalization, tax changes affect the stream of tax payments but not the market price of the house, so this household can escape its higher taxes by selling its house and moving to another location. With capitalization, on the other hand, tax changes are immediately translated into changes in the price of housing and this homeowner has no escape; either she stays in her house and pays the higher stream of taxes or she sells her house and suffers the capital loss caused by the increase in the tax stream. Furthermore, the capital loss is the present value of the entire future tax stream. Remember that with a discount rate of 3%, a $300 increase in the annual tax payment leads to a $300/.03 = $10,000 decrease in house value. With capitalization, therefore, modest changes in tax payments can lead to large gains and losses for current homeowners. If poor information or high search costs lead to incomplete capitalization, a homeowner can escape some of the burden of higher future tax payments.

Capitalization has important implications for the fairness of policies that alter property tax rates. Assessment reform is often motivated, for example, by the observation that some property owners are paying less than their fair share of taxes. With capitalization, however, no one can buy a house with relatively low taxes unless he or she pays a relatively high price for the house; that is, people with relatively low taxes must pay for the privilege. Similarly, people with relatively high taxes paid a relatively low price for their property. Moreover, correcting an assessment error causes an immediate capital gain or loss equal to the present value of all the future consequences of the correction. Assessment reform involves some inequity, therefore, because it generates capital gains for some taxpayers and capital losses for others.

Despite these arguments, assessment reform is desirable under most circumstances. With fixed or inaccurate assessments, the effective property tax rate on a house, which is the property tax payment divided by the market value of the house, changes as the market value of the house changes. In the presence of capitalization, a taxpayer who experiences a decline in the effective tax rate on her house relative to other houses immediately receives a capital gain equal to the present value of the entire future stream of relative tax savings. This property owner can realize this gain by selling her house, so that any future correction of this assessment error will burden future owners. These owners gain nothing from their relatively low property tax rate, even before it is corrected, because they had to pay a relatively high price for the property. Similarly, taxpayers who experience relative tax-rate increases receive a capital loss on their house. These gains and losses, which are generated by assessment errors, are inherently unfair, and assessment reform is needed to prevent them.

Overall, the case for assessment reform depends on the balance between the long-run improvement in fairness from preventing future assessment errors and the short-run loss in fairness from eliminating past assessment errors. If the degree of capitalization is 20%, as we estimate, the short-term gains and losses are modest and the case for reform is strong. We demonstrate in Chapter 7, for example, that few of the houses in one Massachusetts community experience gains or losses from revaluation that are greater than 10%. Moreover, the degree of capitalization will be low if house buyers do not expect assessment errors to persist, so a stated policy to update assessed values regularly, and thereby to eliminate assessment errors, will by itself lower the degree of capitalization and minimize short-term capital gains and losses from reform.

The only type of assessment reform that cannot be justified is a sudden, one-time reform after a long period of inaccurate assessments. In this case, the large pre-revaluation effective tax rate differences are expected to persist, so the degree of capitalization is high, and the reform leads to large capital gains and losses for current homeowners. In addition, a one-time reform does not improve fairness in the long run because it does not prevent arbitrary gains and losses after revaluation, as market values once again diverge from assessed values.

Capitalization also has practical consequences for a tax assessor. A house's tax payment is based on the assessor's estimate of its market value. When assessment reform occurs, the tax payments on some houses go up and the tax payments on other houses go down. These tax changes lead to changes in house values, which in turn lead to further changes in tax payments, and so on. In Chapter 7, we also show how to calculate the "final" market value of a house after this cycle of tax and value changes has been completed.

Finally, property tax capitalization has consequences for the efficiency of the property tax. Without property tax capitalization, the property tax raises the effective price of housing and thereby induces households to buy less of it. This distortion in housing decisions, like a tax-induced distortion of any other decision, represents an inefficient allocation of society's resources. With complete property tax capitalization, on the other hand, the price of housing exactly reflects differences in property taxes across and within communities. As a result, the effective price of housing, that is, the market price plus the property tax payment, does not vary across locations and higher property taxes do not lead to lower housing consumption.

Although complete property tax capitalization eliminates housing-market distortion from variation in the property tax, it does not eliminate housing-market distortion altogether. Even with complete tax capitalization, housing consumption decisions are affected by the average level of property taxes in a metropolitan area. Capitalization only insures that the resulting distortion is the same in every community.[3]

5. HOW IS THIS BOOK ORGANIZED?

Many studies have attempted to estimate the degree of property tax capitalization. We review these studies in Chapter 2. Our review evaluates what has been learned about tax capitalization and focuses on the methodological obstacles confronting previous research, including biases from simultaneity, left-out variables, and misspecification.

In Chapter 3, we present our new approach to estimating intrajurisdictional property tax capitalization. We combine well-known microeconomic tools with the circumstances of revaluation in Massachusetts to derive an equation for estimating the degree of tax capitalization. This equation determines the impact of a change in the effective property tax rate relative to other houses on the percentage change in house value relative to other houses. We also explain how our approach overcomes the methodological obstacles encountered by earlier studies. For example, we account for the simultaneity between house values and tax rates by modeling the behavior of an assessor carrying out a revaluation.

To estimate our capitalization equation, we collected double-sales data for houses in seven communities in Massachusetts. We describe this data in Chapter 4. We explain how we selected the sample communities, outline the characteristics of each community, and list the sources of our double-sales data. In this chapter, we also relate the history of revaluation in two of the communities.

We explain our econometric methodology in Chapter 5. Our estimating equation is nonlinear and involves simultaneity between house value changes and property tax rate changes. We derive a simple linear approximation to this equation, which we can estimate with two-stage least squares, and we discuss the appropriate nonlinear simultaneous equations procedure, which we can estimate with well-known maximization techniques.

We present our results in Chapter 6, focusing on our estimates of the degree of property tax capitalization, as obtained from both our linear approximation and our exact nonlinear form. We examine the importance for estimated capitalization of various control variables and of instruments to correct for the simultaneity between house values and tax rates.

In Chapter 7, we interpret our results and consider the implications of property tax capitalization for public policy. We examine the sources of variation in the degree of capitalization from one community to another, we explain why policy makers should care about capitalization, show how to incorporate capitalization into property tax assessment procedures, demonstrate the impact of capitalization on the gains and losses from assessment reform, and discuss the implications of capitalization for the equity and efficiency of the property tax.

NOTES

[1] Present value formulas and approximations to them are discussed more fully in Chapter 3.

[2] Ignoring monthly compounding, the annual payment on a mortgage equals the amount of the mortgage multiplied by the expression $m/[1 - (1 + m)^{-M}]$, where M is the term of the mortgage in years. With no down payment and a long term, this expression is approximately equal to m.

[3] Curiously, the capitalization of public service quality, unlike the capitalization of taxes, causes housing market distortion that varies from one community to another. If higher service quality leads to higher house values then it must as a direct consequence lead to lower housing consumption; that is, it must distort housing choices. In this book, we do not shed any light on the capitalization of public service quality into house values. We simply note that a complete evaluation of efficiency in the U.S. system of local governments must consider both types of capitalization. For a detailed discussion of the link between service capitalization and efficiency, see Yinger (1985).

2

A Review of Previous Empirical Studies of Property Tax Capitalization

The empirical literature on property tax capitalization dates back to Jensen's 1931 study.[1] Since then, dozens of studies have attempted to estimate the extent to which property taxes are capitalized into house values. This chapter provides a review of this literature.

Three of the authors have already published a detailed review of the literature before 1980. See Bloom, Ladd, and Yinger (1983).[2] In this chapter, we summarize this earlier review and describe in detail the major studies of capitalization that have been carried out since 1980. Some of these studies consider topics other than property tax capitalization, including the determinants of public spending and the capitalization of public service levels into house values. We do not review these other topics, nor do we consider studies of the effect of property taxes on rents, such as Orr (1968), Hyman and Pasour (1973), and Wheaton (1984).

1. THE BASIC CAPITALIZATION EQUATION

All studies of capitalization are based on the simple principle that the value of a house, like the value of any asset, equals the present value of the after-tax flow of services from owning it.[3] We begin by stating this principle in algebraic terms and by examining the econometric problems that arise when it is employed to estimate property tax capitalization.

1.1   The Simple Algebra of Property Tax Capitalization

The asset-pricing equation contains the following terms: V is the market value of a house, R is its annual rental value, T is the property tax payment on the house, and r is households' real discount rate. Market value equals the present value of the rental flow minus the present value of the property tax flow, or

$$V = \frac{R}{r} - \frac{T}{r}. \tag{1}$$

By definition, the effective property tax rate, t, equals T/V. Substituting this definition into Equation (1) yields:

$$V = \frac{R}{r} - \frac{tV}{r}$$

or

$$V = \frac{R}{r+t}. \tag{2}$$

Studies in the tax-capitalization literature attempt to estimate the impact of property taxes on house values using some variant of Equation (1) or (2). If R is assumed to be a linear function of housing and neighborhood characteristics, for example, then (1) can be estimated directly. Minus one times the coefficient of T equals the degree of capitalization divided by the real discount rate. Multiplying the absolute value of the estimated coefficient by an assumed real discount rate therefore yields an estimate of the degree of capitalization.

Alternatively, one can assume that R is a multiplicative function of housing characteristics and take the natural logarithm of (2) to obtain:

$$\ln V = \ln R - \ln(r + t). \tag{3}$$

This equation is nonlinear, but it is often approximated by using $\ln(t)$ as the explanatory variable. The absolute value of the coefficient of this variable is interpreted as the degree of capitalization divided by the discount rate.

1.2   Inherent Econometric Difficulties

Although the asset-pricing equations are simple, any attempt to estimate the degree of property tax capitalization encounters several serious econometric problems.

The first problem is that the property tax variable, whether it is a tax rate or a tax payment, is endogenous. The property tax payment equals the assessed value of the house multiplied by the town's nominal property tax rate. In principle, an assessed value is an assessor's attempt to estimate a house's market value. Hence, a random shock to a house's market value, if observed by the assessor, could boost the house's assessed value and hence both its tax payment and its effective tax rate. The simultaneity problem has another dimension if the effective tax rate is the tax variable: house value is the denominator of the effective tax rate, so the tax variable is endogenous by definition. If jurisdictions, instead of individual houses are the observations, the simultaneity problem takes another form: the property tax rate needed to finance a given public service quality depends on the average house value in a community.

Several studies show that ignoring the endogeneity of the tax variable can lead to a large bias in the estimated degree of capitalization. The direction of this simultaneity bias depends on the tax variable. Within a jurisdiction, the behavioral link between tax payment and house value leads to a positive bias, whereas the definitional link between house value and effective tax rate leads to a negative bias. It follows that ignoring the simultaneity in Equation (1) biases estimated capitalization toward zero. The direction of the bias is indeterminant for Equation (3) because both effects are at work. In most cases, however, the definitional link appears to be stronger so that the simultaneity biases estimated capitalization toward 100%. Across jurisdictions, higher property values allow a given level of services to be provided at a lower property tax rate and therefore bias estimated capitalization upward.

This simultaneity problem is widely recognized, and many studies employ two-stage least squares or some other simultaneous equations procedure to deal with it. Some of the studies with jurisdictions as observations also provide a careful analysis of the behavioral foundation of the simultaneity. These studies combine a house value equation with a model of public expenditure determination, which yields an exogenous prediction of the jurisdiction's desired tax rate. On the other hand, no study with individual houses as observations provides a careful analysis of the behavioral source of the problem, namely assessor behavior. Without an analysis of the source of simultaneity, the selection of instruments for a two-stage least squares procedure is somewhat arbitrary and, as first demonstrated by Pollakowski (1973), estimates of capitalization may be skewed by the use of inappropriate instruments.

The second econometric problem is potential left-out-variable bias. Because assessors employ housing and neighborhood characteristics to determine assessed value, a house's tax payment is correlated with its structural characteristics and the characteristics of its neighborhood. These characteristics are also key explanatory variables in a house-value regression. If any of these characteristics are left out of Equation (1), therefore, the coefficient of the tax payment variable could be biased. In principle, the bias could work in either direction, but because housing characteristics that have a positive impact on house value tend to have a positive effect on assessed value, left-out characteristics are likely to push estimated capitalization toward zero.[4] This problem is not likely to be as severe in Equation (3), because the effective tax rate is not directly correlated with housing and neighborhood characteristics. Nevertheless, left-out-variable bias is still possible in this case because assessment errors, and hence effective tax rates, could be systematically larger (or smaller) for houses with certain characteristics.

The most direct way to insulate a study against this left-out-variable problem is to obtain extensive data on housing and neighborhood characteristics. This requirement makes life difficult for researchers because such data are often difficult to find, particularly when jurisdictions, not individual houses, are the observations. Nevertheless, many studies have demonstrated that left-out variables can lead to large biases in estimates of capitalization.

The third econometric problem is that the form of a capitalization equation is difficult to specify exactly. Equation (1) appears simple enough, but it becomes operational only if one assumes that house value is a linear function of housing characteristics. This assumption is not appealing conceptually, because it does not allow for a declining marginal valuation of a characteristic, and it does not accord with the literature on house-value equations, which finds that multiplicative and other nonlinear forms perform better than linear ones.[5] Furthermore, Equation (1) is more difficult to insulate from left-out-variable bias than is Equation (3), in which the tax variable is nonlinear.

Most of the studies in the literature focus on the effective property tax rate, as does Equation (3). However, virtually every study makes some major compromise to carry out its estimation. Some studies use an approximation, such as $\ln t$ instead of $\ln(r + t)$, and thereby introduce specification biases of unknown magnitude. Others employ a nonlinear estimating technique, but ignore the simultaneity between house values and effective tax rates. One could characterize the literature as a search for the best compromise.

The final key econometric problem is to specify the real discount rate. As noted earlier, both Equations (1) and (3) contain the real discount rate, r, which is reflected in the estimated coefficient of the property tax variable. To obtain an estimate of the degree of capitalization, a study based on Equation (1) must multiply the coefficient of the tax payment variable by the real discount rate. In other words, the estimated degree of capitalization depends on the discount rate.[6] All of the capitalization studies assume a value for the discount rate and calculate the degree of capitalization based on that assumption, although several studies show how the degree of capitalization changes as the assumed discount rate changes.

This problem cannot be avoided. In Equation (1), for example, one cannot separately estimate the discount rate and the degree of capitalization. Nevertheless, the required discount rate assumption has been poorly handled by many studies. Some studies use a nominal rate instead of a real rate and thereby bias upward their estimate of capitalization. A real discount rate is needed because the numerators of Equation (1) and (2) are expressed in real terms; that is, they do not allow for any growth in rental value. Consistency requires that the denominators also be expressed in real terms.[7] In addition, no study brings in outside information to help make the required discount-rate assumption.

Given these inherent econometric difficulties, it is not surprising that researchers have employed a variety of different approaches to estimating property tax capitalization. Our review classifies studies into three broad classes: studies based on aggregate data, that is, data in which jurisdictions are the observations; studies based on a cross-section of individual houses; and studies that examine changes in taxes and house values for a sample of individual houses.

The studies we review are listed in Table 2-1, both by type of study and by year of publication. The first panel of the table lists studies before 1980, which are reviewed in section 2; the second panel lists studies since 1980, which are reviewed in section 3.

2. STUDIES BEFORE 1980

The data, methodologies, and results of tax capitalization studies before 1980 are summarized in Tables 2-2 to 2-4. Most of these studies are reviewed in detail in Bloom, Ladd, and Yinger (1983). Three pre-1980 capitalization studies have come to our attention since Bloom, Ladd and Yinger was published: Noto (1976), Chinloy (1978), and Gronberg (1979). In this section, we discuss these three studies as well as all of the studies covered in the earlier review.

Almost all of the pre-1980 studies find that taxes are capitalized into house values to some degree, with the majority opinion that capitalization is somewhere between 50% and 100%. These estimates depend, of course, on an assumed discount rate. Most of the studies use rates of 5% or 6%, which undoubtedly overstates the real discount rate and therefore leads to an overestimate of the degree of capitalization. For purposes of comparison, we calculate estimated capitalization for each study with a 3% discount rate and an infinite horizon.[8] These calculations are reported in the third row of Tables 2-2 to 2-4.

Table 2-1
Empirical Studies of Property Tax Capitalization

Studies Based on Aggregate Data	Studies Based on Cross-Section Micro Data	Studies Based on Micro Data Describing Tax Changes
Panel A: Studies Before 1980		
Oates (1969, 1973)	King (1973)	Wicks, Little, and
Heinberg and Oates	Church (1974)	Beck (1968)
(1970)	Wales and Weins	Smith (1970)
Pollakowski (1973)	(1974)	Moody (1974)
Edel and Sclar (1974)	Edelstein (1974)	
Gustely (1976)	Case (1978)	
Meadows (1976)	Chinloy (1978)	
McDougall (1976)	Hamilton (1979)	
King (1977)		
Rosen and Fullerton		
(1977)		
Panel B: Studies Since 1980		
Dusansky, Ingber, and	Reinhard (1981)	Gabriel (1981)
Karatjas (1981)	Richardson and	Rosen (1982)
Reinhard (1981)	Thalheimer (1981)	
	Ihlanfeldt and Jackson	
	(1982)	
	Lea (1982)	
	Goodman (1983)	

Table 2-2
Pre-1980 Studies of Property Tax Capitalization Based on Aggregate Data

	Oates (1969 and 1973)	Heinberg and Oates (1970)
Principal Conclusions about Property Tax Capitalization[a]	"Full" capitalization	100%
Assumed Discount Rate and Time Horizon[b]	5%; 40 years	5%; 40 years
Estimated Tax Capitalization with 3% Discount Rate and Infinite Horizon[c]	61%	71%
Study Characteristics:		
Unit of Observation	Municipality	Municipality
Time Period	1960	1960
Location	New Jersey	Boston Area
Sample Size	53	23
Model Specification:		
Dependent Variable	Median house value	Median house value
Property Tax Variable(s)	Log of effective tax rate	Log of effective tax rate
Public Service Variable(s)	Log of school expenditures per pupil; Log of nonschool expenditures per capita	School expenditures per pupil
Number of Housing and Neighborhood Controls[d]	5	3
Estimation Procedure[e]	2SLS	2SLS
Dependent Variables of Other Structural Equations	None	None
Methodological Limitations	Few control variables; Inexact functional form	Few control variables; Inexact functional form

Table 2-2 Continued

	Pollakowski (1973)	Edel and Sclar (1974)
Principal Conclusions about Property Tax Capitalization[a]	Capitalization estimates are sensitive to model specification	50% in 1970; Capitalization attenuates as long-run equilibrium is approached
Assumed Discount Rate and Time Horizon[b]	n.a.	8%; infinite
Estimated Tax Capitalization with 3% Discount Rate and Infinite Horizon[c]	n.a.	20% in 1970
Study Characteristics:		
Unit of Observation	Municipality	Municipality
Time Period	1960	1930, 1940, 1950, 1960, 1970
Location	New Jersey and San Francisco Area	Boston Area
Sample Size	53 and 19	64–78 (depending on year)
Model Specification:		
Dependent Variable	Median house value	Median house value
Property Tax Variable(s)	Log of effective tax rate	Nominal tax rate (all years) Effective tax rate (1970)
Public Service Variable(s)	Log of school expenditures per pupil	School expenditures per pupil; Highway expenditures per square mile
Number of Housing and Neighborhood Controls[d]	5 and 6	4
Estimation Procedure[e]	2SLS	OLS
Dependent Variables of Other Structural Equations	None	None
Methodological Limitations	Few control variables; Inexact functional form	Ignores simultaneity; Few control variables; Inexact functional form; Inappropriate tax variable before 1970.

Table 2-2 Continued

	Gustely (1976)	McDougall (1976)
Principal Conclusions about Property Tax Capitalization[a]	About 65%	"Complete" capitalization
Assumed Discount Rate and Time Horizon[b]	8%; 40 years	5%; infinite
Estimated Tax Capitalization with 3% Discount Rate and Infinite Horizon[c]	34%	62%
Study Characteristics:		
Unit of Observation	Municipality	Census tract
Time Period	1970	1970
Location	Syracuse area	Los Angeles area
Sample Size	100	173
Model Specification:		
Dependent Variable	Median house value	Median house value
Property Tax Variable(s)	Equalized school tax rate; Equalized nonschool tax rate	Equalized tax rate
Public Service Variable(s)	Own-source school expenditures per pupil; Own-source non-school expenditures per capita	12th grade test score crime rate; Fire insurance index; Recreation index
Number of Housing and Neighborhood Controls[d]	6	4
Estimation Procedure[e]	OLS	2SLS
Dependent Variables of Other Structural Equations	None	None
Methodological Limitations	Few control variables; Ignores simultaneity; Inexact functional form	Few control variables; Inexact functional form

Table 2-2 Continued

	Meadows (1976)	King (1977)
Principal Conclusions about Property Tax Capitalization[a]	Capitalization exists in both 1960 and 1970	67%
Assumed Discount Rate and Time Horizon[b]	None	5%; 40 years
Estimated Tax Capitalization with 3% Discount Rate and Infinite Horizon[c]	44% in 1970; 127% in 1960	36%
Study Characteristics:		
Unit of Observation	Municipality	Municipality
Time Period	1960 and 1970	1960
Location	New Jersey	New Jersey
Sample Size	53 (1960) and 44 (1970)	53
Model Specification:		
Dependent Variable	Median house value	Median house value
Property Tax Variable(s)	Equalized tax rate	Median tax payment
Public Service Variable(s)	School expenditures per pupil; Nonschool expenditures per capita	Log of school expenditures per pupil; Log of nonschool expenditures per capita.
Number of Housing and Neighborhood Controls[d]	3	5
Estimation Procedure[e]	2SLS	(1) 2SLS; (2) Ad hoc nonlinear
Dependent Variables of Other Structural Equations	Equalized tax rate; School expenditures per pupil; Nonschool expenditures per capita	None
Methodological Limitations	Few control variables; Inexact functional form	Few control variables; Functional form subject to left-out-variable bias (1); Inappropriate estimating procedure (2); No hypothesis test (2)

Table 2-2 Continued

	Rosen and Fullerton (1977)	Gronberg (1979)
Principal Conclusions about Property Tax Capitalization[a]	88%	No capitalization
Assumed Discount Rate and Time Horizon[b]	6 years; 40 years	None
Estimated Tax Capitalization with 3% Discount Rate and Infinite Horizon[c]	58%	0%
Study Characteristics:		
Unit of Observation	Municipality	Municipality
Time Period	1960 and 1970	1970
Location	New Jersey	Chicago Area
Sample Size	53	83
Model Specification:		
Dependent Variable	Median house value	Median house value
Property Tax Variable(s)	Log of effective tax rate	Nominal municipal tax rate; Nominal school tax rate
Public Service Variable(s)	4th grade test scores	Municipal expenditures per capita; School expenditures per pupil
Number of Housing and Neighborhood Controls[d]	5	3
Estimation Procedure[e]	2SLS	2SLS
Dependent Variables of Other Structural Equations	None	Municipal and school tax rates; Municipal and school expenditures; Median income
Methodological Limitations	Few control variables; Inexact functional form	Few control variables; Inexact functional form; Inappropriate tax variable

[a] A "cap. ratio" is the degree of capitalization divided by the discount rate.
[b] The entry "none" indicates that no discount rate was selected.
[c] As calculated by the authors of this book.
[d] Does not include squared terms or other variables that simply reflect functional form choices.
[e] OLS = ordinary least squares; 2SLS = two-stage least squares.
n.a. = not applicable.

Table 2-3
Pre-1980 Studies of Property Tax Capitalization Based on Micro Data

	King (1973)	Church (1974)
Principal Conclusions about Property Tax Capitalization[a]	30%–50%	"Over" capitalization
Assumed Discount Rate and Time Horizon[b]	5%–8%; 40 years	5%; 60 years from date of construction
Estimated Tax Capitalization with 3% Discount Rate and Infinite Horizon[c]	18%	Unable to calculate due to misspecification
Study Characteristics:		
Unit of Observation	House sale	House sale
Time Period	1967 to 1969	1967 to 1970
Location	New Haven Area (10 jurisdictions)	Martinez, CA
Sample Size	1892	957
Model Specification:		
Dependent Variable	Sales price	Log of sales price
Property Tax Variable(s)	Actual tax payment minus predicted payment in low-tax town given current assessment	Log of (discount rate plus effective tax rate)
Public Service Variable(s)	Student test scores; Perceived school quality from a questionnaire; Perceived quality of other services; Public provision of water, sewage disposal or garbage collection	None
Number of Housing and Neighborhood Controls[d]	20	8 composite variables constructed using principal components
Estimation Procedure[e]	OLS	2SLS
Dependent Variables of Other Structural Equations	None	None
Methodological Limitations	Ignores simultaneity; Functional form subject to left-out-variable bias	Incorrect functional form

Table 2-3 Continued

	Edelstein (1974)	Wales and Wiens (1974)
Principal Conclusions about Property Tax Capitalization[a]	Cap. ratio is 7.75 for 4 bedroom house and 15.5 for 2 bedroom house.	No capitalization
Assumed Discount Rate and Time Horizon[b]	None	None
Estimated Tax Capitalization with 3% Discount Rate and Infinite Horizon[c]	23% for 4 bedroom house 47% for 2 bedroom house	Unable to calculate
Study Characteristics:		
Unit of Observation	House sale	House sale
Time Period	1967 to 1969	1970
Location	Philadelphia area (6 jurisd.)	Surrey, British Columbia
Sample Size	2143	1828
Model Specification:		
Dependent Variable	Sales price	Sales price
Property Tax Variable(s)	Property tax payment per bedroom	Effective tax rate
Public Service Variable(s)	3 dummy variables for groups of communities	None
Number of Housing and Neighborhood Controls[d]	5	15
Estimation Procedure[e]	2SLS	Ad hoc simulation
Dependent Variables of Other Structural Equations	Property tax payment	None
Methodological Limitations	Few control variables; Functional form subject to left-out-variable bias.	Incorrect estimating procedure

Table 2-3 Continued

	Noto (1976)	Case (1978)
Principal Conclusions about Property Tax Capitalization[a]	"More than full"	Interjurisdictional cap. ratio = 8.8; Intrajurisdictional cap. ratio = 16.6 in one case, insignificant in another case
Assumed Discount Rate and Time Horizon[b]	Inferred to be equivalent to 11.4%, infinite	7%; 20–30 years
Estimated Tax Capitalization with 3% Discount Rate and Infinite Horizon[c]	31% (excluding interaction terms)	26% (interjurisdictional); 50% and zero (intrajurisdictional)
Study Characteristics:		
Unit of Observation	House sale	House sale
Time Period	1971–1973	1971 and 1972 to 1975
Location	San Mateo Co., CA (18 municipalities and school districts)	Boston Area (13 jurisdictions) and Hanford, CA
Sample Size	17,000	2195 and 1014
Model Specification:		
Dependent Variable	Sale price per square foot	Sales price
Property Tax Variable(s)	Nominal tax rate (t) and t interacted with percentage change in population and with percentage of units for sale	Boston: Town effective tax rate; Actual and predicted assessed value; Hanford: Neighborhood effective tax rate (or payment)
Public Service Variable(s)	Elementary school expenditures; Elementary achievement score; Fire insurance rating; Burglary rate	School expenditures per pupil; sewer tie-in; paved road
Number of Housing and Neighborhood Controls[d]	36	27 (Boston); 23 (Hanford)
Estimation Procedure[e]	OLS	OLS and Ad hoc
Dependent Variables of Other Structural Equations	None	None
Methodological Limitations	Ignores simulteneity; Inappropriate functional form; Inappropriate tax variable	Tax rate equations: Ignores simultaneity; Inexact functional form Tax payment equations: Inappropriate estimating procedure; Functional form subject to left-out-variable bias

Table 2-3 Continued

	Chinloy (1978)	Hamilton (1979)
Principal Conclusions about Property Tax Capitalization[a]	None	Intrajurisdictional cap. ratio = 16.8; Interjurisdictional cap. ratio = 9.37 (based on fiscal surplus)
Assumed Discount Rate and Time Horizon[b]	5%; 40 years	None
Estimated Tax Capitalization with 3% Discount Rate and Infinite Horizon[c]	0%	Intrajurisdictional: 50% Interjurisdictional: 28%
Study Characteristics:		
Unit of Observation	Household	House sale
Time Period	1974	1961
Location	London, Ontario	Toronto Area (10 jurisdictions)
Sample Size	1224	410
Model Specification:		
Dependent Variable	Owner estimate of market value	Sales price
Property Tax Variable(s)	Effective tax rate minus rate of income tax credit	Estimated random assessment error; Community fiscal surplus (expenditure minus tax payment)
Public Service Variable(s)	None	Education spending per pupil
Number of Housing and Neighborhood Controls[d]	9	16
Estimation Procedure[e]	2SLS	Nonlinear least squares
Dependent Variables of Other Structural Equations	None	None
Methodological Limitations	Incomplete correction for simultaneity; Inappropriate functional form	Ignores simultaneity; Inappropriate treatment of public services; Inappropriate functional form.

See notes to Table 2-2.

Table 2-4
Pre-1980 Studies of Property Tax Capitalization Based On Tax Changes

	Wicks, Little and Beck (1968)	Smith (1970)
Principal Conclusions About Property Tax Capitalization[a]	Cap. ratio = 17	Cap. ratio = 14.5; Tax changes from revaluation are anticipated.
Assumed Discount Rate and Time Horizon[b]	None	None
Estimated Tax Capitalization with 3% Discount Rate and Infinite Horizon[c]	50%	44%
Study Characteristics:		
Unit of Observation	House sale	House sale
Time Period	1965	1966 to 1968
Location	Missoula, Montana	San Francisco
Sample Size	64	301
Model Specification:		
Dependent Variable	Observed minus predicted sales price	Observed minus predicted sales price
Property Tax Variable(s)	Change in tax payment	Change in tax payment; Proximity to revaluation (to measure anticipation)
Public Service Variable(s)	None	None
Number of Housing and Neighborhood Controls[d]	None	One
Estimation Procedure[e]	Tabular comparisons	OLS
Dependent Variables of Other Structural Equations	None	None
Methodological Limitations	Biased prediction of post-reassessment sale price; Inexact controls for non-tax variables	Inexact controls for non-tax variables

Table 2-4 Continued

	Moody (1974)
Principal Conclusions About Property Tax Capitalization[a]	Cap. ratio = $18-22$
Assumed Discount Rate and Time Horizon[b]	Unknown
Estimated Tax Capitalization with 3% Discount Rate and Infinite Horizon[c]	About 60%
Study Characteristics:	
Unit of Observation	House sales
Time Period	1963
Location	San Francisco Area (2 jurisdictions)
Sample Size	518
Model Specification:	
Dependent Variable	Deviation of sales price from pre-1963 trend in the jurisdiction
Property Tax Variable(s)	Dummy variable for location in the jurisdiction with a transit tax increase
Public Service Variable(s)	Access to new transit station
Number of Housing and Neighborhood Controls[d]	None
Estimation Procedure[e]	Difference-of-means test
Dependent Variables of Other Structural Equations	None
Methodological Limitations	Inexact controls for non-tax variables

See notes to Table 2-2.

2.1 Aggregate Studies

Let us begin with a look at the aggregate studies. Several of these studies, including Oates (1969 and 1973), Heinberg and Oates (1970), McDougall (1976), and Rosen and Fullerton (1977) are careful and appealing. Nevertheless, all of the aggregate studies run into three problems: they have few controls for housing and neighborhood characteristics; they misspecify the capitalization equation, usually by regressing house value on the property tax rate (or its log); and, except for Meadows (1976) and Gronberg (1979), they do not fully analyze the behavioral foundations of the simultaneity in their equations. A few studies, namely Edel and Sclar (1974), Gustely (1976) and King (1977), do not correct for simultaneity at all. Moreover, Pollakowski (1973) shows that the results of these studies can change greatly with small changes in specification.

Because of data limitations, several of the aggregate studies encounter potential errors-in-variables bias, in addition to the four basic econometric problems. Edel and Sclar (for results before 1970) and Gronberg use nominal property tax rates, thereby ignoring variation across communities in assessment – sales ratios. The choice of public service variables also appears to have some effect on estimated capitalization. In making bids on housing, people care about service quality, so measures of service quality are preferable to measures of public spending. Only McDougall and Rosen and Fullerton employ such measures.

2.2 Micro Studies

Many of the pre-1980 micro studies include careful investigations of both inter- and intrajurisdictional tax capitalization, with extensive controls for housing and neighborhood characteristics. Nevertheless, all of these studies founder, to some degree, on the methodological difficulties inherent in estimating capitalization.

With the exception of Edelstein (1974), the micro studies have adequate, and sometimes extensive, sets of housing and neighborhood control variables. Nevertheless, King (1973) estimates Equation (1), and as explained below, Edelstein and Case (1978) use versions of Equation (1), so that these studies may be subject to left-out-variable bias.

The most common methodological limitation of the micro studies is a misspecification of the tax capitalization equation. We now describe and evaluate the specifications used by Church (1974), Edelstein (1974), Noto (1976), Case (1979), Chinloy (1978), and Hamilton (1979).

Church interprets the coefficient of $\ln(r + t)$ in Equation (3), instead of the nonlinear coefficient of t alone, as the degree of capitalization. In fact, however, this coefficient reflects the impacts of both the discount rate and the effective tax rate on house values and restricts these two impacts to be the same. This restriction is particularly troublesome because Church assumes a nominal instead of a real discount rate.

Edelstein regresses house value on tax payment per bedroom and several control variables. Because the number of bedrooms is not included as a separate control variable, the negative coefficient on the "tax" variable could be interpreted as the impact of another bedroom, holding taxes constant. In addition, this specification is subject to the same potential left-out-variable problem as Equation (1), which is a particularly troublesome problem in light of the fact that his data set contains only a few control variables.

Noto is the one of the few authors to investigate whether the degree of capitalization is different under different circumstances. Her data cover a large sample of house sales in 18 cities. She interacts the property tax rate with the percentage change in city population (a proxy for increasing house supply) and the percentage of the city's housing units for sale (a proxy for excess housing supply). She hypothesizes that capitalization will be lower in locations with increasing or excess supply, but finds the opposite to be true. These results are difficult to interpret, in large part because of Noto's basic specification. She regresses house value per square foot on the nominal property tax rate. To gain insight into this specification, let us divide Equation (1) by the number of square feet in the house. The tax term becomes tax payment per square foot, which is the same as the nominal tax rate multiplied by assessed value per square foot. In other words, Noto's specification is equivalent to Equation (1) with a systematic error in the tax variable. Even if assessed value per square foot is constant, so that this specification does not involve a classic errors-in-variables problem, the degree of capitalization equals the coefficient of the nominal tax rate divided by assessed value per square foot — not, as Noto assumes, the coefficient itself.

Case also has a sample of houses in several communities and carefully distinguishes between inter- and intrajurisdictional tax capitalization. He estimates interjurisdictional capitalization by regressing house value on two different tax variables. The first variable is simply the community effective tax rate. The second is a predicted tax bill, which is house value predicted from an equation without taxes included, multiplied by the community tax rate. As Case recognizes, the first variable involves a misspecification of Equation (1). The regression based on the second tax variable is difficult to interpret because it is ad hoc. This regression is similar to two-stage least squares, except that it does not involve an additional exogenous instrument to identify the tax coefficient and does not include the tax rate in the dependent variable of the first-stage regression. Moreover, as Case recognizes, his approach, which is a version of Equation (1), is vulnerable to left-out-variable bias. We suspect, therefore, that this approach does not yield consistent estimates. Case employs similar ad hoc procedures to estimate intrajurisdictional tax capitalization and finds the left-out-variable problem to be particularly severe. In his California sample, the data set contains inadequate controls for neighborhood quality; and in his Massachusetts sample, left-out-variable bias leads to the wrong sign for the tax variable.

Chinloy studies tax capitalization in Canada, where homeowners receive an income tax credit for property taxes. His study is distinguished by its careful analysis of the capitalization of this credit. Unfortunately, however, Chinloy makes two specification errors. First, he assumes that property taxes apply to the before-tax asset price of housing, not to market value. Second, he restricts capitalization to be the same for tax payments and tax credits, despite his own argument that the two coefficients are likely to be different.

Hamilton carefully distinguishes between the capitalization of random assessment errors within a community and the capitalization of differences in services and taxes across communities. He employs an elaborate methodology to identify random assessment error and derives an estimating equation similar to Equation (2) that includes both random and inter-community tax differences.[9] To estimate interjurisdictional capitalization, he assumes that everyone is willing to pay $1 for $1 of public spending. On the basis of this assumption, he defines the "fiscal surplus" as the difference between per-capita spending and the property tax payment and estimates the extent to which differences across communities in this fiscal surplus are capitalized into house values. The assumption that $1 of spending is worth $1 is inappropriate on two counts: it ignores both the declining marginal rate of substitution between public service quality and other goods and the variation across jurisdictions in the cost of providing public services.[10]

Inappropriate or nonexistent corrections for the simultaneity between house values and tax rates raise questions about several other studies. Wales and Weins (1974) devise an elaborate simulation method to account for this simultaneity and conclude that capitalization does not exist. This conclusion is not credible, however; as shown by Bloom, Ladd, and Yinger, the Wales and Weins method biases estimated capitalization toward zero. Chinloy employs two-stage least squares, but the instruments in his first stage only account for the simultaneity between house value and the credit, not for the simultaneity between house value and the tax rate. King and Hamilton do not correct for simultaneity at all.

Finally, the choice of public service variables is also relevant for the four micro studies (King, Edelstein, Case, Hamilton, Noto) that cover more than one community. King and Noto are the only authors to employ extensive service quality measures. Data limitations force the other authors to compromise. Edelstein picks up services differences with dummy variables that combine several communities. Case and Hamilton use school spending per pupil.

2.3 Micro Studies Based on Tax Changes

The micro studies based on tax changes are clever attempts to take advantage of unusual market circumstances. Wicks, Little, and Beck (1968) and Smith (1970) study jurisdiction-wide revaluations to see if changes in tax payments lead to changes in house values. These studies observe sales prices before revaluation and predict sales prices after revaluation. The fact that post-revaluation sales prices must be predicted injects some uncertainty into their approach. In fact, it can be shown that the prediction method employed by Wicks, Little, and Beck leads to an underestimate of capitalization.[11] Both of these studies find evidence for substantial tax capitalization. In addition, Smith finds that anticipated tax changes also are capitalized; house values decline after tax increases are announced but before they are implemented.

Moody (1974) studies a peculiarity in the financing of a rapid transit station that opened in 1963. This station provided benefits to nearby residents of San Francisco and Daly City, but the tax increase to pay for the station fell only on the residents of San Francisco. Moody's approach yields a compelling estimate of capitalization despite a lack of direct controls for housing and neighborhood characteristics. For each city, Moody observes the housing price trend before 1963 and predicts the average house price in 1963 on the basis of this trend. Then, using a sample of houses that sold near the station in 1963, he computes the deviation of the average sales price in each city from the predicted house price. His evidence for capitalization is that sales prices were much farther above the prediction in Daly City than in San Francisco. He finds a capitalization ratio of about 20, which corresponds to 60% capitalization with a 3% discount rate.

3. STUDIES SINCE 1980

In this section, we provide a detailed review of eight capitalization studies published since 1980. The data, methodologies, and results of these studies are summarized in Tables 2-5 to 2-7. As before, we divide the studies into those based on aggregate data, those based on micro data, and those based on tax changes. One study, Reinhard (1981), examines both aggregate and micro data and is considered at the end of the section on aggregate studies.

Table 2-5
Post-1980 Studies of Property Tax Capitalization Based on Aggregate Data

	Dusansky, Ingber, and Karatjas (1981)	Reinhard (1981, aggregate data)
Principal Conclusions about Property Tax Capitalization[a]	43%–96%, depending on time horizon	Functional form matters
Assumed Discount Rate and Time Horizon[b]	5%; 10–40 years	Real rate; 40 years
Estimated Tax Capitalization with 3% Discount Rate and Infinite Horizon[c]	22%	107%
Study Characteristics:		
Unit of Observation	School district	Municipality
Time Period	1970	1960
Location	Suffolk County, NY	New Jersey
Sample Size	62	53
Model Specification:		
Dependent Variable	Median house value	Median house value
Property Tax Variable(s)	Equalized tax rate	Effective tax rate
Public Service Variable(s)	School expenditures per pupil	School expenditures per pupil; Nonschool expenditures per capita
Number of Housing and Neighborhood Controls[d]	3	5
Estimation Procedure[e]	3-stage least squares	Ad hoc, nonlinear, simultaneous equations
Dependent Variables of Other Structural Equations	School expenditures per pupil; Effective property tax rate; Median gross rent.	None
Methodological Limitations	Few control variables; Inexact functional form	Few control variables; Inappropriate econometric technique; No hypothesis tests

See notes to Table 2-2.

Table 2-6
Post-1980 Studies of Property Tax Capitalization Based on Micro Data

	Reinhard (1981, micro data)	Richardson & Thalheimer (1981)
Principal Conclusions About Property Tax Capitalization[a]	100%	73%
Assumed Discount Rate and Time Horizon[b]	3.6%; Infinite	8%; 10 years
Estimated Tax Capitalization with 3% Discount Rate and Infinite Horizon[c]	120%	15%
Study Characteristics:		
Unit of Observation	House sale	House sale
Time Period	1969–1970	1973–1974
Location	San Mateo Co., CA	Fayette Co., KY
Sample Size	1453	861
Model Specification:		
Dependent Variable	House value	Log of house value
Property Tax Variable(s)	Effective tax rate	Dummy variable for location in the city
Public Service Variable(s)	School expenditure per pupil; Reading test score; crime rate; Fire insurance rate; Recreation expenditure per capita; Road expenditure per capita	Sanitary sewers
Number of Housing and Neighborhood Controls[d]	14	27
Estimation Procedure[e]	Nonlinear least squares	OLS
Dependent Variables of Other Structural Equations	None	None
Methodological Limitations	Ignores simultaneity; No hypothesis tests.	Inexact controls for service quality; Inappropriate sample selection; Ignores possible endogeneity of annexation.

Table 2-6 Continued

	Ihlanfeldt and Jackson (1982)	Lea (1982)
Principal Conclusions About Property Tax Capitalization[a]	Cap. ratio of 22 for systematic assessment errors; Larger but insignificant ratio for random assessment errors	Taxes capitalized to a lesser extent than services
Assumed Discount Rate and Time Horizon[b]	Real rate; 40 years	None
Estimated Tax Capitalization with 3% Discount Rate and Infinite Horizon[c]	66% (for systematic errors)	26%
Study Characteristics:		
Unit of Observation	Single-family house	Family
Time Period	1976	1968
Location	St. Louis, MO	Nation
Sample Size	1321	680
Model Specification		
Dependent Variable	Owner estimate of market value (or its log)	Owner estimate of market value
Property Tax Variable(s)	Systematic assessment error; Random assessment error	Average effective tax rate in county
Public Service Variable(s)	None	Average expenditure per capita in county
Number of Housing and Neighborhood Controls[d]	20	10
Estimation Procedure	Ad hoc	2SLS
Dependent Variables of Other Structural Equations	Assessment errors	Average expenditure per capita in county
Methodological Limitations	Incorrect estimating procedure	Ignores simultaneity between house value and tax rate; Severe data limitations; Inappropriate functional form

Table 2-6 Continued

Goodman (1983)

Principal Conclusions About Property Tax Capitalization[a]	Intrajurisdictional: 10–122%; (based on fiscal surplus)
Assumed Discount Rate and Time Horizon[b]	5%; 40 years
Estimated Tax Capitalization with 3 Percent Discount Rate and Infinite Horizon[c]	Intrajurisdictional: about 65%; Interjurisdictional: about 25%
Study Characteristics:	
Unit of Observation	House sale
Time Period	1967–1969
Location	New Haven Area (10 jurisdictions)
Sample Size	1835
Model Specification:	
Dependent Variable	Box-Cox transformation of sales price
Property Tax Variable(s)	Effective tax rate; community average effective tax rate
Public Tax Variable(s)	Average house price in the jurisdiction (= tax base proxy); Percentile reading score
Number of Housing and Neighborhood Controls[d]	15
Estimation Procedure[e]	Box-Cox
Dependent Variables of Other Structural Equations	None
Methodological Limitations	Ignores simultaneity; Inappropriate treatment of public services.

See notes to Table 2-2.

Table 2-7
Post-1980 Studies of Property Tax Capitalization Based on Tax Changes

	Gabriel (1981)	Rosen (1982)
Principal Conclusions about Property Tax Capitalization[a]	Cap. ratio = 12	Cap. ratio = 7.3
Assumed Discount Rate and Time Horizon[b]	None	None
Estimated Tax Capitalization with 3% Discount Rate and Infinite Horizon[c]	36%	22%
Study Characteristics:		
Unit of Observation	Municipality	Municipality
Time Period	1978–1979	1978–1979
Location	San Francisco Area	San Francisco Area
Sample Size	30	64
Model Specification:		
Dependent Variable	Change in mean house value	Change in mean house value
Property Tax Variable(s)	Change in mean tax payment	Change in mean tax payment
Public Service Variable(s)	None	None
Number of Housing and Neighborhood Controls[d]	5	5
Estimation Procedure[e]	OLS	OLS
Dependent Variables of Other Structural Equations	None	None
Methodological Limitations	Inexact controls; Ignores possible simultaneity	Ignores possible simultaneity

See notes to Table 2-2.

3.1 Aggregate Studies

Dusansky, Ingber, and Karatjas (1981) is distinguished by an attempt to model the simultaneous determination of rents, land values, house values, and educational spending. The authors employ data from 62 school districts in Suffolk County, New York in 1970 and estimate their equations with three-stage least squares.

Whatever its value as a model of this system of equations, this study falls short of providing a compelling estimate of tax capitalization. The tax-capitalization equation contains only five control variables: median number of rooms, predicted rental value of housing, predicted school expenditures, median income, and the ratio of owners to renters. Although simultaneity is treated with some care, the specification is not: the effective tax rate variable appears in a linear house-value regression.[12]

The authors present estimated capitalization rates for several time horizons with a 5% discount rate. Their preferred estimate, 96%, is based on a 10 year horizon. More appropriate assumptions, such as a 3% rate and an infinite horizon, would lower their estimate of capitalization to 22%.

Reinhard (1981) pays careful attention to functional form and obtains estimates of capitalization in Oates's (1969 and 1973) sample of New Jersey communities and in a sample of 1453 single-family houses in San Mateo, California in 1969–1970. Reinhard assumes that rental value is a linear function of housing and neighborhood characteristics, substitutes this assumption into Equation (2), and estimates the result with an iterative nonlinear technique. He also recognizes that a real discount rate should be used.

Reinhard finds that correcting for the nonlinear effect of the tax rate does matter in the Oates sample; assuming a 3% discount rate, Reinhard's approach implies that capitalization is 107%, whereas Oates's approach implies that it is 61%. Although Reinhard's specification is a step in the right direction, he employs an ad hoc econometric procedure, the properties of which are not known. The technique is to assume a value for the coefficient of the tax variable and estimate the equation with two-stage least squares conditional on this assumption. The assumption that yields the highest F-statistic is selected as the estimate of capitalization (divided by r). In the case of a single equation with normal error terms, any procedure that minimizes the sum of squared errors is a maximum likelihood procedure. Because the F-statistic is proportional to the sum of squared errors, Reinhard's approach would be appropriate for a single equation. This theorem does not carry over, however, to a simultaneous equations system. Reinhard's approach is an easy way to account for the nonlinear effect of the tax rate, but it probably does not yield consistent estimates.[13] Moreover, Reinhard presents no evidence to indicate whether his estimates of capitalization are significantly different from zero.

The San Mateo data set includes an extensive list of housing, neighborhood, and service-quality variables, but no instruments to identify the effect of house values on tax rates. Application of Reinhard's nonlinear technique to this data set without a correction for simultaneity indicates that capitalization is 100% if the discount rate is 3.6%. This estimate probably is biased upward by simultaneity.

3.2 Micro Studies

Richardson and Thalheimer (1981) make clever use of an unusual situation in Fayette County, Kentucky. The county contains two taxing districts, the City of Lexington and parts of the county that have not yet been annexed by the city. Both taxing districts belong to the same school district and pay the same school property tax rate, but the property tax rate is significantly higher in Lexington than in the rest of the county. Arguing that there is no significant service difference between the city and the rest of the county, Richardson and Thalheimer interpret housing price differences between the two taxing districts, controlling for housing and neighborhood variables, as a reflection of property tax capitalization.

The study is based on 861 single-family house sales in 1973–1974. The specification is carefully worked out and the data set contains a long list of housing and neighborhood control variables. Richardson and Thalheimer find that the average housing price difference between the two jurisdictions is $682. By assuming an 8% discount rate and a 10-year time horizon, they conclude that this difference implies a capitalization rate of 73%.[14] This discount rate is too high and this time horizon is too low. More realistic assumptions would cut this estimate of capitalization considerably. Richardson and Thalheimer show that rising the horizon to 15 years cuts the estimated rate to 57%. A 3% rate and an infinite horizon, which are even more realistic, would cut the rate to 15%.

Richardson and Thalheimer show that with only two tax rates to consider, Equation (3) can be estimated with a dummy variable that indicates the taxing district. Although this approach is simple, it magnifies the potential problem from left-out variables; any difference between the two districts that affects house values and is not explicitly controlled for will influence the coefficient of the dummy variable. The most likely left-out variables are measures of service quality. Richardson and Thalheimer present some evidence that service quality is the same in the two districts. Although the districts have different police and fire departments, they find "no evidence of a perceived difference in services received in either district" (p. 677). The City picks up trash and provides street lights, whereas the County does not. "Both trash pickup and street lighting are probably capitalized to some extent but we would not expect these differences in benefits to greatly counteract the degree of capitalization that might be expected from the difference in tax rates mentioned above" (p. 677). The authors also offer two reasons why service quality may be the same in the city and the rest of the county, even if spending is not. First, "Many county residents were receiving benefits, such as libraries, police and maintenance of the central city district, from the city without paying for them in property taxes."[15] Second, higher spending may reflect "inefficiency" in the City government. The authors do not present any evidence, however, that these factors are sufficient to explain why the nonschool tax rate is almost four times as high in the city as in the rest of the county.

Two other potential problems arise in this study. First, the sample selection criterion is not appropriate. The authors exclude observations from older portions of the city "because we have found it difficult to explain high proportion of the variation in sales in these areas using the attribute measurements that were available" (p. 677). Older portions of the city are likely to have smaller property values so this sample selection criterion could inject truncation bias into the results. Second, the authors make no correction for simultaneity. The nature of the simultaneity problem here is quite different that in other studies, because property taxes are represented by a dummy variable. Nevertheless, the annexation process itself may be endogenous. Places with high property values, for example, might be the first ones to be annexed, so that the dependent variable may in fact influence the district dummy. Without knowing the factors that cause annexation, one cannot rule out the possibility of simultaneity bias.

Ihlanfeldt and Jackson (1982) are aware of the specification errors that have bedeviled many tax capitalization studies and attempt to avoid them with a complex new methodology, which, among other things, distinguishes between systematic and random assessment errors. They apply this methodology to a sample of 1321 single-family houses in St. Louis. This sample comes from the 1976 Annual Housing Survey. They are also aware that a real discount rate should be used; with a 3% rate, their result implies that tax differences caused by systematic assessment errors are capitalized at a 66% rate.[16]

As the authors recognize, the Annual Housing Survey data has strengths and weaknesses. It provides extensive information on the structural characteristics of houses but little objective information on the characteristics of neighborhoods. Moreover, the market value of a house is measured by an owner's estimate, not by an actual sale price. These data limitations do not appear to be a major problem for the study. The authors present some evidence, for example, that owners' estimates are reasonably accurate measures of market values.

Unfortunately, however, the methodology of the paper is seriously flawed. The methodology proceeds in four steps. The first step is to estimate house values as a function of housing characteristics without using a tax variable on the right side of the equation. Suppressing the observation subscripts for simplicity, this regression is

$$\ln V = \sum a_j X_j + \epsilon. \tag{4}$$

Note that $\hat{V}$ is the predicted value of V from this regression. The second step is to calculate assessment errors, which are defined as the difference between actual and "fair" tax payments, or

$$AE = T - \bar{t}V, \tag{5}$$

where T is tax payment and $\bar{t}$ is the average effective property tax rate in the sample. Step three is to regress assessment errors on $\hat{V}$:

$$AE = b_0 + b_1\hat{V} + \phi. \tag{6}$$

The predicted value from this regression is defined to be the systematic assessment error, SAE, and the residual is defined to be the random assessment error, RAE. The final step is to determine whether the residual from the regression in the first step is influenced by SAE and RAE. This step involves the following regression:

$$V - \hat{V} = \gamma_0 + \gamma_1 SAE + \gamma_2 RAE + \theta. \tag{7}$$

As the authors point out, Equation (4) may yield biased results because the tax variable is left out. If so, then the rest of the steps do not make sense. So the authors carry out a specification test to see if such a bias is present. The results of this test convince them that it is not. The trouble is that they carry out the wrong test. As shown in Equation (1) and Equation (7) (Ihlanfeldt and Jackson's step four), tax payment has a linear effect on house value. However, their specification test looks for a bias when the tax payment is left out of Equation (4), which has the log of house value on the left side. The log of house value is a function of the effective tax rate, as in Equation (3), but not of the tax payment. In effect, their specification test is itself misspecified, and does not show that the coefficients in Equation (4) are unbiased.

This problem goes beyond the particular specification test they use. Their methodology would not be appropriate even if the right specification test indicated no bias in Equation (4). Without the inappropriate mixing of a nonlinear form, Equation (4), and a linear form, Equation (7), their methodology would not be able to identify the tax capitalization parameter. If these two equations were both linear, their method would collapse to Equation (1); if they were both nonlinear, it would collapse to Equation (2).[17] In both cases the coefficient of the tax variable would be $\gamma_2/(1 + \gamma_2 t)$ and the parameter for systematic assessment errors, γ_1, would not be identified. The potential for an identification problem was first pointed out in a comment by Gerking and Dickie (1985). As noted in a reply by Ihlanfeldt and Jackson (1986), however, this identification problem does not exist given their assumptions. The problem is that the assumptions themselves are contradictory, and any attempt to make them consistent leads to the identification problem. Without this contradiction, there is no way to separate the direct effect of housing characteristics on house values from the indirect effect of $\hat{V}$ on house values through systematic assessment errors, because $\hat{V}$ is a linear combination of these housing characteristics.[18]

Lea (1982) provides a careful analysis of the simultaneity between house values and public spending. His two-equation model is applied to data on 680 individual families from the 1968 Panel Study of Income Dynamics, combined with tax and expenditure data from the 1967 Census of Governments. In presenting his results, he combines tax and expenditure capitalization and does not state tax capitalization separately. But his results imply 26% tax capitalization with a 3% real discount rate and an infinite time horizon.

As Lea recognizes, his data set has severe limitations, which cast doubt on the accuracy of his estimate of capitalization. The tax and expenditure variables are county-wide averages and therefore ignore both inter- and intrajurisdictional variation within a county. Only ten housing and neighborhood control variables are available. Many observations were eliminated because of a lack of complete tax data.

Although Lea models the simultaneity between house values and expenditures, he ignores the simultaneity between house values and tax rates.[19] Moreover, he includes the effective tax rate in a linear house value regression. As several other studies have shown, either of these flaws can seriously bias an estimate of capitalization.

Goodman (1983) estimates a house value regression with a Box-Cox technique and carefully distinguishes between inter- and intrajurisdictional tax rate difference. His sample of 1835 single-family houses in 10 communities in the New Haven metropolitan area in 1967–1969 is the same sample used by King (1973). Assuming a 5% rate and a 40-year horizon, he concludes that intrajurisdictional differences are capitalized at slightly more than 100% in most communities. He combines tax and expenditure capitalization and therefore does not present estimates of interjurisdictional tax capitalization. We calculate that with a 3% rate and an infinite horizon, Goodman's results imply intrajurisdictional tax capitalization of about 65% and capitalization of interjurisdictional fiscal residuals, to be defined below, of about 35%.

In discussing tax capitalization, Goodman begins with Equation (2). He then argues that the numerator of this equation equals benefits from housing services plus the benefits from public services. On the assumption that $1 of public spending yields benefits worth $1, which is the assumption also made by Hamilton (1979), he argues that for a community as a whole total benefits must equal total revenues. Total revenues in turn equal the community average effective tax rate, $\bar{t}$, multiplied by the community tax base, B, so Goodman substitutes $\bar{t}B$ for the benefits from public services in the numerator of Equation (2). To distinguish between inter- and intrajurisdictional tax capitalization, Goodman also decomposes the tax rate variable into $\bar{t}$ and $(t - \bar{t})$.

After this conceptual development, Goodman estimates a house value regression using the Box-Cox approach. The two tax variables, t and $\bar{t}$, and the community tax base, B, are included as explanatory variables. The functional form relating tax rates to house values is determined by the Box-Cox procedure, not by assumption, so that it does not correspond to either Equation (1) or Equation (3). This fact makes the specification difficult to interpret. The Box-Cox procedure may be an excellent way to select a functional form when economic theory does not suggest the appropriate form; indeed, this is the reason why this procedure has been employed so often, by Goodman (1978) and others, in estimating house value regressions. But does the Box-Cox procedure represent an improvement when economic theory does suggest a particular functional form? To put it another way, why does Goodman so carefully derive a functional form for the capitalization equation only to overrule this form by employing a Box-Cox technique? If the theoretically derived form is correct, then the Box-Cox procedure may be a source of bias.

Two other features of Goodman's study cast some doubt on his conclusions. First, as the author recognizes, the assumption that $1 of spending yields benefits worth $1 to households is extreme. Moreover, the tax-base variable itself is incomplete; Goodman points out that it does not reflect commercial and industrial property or intergovernmental aid. Goodman implicitly reveals the limits of his tax-base variable by including one public service, a school test score; by Goodman's own argument, the tax base is a replacement for measures of service quality. A comprehensive set of public service quality variables, such as those used by King for the same data set, would be more appropriate controls than a partial property tax base and a single service quality measure.

Second, Goodman makes no correction for simultaneity. This correction is particularly important for his data set, which involves simultaneity through both assessor behavior and through the process of public expenditure determination. Many studies have demonstrated the potential bias from ignoring this simultaneity.

3.3 Studies Based on Tax Changes

Two studies take advantage of the large property tax changes induced by Proposition 13 in California to study interjurisdictional tax capitalization in the San Francisco area in 1978–1979: Gabriel (1981) and Rosen (1982).

Both of these studies estimate Equation (1) in change form. The authors collect data on individual house sale prices and property tax payments over two years, calculate the mean change in house price and in property tax payment in each community, and regress this change in house price on the change in tax payment, controlling for factors that influence the change in the pre-tax rental value of housing. Gabriel estimates that the capitalization ratio is about 12; Rosen estimates that it is 7.3. With a 3% discount rate, these estimates imply that the degree of capitalization is 36% and 22%, respectively.

Because of the circumstances surrounding Proposition 13, neither author controls for changes in public service quality. The rules of the Proposition are as follows: for people who owned their houses in 1975, 1979 assessed values were rolled back to their level in 1975; after 1979, assessed values can increase by no more than 2% per year unless the property sells, in which case the assessed value is set at the market value; and the effective property tax rate in a community cannot exceed 1%. Moreover, Proposition 13 was accompanied by large changes in state aid to localities. The State Government had a large surplus at the time of the Proposition, and these aid changes were designed to fully compensate communities for their property-tax losses from Proposition 13. The State bail-out, in other words, prevented any change in service quality. Even if the bail-out was not exact, so that service quality did change to some degree, the factors determining the change in a community's property taxes appear to be largely uncorrelated with the factors determining its change in service quality, so leaving out service-change variables may not lead to biased results. As both authors point out, however, the bail-out was widely regarded as a short-term solution and housebuyers may have believed that likely long-term changes in service quality were correlated with changes in property taxes.

Although both studies employ the same basic methodology, the Rosen study has three advantages. First, Rosen employs a larger and more representative sample of communities. Second, Rosen employs changes in housing characteristics as control variables, as dictated by theory, whereas Gabriel employs levels of housing characteristics in 1979. Third, Rosen recognizes and corrects for the possibility that this approach may involve heteroskedasticity because the underlying samples of house sales are larger in some communities than in others.[20]

Neither Gabriel nor Rosen accounts for simultaneity between changes in house values and changes in tax rates. Their approach can be defended by the argument that changes in property taxes are determined by the rules of Proposition 13, not by changes in house values. Nevertheless, an indirect link between changes in house values and changes in tax payments could exist. Suppose long-term changes in some unobserved variable are partly responsible for relatively rapid growth in house values in some communities both before and after the Proposition was passed. Assessed values therefore grew more between 1975 and 1978 in these communities than in other communities, so according to the rules of Proposition 13, the rollback in assessed values to 1975 levels resulted in larger tax cuts in these communities than in others. In other words, this unobserved variable is part of the error term in their regressions and is correlated with the change in property taxes. In principle, this correlation could result in biased coefficients.

3.4 Summary

Tax capitalization studies published since 1980 have extended the range of econometric techniques applied to this topic and have taken advantage of some extensive data sets and some unusual property-tax circumstances. Like their predecessors, the studies based on aggregate data employ few control variables. In addition, one of these studies (Dusansky, Ingber and Karatjas (1981)) uses an inappropriate functional form and the other (Reinhard (1981)) uses an inappropriate econometric technique. Most of the studies based on micro data, namely Reinhard (1981), Lea (1982), and Goodman (1983), fail to consider the simultaneity between house values and tax rates. Moreover, Ihlanfeldt and Jackson (1982) make contradictory assumptions in their correction for simultaneity, and Richardson and Thalheimer (1981) do not address the possible endogeneity of annexation. Inappropriate functional forms are employed by three of the micro studies (Ihlanfeldt and Jackson (1982), Lea (1982), and Goodman (1983)) and a fourth study (Richardson and Thalheimer (1981)) may be subject to left-out-variable bias. The two studies based on the tax changes caused by Proposition 13 (Gabriel (1981) and Rosen (1982)) yield particularly compelling results, although they too may be subject to simultaneity bias.

After restating the results of these studies with a common 3% discount rate, the range of capitalization estimates is still quite large, from 15% to 120%. These estimates are presented in the third row of Tables 2-5 to 2-7. Three studies (Richardson and Thalheimer (1981), Gabriel (1981), and Rosen (1982)) take advantage of unusual circumstances to help overcome the methodological obstacles inherent in estimating tax capitalization. Among these three studies, the range of estimates is much smaller, from 15% to 36%.

4. CONCLUSIONS

Four principal conclusions emerge from this literature review. The first conclusion is that virtually every study of tax capitalization, regardless of its methodological flaws and data limitations, finds statistically significant capitalization. Because the various studies differ so much in both their strengths and weaknesses, this almost-universal finding provides strong evidence that capitalization really does exist.

The second conclusion is that despite the apparent simplicity of Equations (1) and (3), accurate estimates of property tax capitalization have proved to be remarkably difficult to obtain. The four inherent methodological problems — simultaneity, left-out-variable bias, specification error, and discount rate selection — combined with the data limitations and methodological quirks of individual studies make it difficult to find a study without a significant flaw. Many of the studies are careful and clever, but the methodological obstacles and data limitations they confront are very severe; no study of which we are aware, for example, fully considers both the simultaneity and the nonlinearity in the relationship between effective property tax rates and house values. Our task in this book is to overcome these obstacles.

Third, we conclude that most, but not all, of the studies in the literature overstate the estimated degree of capitalization by employing a nominal discount rate instead of a real discount rate. The degree of overstatement can be large. Most studies assume a 6% rate, which doubles the estimated degree of capitalization compared to the more realistic rate of 3%. Although many studies claim to find capitalization rates near 100%, only two studies, Meadows (1976) and Reinhard (1981), find a capitalization rate above 75% with a reasonable real discount rate.

Finally, once differences in assumptions about the discount rate have been removed, we find no pattern in the variation across studies in the estimated degree of capitalization.[21] It is not true, for example, that estimates of interjurisdictional tax capitalization tend to be higher than estimates of intrajurisdictional tax capitalization, or vice versa. In our view, studies that take advantage of unusual property-tax situations often yield particularly compelling results, but the best of these studies (Smith (1970), Moody (1974), Richardson and Thalheimer (1981), and Rosen (1982)) yield estimates of the degree of capitalization that range from 15% to 60%, assuming a 3% discount rate. Overall, the literature does not support the proposition that the degree of capitalization is the same in every case, but it also does not shed much light on the factors that cause the degree of capitalization to vary.

NOTES

[1] Apparently, theoretical discussions of tax capitalization date back even farther, to 1735. See Seligman (1932).

[2] This review did not examine early studies of capitalization, namely Jensen (1931), Daicoff (1962), and Woodard and Brady (1965), because of large methodological advances that

have taken place since these studies were carried out. This review did present preliminary estimates of capitalization based on our Massachusetts data. Because of conceptual and econometric flaws, these preliminary estimates proved to be incorrect and should be ignored.

[3] This principle is examined in more detail in Chapter 3.

[4] More formally, the bias in the coefficient of an included variable equals the sum across left-out variables of the true effect of the left-out variable multiplied by the partial correlation between the included and left-out variable. In some cases, the distinction between the first two econometric problems is blurred. A "random shock" to house value can be interpreted as a housing or neighborhood characteristic that the assessor observes but the researcher does not.

[5] See, for example, Halvorsen and Pollakowski (1981). Of course, housing characteristics can be transformed to help break the linearity; for example V could be a function of X and X-squared or of log X. And housing characteristics can be interacted with each other. But the advantages of a multiplicative form (declining marginal valuations and full interaction) cannot be achieved without consuming many degrees of freedom, often more than are available.

[6] Strictly speaking, the estimated degree of capitalization also depends on the buyer's time horizon and a variety of income tax provisions. A detailed discussion of these issues is provided in Chapter 3.

[7] In Chapter 3, we explain more fully the need for a real discount rate. Three of the authors hereby confess that we were not fully aware of this problem in our earlier literature review: Bloom, Ladd, and Yinger (1983).

[8] These calculations are based on the estimated tax coefficient and functional form and on the techniques that are found in the literature. The calculations are straightforward for most articles, but questions of interpretation sometimes arise. In such cases, we have attempted to employ all relevant information in the article to come up with a calculation that is consistent with the author's approach and with the basic theory of capitalization.

[9] Hamilton appears to make two errors in his derivation. First, his decomposition depends on an incorrect statistical argument in his footnote 13. He assumes that the probability limit of an expression equals zero even though he knows the expected value of this expression is not zero. These assumptions are contradictory; as shown by Goldberger (1964, p. 118), if the probability limit of X equals X^*, then the expected value of X also equals X^*. Second, his article contains an algebraic error. In his version of Equation (1), he replaces T with its systematic and random components and derives his version of Equation (2). But in the result (his Equation (11)) the determinants of rental value are not divided by $(r + t)$.

[10] In implementing his approach, Hamilton substitutes education spending per pupil for total spending per capita. Even if his assumption about the value of $1 of spending is correct, this substitution introduces a new parameter onto the benefit side of fiscal surplus but not onto the tax side. This parameter invalidates Hamilton's restriction that the coefficients of the benefit and tax sides are the same.

[11] See Bloom, Ladd, and Yinger (1983).

[12] Because this is clearly an inappropriate specification, both in form and in number of controls, the use of three-stage least squares is troublesome; without the right specification, this procedure will not yield consistent estimates. See Hausman (1978).

[13] Because it does not meet the conditions of the usual consistency proof for two-stage least squares, we suspect that it does not yield consistent estimates. Note that although his technique accounts for the nonlinearity of the tax rate, it does not account for the nonlinear effect of housing characteristics on house values.

[14] Richardson and Thalheimer also estimate capitalization with a linear specification. Although this estimate varies with house value, it is similar to the result in the text.

[15] Sewer service also differs from one house to another. This difference, which is not perfectly correlated with taxing district, is carefully controlled for by the authors.

[16] Although Ihlanfeldt and Jackson clearly explain that a real discount rate should be used, their numerical illustration of this rate does not make sense. They say, "if $\dot{V}$ [the expected percentage change in house values] is assumed to equal 8% and the typical mortgage term of 30 years is employed as n [the buyer's time horizon], full capitalization coefficients equal to 40 or larger are obtained for r [the nominal discount rate] less than or equal to 6.4%" (p. 424). But the real rate is the nominal rate less anticipated price growth, so this example implies a negative real discount rate, which has the nonsensical implication that the sign of the capitalization coefficient is reversed.

[17] To be more precise, they collapse to these other equations if one assumes, as Ihlanfeldt and Jackson do (1986, p. 838) that the estimated coefficients equal the true parameters of Equation (4).

[18] Part of the methodological trouble is that $\hat{V}$, not the X's themselves, are included in Equation (6). If the coefficients of individual X variables could be different in Equations (4) and (6), this identification problem would not arise. This methodological problem should not be confused with the philosophical question of the best way to define a systematic assessment error. Ihlanfeldt and Jackson include $\hat{V}$ because they want to focus on the vertical equity of assessment errors: Gerking and Dickie would prefer a more general definition of "systematic." But even if one agrees with Ihlanfeldt and Jackson on philosophical grounds, one cannot avoid the identification problem inherent in their approach.

[19] Lea argues (in his footnote 10) that the tax rate is predetermined by the expenditure level (and the tax base). This argument is correct, but he does not implement it; the tax rate is still endogenous in his regression because he does not predict it on the basis of his expenditure equation combined with a community budget constraint.

[20] An alternative approach would be to retain individual houses as observations, but this approach requires data on the characteristics of individual houses, which were not available to either author.

[21] The only generalization we can see is a more negative one: all the studies that report an extreme degree of capitalization, either zero or greater than 100%, appear to have severe methodological limitations, usually due to an inappropriate functional form or an ad hoc and inconsistent econometric technique or both.

3

A Theoretical Analysis of Intrajurisdictional Property Tax Capitalization

Revaluation of all the property in a town is an "experiment" that provides an unusual opportunity to estimate the degree of property tax capitalization. This type of experiment, which has been studied by Wicks, Little and Beck (1968) and by Smith (1970), generates large changes, positive and negative, in property taxes. By observing house sales before and after revaluation, a researcher can determine the extent to which an increase in a house's property taxes leads to a decrease in its market value. In this chapter, we present the theory of property tax capitalization, describe the circumstances of revaluation in Massachusetts, and show how we combine theory and circumstance to estimate the degree of capitalization. In the following three chapters, we describe our data, explain our econometric methodology, and present our results for seven communities in Massachusetts.

1. OVERVIEW

Our research design has three key characteristics. First, we examine *intra*jurisdictional property tax capitalization. This focus is both a strength and a limitation of our approach. It is a strength because it rules out the need to control for public services and other non-tax factors that vary across jurisdictions—factors which have bedeviled many previous studies and caused left-out-variable biases of unknown magnitudes. It is a limitation because we cannot determine whether our results apply to property tax differences across jurisdictions. In the abstract, a $1.00 difference in property taxes should affect households' bids for a house in the same way whether the difference is relative to other houses in the same jurisdiction or relative to houses in other jurisdictions. We will see, however, that expectations and institutional factors might lead to different degrees of capitalization in these two cases. Our method does not allow us to measure such differences.

Second, our approach focuses on relative property tax changes generated by jurisdiction-wide revaluations in several Massachusetts communities. In these communities, reassessments had not occurred for many years, even for houses that had sold, and assessment–sales ratios (and hence effective property tax rates) varied widely from one house to the next. In a revaluation, an assessor attempts to bring all houses to the same assessment–sales ratio. A house with a low ratio before revaluation experiences an increase in its property taxes relative to other houses, and a house with high ratio before revaluation experiences a cut in its property taxes relative to other houses. We collect data on houses that sold twice. These data allow us to estimate the relationship between *changes* in property tax rates and *changes* in house values.[1] In particular, our intrajurisdictional focus leads us to estimate the impact of a change in property tax rate relative to other houses in the jurisdiction on the change in house value relative to other houses in the jurisdiction.

This focus on changes caused by revaluation has three advantages. First, it minimizes the danger of bias from left-out housing and neighborhood characteristics. In a regression of house values on property taxes, the coefficient of the tax variable will be biased unless all housing and neighborhood characteristics that both influence value and are correlated with the tax variable are included as explanatory variables. Many characteristics meet these conditions, so it is difficult to eliminate bias from this type of regression. Switching to changes, however, breaks the correlation between the tax variable and housing characteristics, and therefore lowers the potential bias.

Thanks to the infrequent reassessment before revaluation, houses with histories of rapid value growth had relatively low effective tax rates whereas houses with relatively slow value growth had relatively high effective tax rates. The impact of revaluation on a particular house therefore depends on the events, often far in the past, that determined its value growth and hence its effective tax rate before revaluation. Changes in housing or neighborhood characteristics or in the market's valuation of these characteristics might lead to a change in house value, but this relationship is confined to the time period surrounding the revaluation, when our double sales took place. Hence, the events that affect our tax change variable and the market events that influence house values occur at different times. This lack of coincident timing weakens the link, and hence the correlation, between the tax variable and housing or neighborhood characteristics.

It must be pointed out, however, that our approach does not rule out altogether the possibility of left-out-variable bias. Continuing long-term trends in the market valuation of certain housing characteristics could contribute to varying effective tax rates before revaluation and affect house values after revaluation. Furthermore, some houses may receive renovations or additions that both influence their relative values and their relative change in property taxes. As a result, we employ an extensive set of housing and neighborhood control variables, including types of additions and renovations, as insurance against this possible left-out-variable bias.

The second advantage of a focus on tax changes caused by revaluation is that revaluation causes large changes, positive and negative, in relative property tax rates. This extensive variation should help to estimate intrajurisdictional tax capitalization with precision.

The third advantage is that revaluation provides a conceptual handle on the causes of the changes in relative property taxes, namely assessors' attempts to set equal assessment–sales ratios. As a result, we are able to specify and estimate, in a more precise way than any previous study, the simultaneous relationship between a change in relative house value and a change in relative property taxes.

The final distinguishing feature of our approach is that we rely heavily on microeconomic theory in deriving an estimating equation. As shown in Chapter 2, many previous studies have been led astray by using ad hoc or even incorrect assumptions about functional forms. We minimize the chance of misspecification by deriving our estimating equation from theories that have been widely used in studying financial markets and markets for income-producing property.

After developing the basic theory of property tax capitalization and describing the setting in Massachusetts from which the data are drawn, we derive a capitalization equation based on tax changes, show how to isolate intrajurisdictional tax capitalization, account for mortgage provisions and income tax deductions, consider anticipation of revaluation, show how to control for housing and neighborhood characteristics, and account for simultaneity by modeling assessor behavior.

2. THE BASIC THEORY OF PROPERTY TAX CAPITALIZATION

Property taxes are capitalized into house values because, all else equal, a household is willing to pay more for a house the lower the property taxes on that house. This relationship can be formalized with an asset-pricing model or with an analysis of household utility maximization.

2.1   House Values, Rental Flows, and Property Taxes

The market value of an asset equals the present value of the net flow of services derived from owning it. This hypothesis has been widely employed, and widely supported by the evidence, in the study of financial markets. Furthermore, this hypothesis is the intellectual foundation of the income approach to property assessment, which is one of the principal methods used to assess rental housing and other forms of income-producing property.[2]

The price paid for an asset today is based on the future flow of services from that asset and therefore reflects the purchaser's expectations about that flow. We assume static expectations: people expect this year's rental flows to continue into the future. This approach can be implemented with available data and rules out the need for a complex analysis of risk and risk aversion. Static expectations do not imply zero growth; as we will see, steady growth in rents and values can easily be incorporated into this approach.

Consider a single-family house containing H units of housing services with a before-tax rental value of \$$R$ per unit. The rental flow for this house is \$$RH$ per year.[3] We make the convenient, but inessential, assumption that H depends on the structural characteristics of the house, such as the number of rooms and the quality of construction, whereas R depends on the level of public services and of locational amenities, such as access to employment and recreation.[4] By definition, the annual property tax payment on this house, T, equals the effective tax rate, t, multiplied by the house's market value, V; that is,

$$T = tV. \tag{1}$$

Now suppose that i is the discount rate facing the buyer of a single family house and that N is the house's expected lifetime. Then with static expectations, the current rental value and property tax payment are expected to continue, and the market value of the house equals the present value, calculated with discount rate i, of the stream of rental services from the house minus the present value of the stream of property taxes levied on it. In symbols,

$$V = \sum_{n=1}^{N} \frac{RH - T}{(1 + i)^n} = \sum_{n=1}^{N} \frac{RH - tV}{(1 + i)^n}. \tag{2a}$$

A purchaser may anticipate selling the house before year N. This possibility does not change this formula because the sale price is simply the present value of the rental services in the years after the resale.[5] Equation (2a) can be simplified to yield

$$V = \frac{RH - T}{i'} = \frac{RH - tV}{i'}, \tag{2b}$$

where

$$i' = \frac{i}{1 - (1 + i)^{-N}}. \tag{3}$$

The term i' can be interpreted as the infinite-horizon discount rate that is equivalent to discount rate i with horizon N. Solving (2b) for V yields the basic capitalization equation:

$$V = \frac{RH}{i' + t}. \tag{4}$$

With a long expected lifetime for housing, say 100 years, i' is approximately equal to i.[6] For the moment, therefore, we simply ignore the prime in Equation (4).

A capitalization equation can also be derived with steady growth in rents and values. Suppose that rents are expected to grow at a steady annual rate, π; that is, $R_n = R_0(1 + \pi)^{n-1}$. This growth in R implies a steady expected growth in V, that is, housing appreciation; in symbols, $V_n = V_0(1 + \pi)^{n-1}$. Substituting R_n for R and V_n for V in the right side of Equation (2a) and re-deriving (4) yields:

$$V_0 = \frac{R_0 H}{i - \pi + t} = \frac{R_0 H}{r + t}, \tag{5}$$

where $r = (i - \pi)$ is the real interest rate.[7] To interpret this result, note that with R_n and V_n in Equation (2a), both the numerator and denominator are expressed in nominal terms. In (5), on the other hand, both the numerator and denominator are in real terms: R_0 is the real rent level (in year-o dollars) and r is the real interest rate. As in any discounting problem, one can use nominal or real values, as long as one is consistent.

In determining the present value of a house, households discount the flow of net rents at the rate of return they could obtain on an alternative investment with characteristics similar to housing. This rate of return is the i in Equation (5). During the sample period, 1960 to 1977, housing was widely seen as a safe investment with a steady rate of return. U.S. Treasury bonds with long maturities were a widely accessible alternative investment with these same characteristics. Diversified investment alternatives, such as stock or bond funds, were not available to most households during this period. Thus, we employ the rate of return on 10-year Treasury bonds as a measure of i.

Measuring π is more difficult. Remember that π is the expected rate of growth in rents and house values or of housing appreciation. This rate has two components: the expected inflation rate and the expected rate of net housing appreciation over and above inflation. This housing appreciation rate is net of housing maintenance.[8] We assume that net rents are expected to grow at the inflation rate, so that π can be interpreted as the expected rate of growth in the overall price level. As explained more fully in Chapter 5, we rely on Gramlich's (1983) careful study of households' inflation expectations to obtain an estimate of π as a function of past inflation.

We are not aware of any direct estimate of the expected lifetime of single-family houses, N, but this expectation must be related to the rate at which these houses depreciate. Most studies conclude that the average depreciation rate for single-family houses is less than 1% per year. Malpezzi, Ozanne, and Thibodeau (1987) review this literature and present their own careful estimates of housing depreciation in 59 metropolitan areas. They find that the average depreciation rate for single-family houses is 0.93 percent in a house's first year and declines to 0.43 percent by the house's 10th year. These are compound depreciation rates, that is, they apply to a base that declines every year, but one can obtain a lower bound estimate of a house's economic life by assuming that they are straight-line rates, that is, that they apply to the house's original value. A house that loses 0.93% (0.43%) of its original value per year will last 107 (233) years. It seems reasonable to suppose, therefore, that most homeowners, even those in 20- or 30-year-old houses, expect their house to last indefinitely, and we assume that homeowners act as if the expected lifetime of their house were infinite.

Equation (3) provides some perspective on this assumption. For example, the infinite-horizon discount rate that is equivalent to a 3% rate with a 100-year horizon is 3.16%. If the actual expected lifetime is 100 years, in other words, employing an infinite lifetime introduces a very small error, 0.16 percentage points, into the analysis. Although we assume an infinite horizon, Equation (3) can be used to restate our results with any other expected lifetime.

Another point worth emphasizing is that Equations (4) and (5) focus on the effective property tax rate, t, not the annual property tax payment, T. Equation (2b) provides an alternative capitalization equation based on tax payments. At one level, the capitalization of tax payments into house values is equivalent to the capitalization of tax rates into house values; the definition (1) switches one back and forth between (2b) and (4).[9] As we will see, however, a focus on tax rates has several conceptual and econometric advantages, and our estimating equation is based on (4), not (2b). One advantage is discussed in Chapter 2; it is more difficult to eliminate left-out-variable bias in a tax-payment model than in a tax-rate model.

2.2 The Household Utility Maximization Problem

Equation (4) can also be derived from a household utility maximization problem. In choosing a residential location, a household considers the effective property tax rate, t, the level of local services per household, E, and the level of other locational amenities, L, at alternative locations. The amount, P, a household is willing to pay per year for a unit of housing services is a function of these three variables; that is, $P = P(t, E, L)$. The form of this so-called bid function is determined by household utility maximization. Following the logic of the previous section, this annual bid function translates directly into a house-value equation. A household that buys a house containing H units of housing services is willing to pay $P(t, E, L)H$ per year to live in that house. With a discount rate i and a long expected lifetime, the value of the house is, approximately, $V(t, E, L, H) = P(t, E, L)H/i$.

Now let us derive $P(t, E, L)$. For a more complete discussion, see Yinger (1982). A household's utility, U, is a function of H, E, L, and a composite consumption good G, and its income must be spent on H, property taxes, and on G, which is scaled so that its price is unity. Combining the definition (1) with the above expression for house value indicates that the households property tax payment, T, equals tPH/i. Thus, the household's problem is to

$$\text{Maximize} \quad U(G, H, E, L)$$
$$G, H, E, L, t$$
$$\text{Subject to} \quad Y = G + P(t, E, L)H\left(1 + \frac{t}{i}\right). \tag{6}$$

The choice of a residential location is implicit in this problem. A household determines its optimal combination of t, E, and L, and then moves to the location that provides that combination.[10]

Property tax capitalization arises because households compete against each other for houses in desirable locations, such as jurisdictions with low property tax rates. Each household wants to live in a jurisdiction with the effective tax rate that maximizes its utility. Differentiating (6) with respect to t yields

$$\frac{\partial P}{\partial t}(i + t) + P = 0. \tag{7}$$

This condition indicates the tax rate that a household would prefer if the response of market prices to tax rates, $(\partial P/\partial t)$, were known. Note that this condition is the same for all households. It depends only on i, t, and the market function P. Hence, no matter what household utility functions look like, all households will want to move into the same jurisdictions — namely the jurisdictions with values of t that satisfy (7).

How can all households move into the same jurisdictions? The answer is that market prices, P, adjust until Equation (7) holds everywhere. If housing prices do not satisfy (7), some locations will be more attractive than others and all households will want to live in those locations. As a result, housing prices in those locations will be bid up until (7) is satisfied. In other words, Equation (7) can be interpreted as a equilibrium condition for the market price of housing. Because households compete against each other for access to housing in jurisdictions with low tax rates, jurisdictions with relatively low tax rates will have relatively high house values, and vice versa. In equilibrium, households must be exactly compensated for higher property tax rates by lower housing prices.[11]

It follows that the housing-price function that keeps households in equilibrium with respect to property taxes is the solution to the differential Equation (7). This solution is:

$$P(t, E, L) = \frac{C(E, L)}{i + t}, \tag{8}$$

where C is a constant of integration that depends, through the other first-order conditions of Problem (6), on E and L. Translating this annual price per unit of H into an asset value yields:

$$V(t, E, L, H) = \frac{\dfrac{C(E, L)H}{i}}{i + t}. \tag{9}$$

This equation describes the capitalization of effective property tax rates into house values.[12] It obviously is equivalent to (4), with $C(E,L)/i = R$; that is, the constant of integration in (8) can be interpreted as the before-tax rental value of housing services multiplied by i. Thus, both household utility maximization and the asset-pricing approach yield the same relationship between effective tax rates and house values. Moreover, expected growth in R (or C) has the same effect on (9) as on (4); it leads to the replacement of the nominal interest rate, i, with the real interest rate, r.

The household maximization problem, like the asset-pricing model, can be formulated in terms of tax payments or tax rates. Substituting Equation (1) into the budget constraint of (6) and solving for the equilibrium housing-price function yields Equation (2b). This observation solves a mystery that is sometimes raised in discussing intrajurisdictional tax capitalization: How can a household determine its bid on the basis of t when t depends on its bid? Substituting (2b) into (1) yields

$$t = \frac{Tr}{RH - T}.$$ (10)

Thus, a knowledge of T, r, R, and H is sufficient for a household to determine t and hence to make a bid on a house as described by Equation (9).[13]

2.3   The Degree of Capitalization

One might say that Equations (4), (5) and (9) imply complete capitalization; differences in property taxes are reflected, dollar for dollar, in house values. Intrajurisdictional property tax capitalization may not be complete, however, for three reasons.[14]

First, households may have imperfect information. A household is likely to know the tax payment (and hence the effective tax rate) on any house it wants to purchase, but it may not have good information about the taxes on other houses and hence about the town average tax rate. As explained by Case (1978) and Ihlanfeldt and Jackson (1982), this lack of information could arise for several different reasons. In some cases, the scale of the relevant housing market may be so small that information on comparable sales simply does not exist. In other cases, the scale or complexity of the market may swamp the ability of buyers and housing intermediaries to collect accurate, complete information. With imperfect information about the town average tax rate, for example, a household cannot accurately determine the tax rate on the house it wants to purchase relative to the town average, so relative tax rates may not be exactly reflected in bids for housing or in relative house values.

Although imperfect information could lead to over- or under-capitalization, we suspect that it is most likely to push the coefficient of t toward zero. From the perspective of a household, setting bids on housing as a function of effective tax rates is like running a regression of house values on tax rates. The true coefficient of the tax rate is unity, but households measure this variable with error; thus, according to the well-known errors-in-variables theorem, the household's estimated coefficient is biased toward zero. In other words, household bids on housing do not fully reflect actual effective tax rate differences. The errors-in-variables problem appears in the household's regression problem — not in ours. We know the effective tax rate on a house relative to the town average and therefore measure this variable without error. If imperfect information leads to household bids that undercapitalize relative tax rate differentials, then we will estimate this undercapitalization without bias. This analogy suggests, but does not prove, that the bias in the households "regression" is toward zero. Strictly speaking, the sign of the bias is known only in a linear bivariate problem. Our problem is nonlinear and multivariate, and households may have imperfect information about other variables in Equation (9).[15]

Second, supply-side factors may pull housing prices away from the levels dictated by full capitalization and, because housing search is costly, households may be willing to pay the amounts that suppliers ask. Even if households have full information about relative property taxes, therefore, capitalization may not be complete.[16]

Several factors might pull housing prices away from the relationship described by Equation (9). If houses in one neighborhood are systematically underassessed relative to houses in other neighborhoods, then with tax capitalization, houses in that neighborhood will sell for more than comparable houses elsewhere. To the extent possible with available land, builders in search of profits will want to expand the supply of housing in that neighborhood. Any expansion in supply will drive down the price there, at least in the short run.[17] Another possibility is that sellers do not include property tax changes in their asking prices. When assessments are fixed, as in Massachusetts, a decrease in house value relative to other houses, for reasons unrelated to property taxation, leads to an increase in effective property tax rate relative to other houses. Full capitalization of this tax-rate increase would lead to an additional decrease in house value. Asking prices may not reflect this additional decrease.

If housing search were not costly, buyers would not agree to asking prices that did not fully reflect relative property tax rates. In fact, however, housing search involves considerable time and effort. Suppose a household finds a house that it would be willing to buy at the asking price if that price were adjusted to fully reflect relative property taxes. This household may not expect to find, without extensive searching, another house with equally desirable structural characteristics or in an equally desirable neighborhood, and may therefore decide to pay the asking price, even though it is "too high." This outcome may not be a long-run equilibrium, but existing analyses of housing search, such as Courant's work (1978) on housing discrimination, have shown that this type of disequilibrium can persist for a long time.

Third, even if households are aware of relative property tax rates and face low housing search costs, they may not expect tax rate differences that exist at the time of first sale to persist indefinitely. This point has been made by Ihlandfeldt and Jackson (1982) and Goodman (1983). House values reflect the present value of the expected future stream of property tax payments, so any house value calculation requires a property tax forecast. We assume static expectations in deriving Equation (3); that is, the household expects the current property tax rate on its house to persist indefinitely. Two alternative assumptions are possible.

The first assumption is that households expect that assessment errors eventually will be corrected, so that all houses within a town will converge toward the same effective tax rate over time. This assumption is consistent with the situation in Massachusetts during the sample period when, as explained below, revaluation was in the wind. According to this assumption, current tax rate differentials will not be fully capitalized because households do not believe that they will persist.

As explained more fully below, this argument can be tested directly once a revaluation is announced. This announcement gives households some information about their likely future tax rates and they may incorporate this information into their bids. Smith (1970) provides some evidence to support this possibility, and we account for it in our estimating equation. However, we cannot incorporate household forecasts that occur before a revaluation is announced, except by determining whether current taxes are fully capitalized.

The second assumption is that households expect the factors that lead to their current relative effective tax rate to continue to operate. In the Massachusetts situation, assessed values were essentially fixed before revaluation, so the relative assessment – sales ratios, and hence relative effective tax rates, depend on changes in relative house values. Houses with relatively rapid (slow) value growth have relatively low (high) assessment – sales ratios and hence relatively low (high) effective tax rates. If households believe that assessments will stay fixed and that past relative value growth will continue, then current tax rate differentials understate expected future tax rate differentials. With this type of expectation, which seems unlikely in Massachusetts because of the long-standing discussion of revaluation, current tax rate differentials will be overcapitalized into house values.

In Massachusetts, therefore, current differences in effective property tax rates could be over- or under-capitalized. The most likely outcome of imperfect information, imperfect mobility, or expected tax rate changes is the under-capitalization of current tax rate differentials, although over-capitalization is conceptually possible.

It should be emphasized that these arguments about the degree of capitalization are specific to the situation within Massachusetts cities and towns during our sample years. These arguments do not necessarily apply, for example, to interjurisdictional capitalization. Clearly, imperfect information and imperfect mobility can exist across jurisdictions as well as within them. However, the extent of misinformation or the magnitude of the search costs may be different across towns than within towns. Furthermore, expectations about future reassessments are strictly an intrajurisdictional matter, although other sources of expectations might affect capitalization in other circumstances. This discussion reveals, therefore, that the degree of capitalization may be different for inter- and intrajurisdictional property tax differences. In addition, expectations about future reassessments could vary from one town to the next so that the degree of intrajurisdictional capitalization may not be the same in every town.

These arguments also depend on assessment practices in Massachusetts, and in particular on the fact that houses were not reassessed upon sale. Before revaluation, households had to make long-range forecasts of what would happen to their assessments, not predictions of how the assessor would respond to their sale price. The situation is quite different in California under Proposition 13, where houses always are reassessed upon resale and the growth in assessed values between sales is strictly limited. Under these circumstances, long-run forecasts about assessor behavior and their impact on the estimated degree of capitalization are irrelevant.

In short, our objective is to estimate the degree of capitalization in Massachusetts towns and to test the associated hypothesis that capitalization is complete. Let β measure the degree of capitalization. Then we can rewrite (2b) as

$$V = \frac{RH - \beta T}{i}. \tag{11}$$

A value of 1.0 for β implies that capitalization is complete; a value of 0.5 implies that a \$1.00 increase in the present value of the stream of property taxes (relative to other houses) leads to a \$0.50 decrease in V; and so on.

Substituting (1) into (11) and solving for V yields

$$V = \frac{RH}{i + \beta t}. \tag{12}$$

Because (11) and (12) are algebraically equivalent, β is interpreted in exactly the same way in both equations. Although (12) contains an effective tax rate not a tax payment, β still measures the impact on V of a \$1.00 increase in the present value of property tax payments.

Expectations about the persistence of tax differences can be formally introduced into this formulation. Suppose the expected lifetime of housing is so long that assuming an infinite lifetime is a close approximation, but that house buyers expect property tax differentials to persist for only N' years.[18] Let $\bar{t}$ stand for the average effective property tax rate (either within a jurisdiction or within a metropolitan area) and let $t^* = (t - \bar{t})$ stand for the deviation between a house's effective tax rate and this average. As shown formally in Section 4.2, the effect of the $\bar{t}$ can be extracted from V and R, so that we can examine the effect of tax deviations, t^*, on house values. Finally, suppose that β' is the degree of capitalization resulting from imperfect information and high search costs. Then, using a real discount rate, Equation (2) becomes

$$V = \sum_{n=1}^{\infty} \frac{RH}{(1+r)^n} - \sum_{n=1}^{N'} \frac{\beta' t^* V}{(1+r)^n}$$
$$= \frac{RH}{r} - \frac{\beta' t^* V}{r'}, \tag{13}$$

where r' is the infinite-horizon discount rate that is equivalent to rate r with horizon N', as defined by Equation (3). Solving Equation (13) for V yields

$$V = \frac{RH}{r + \dfrac{r}{r'} \beta' t^*}; \tag{14}$$

that is,

$$\beta = \frac{r}{r'} \beta' = \beta'[1 - (1+r)^{-N'}]. \tag{15}$$

Suppose, for example, that, because of perfect information and no search costs, β' equals 1; that r is 3%; and that tax differentials, which arise, say, because of out-of-date assessments, are expected to persist for 10 years. Then $\beta = 1 - (1.03)^{-10} = .26$. In this example, therefore, current tax differentials are capitalized into house values at a rate of 26%. Expectations clearly can have a dramatic effect on the capitalization of current tax differentials.

3. THE SETTING: REVALUATION IN MASSACHUSETTS

Ordinarily, it would be difficult to estimate intrajurisdictional property tax capitalization using Equation (12) because of all the econometric difficulties discussed in Chapter 2. It is difficult to account for simultaneity, for example, when the source of simultaneity, namely assessor behavior, contains a large random component. Fortunately, however, systematic revaluation of all the houses in a town, which has occurred in many cities and towns in Massachusetts over the last twenty years, generates varied changes in effective tax rates and represents a type of assessor behavior that can be readily modeled. This study is designed to make use of the particular circumstances of revaluation to estimate the degree of intrajurisdictional property tax capitalization.

In Massachusetts, as in some other states, the assessed value for a house is determined when the house is built or on the rare occasions when the entire town is reassessed. In the jurisdictions in our sample, assessed values are not updated when a house is sold. The only significant changes in assessed values are made to account for major renovations or additions, changes we correct for.

Tax payment, T, equals a nominal tax rate or mill rate, m, multiplied by an assessed value, A. Because the mill rate is the same for all houses in a town, A determines a house's tax payment relative to other houses in the town. And because A does not change over time, relative tax payments also do not change.

Relative house values do not remain constant over time, however. Some types of houses or houses in some locations appreciate faster than other houses. Hence, over time the effective tax rate, mA/V, on one house may change relative to the average effective tax rate in the town. Because assessed values are altered so seldom, gradual change in relative house values may result in dramatic variation in effective tax rates within a single jurisdiction.

Largely because of widespread disparities in effective tax rates within many jurisdictions, the Massachusetts Supreme Judicial Court ruled, in the 1961 Springfield case and the 1974 Sudbury case, that all cities and towns must assess all property at full market value. Many cities and towns responded to these decisions by reassessing all their property.[19] Case histories of revaluation in two of the seven towns in our sample are presented in Chapter 4.

In most cases of revaluation, a jurisdiction hires a private firm to estimate the full market value of all property in the jurisdiction. The techniques used by these firms provide a reasonably objective and accurate estimate of market value.[20] Hence, these revaluations represent a change from a situation in which effective tax rates differ widely within a jurisdiction to one in which effective tax rates are approximately the same for all houses. After revaluation, the effective tax rates within the town begin to spread out again, but this process is gradual and it takes many years to restore the pre-revaluation dispersion in effective tax rates. In fact, revaluations are now supposed to take place every three years, so it is unlikely that the wide dispersion that existed before the first revaluation will ever be replicated.

Thus, revaluation generates large changes in effective tax rates, changes that differ widely from house to house. We make use of this fact by collecting data on houses that sold twice, once before and once after revaluation. These data allow us to determine changes in house values and in effective tax rates.

The sample of houses that sold before and after revaluation is not a random sample of all houses that sold during the sample period. In particular, houses that sold only once are not included in our sample. Nevertheless, houses that sold twice appear to make up a large share of houses that sold, and we have no reason to believe that capitalization is different for house sales in and out of our sample.[21] We believe, but cannot prove, that sample-selection bias is unlikely to be a serious problem in our data.

In the process of identifying houses that sold before and after revaluation, we also identified many houses that sold twice either before or after revaluation. Because the effective tax rate does not change significantly for these nonstraddling observations, these data cannot be expected to yield precise estimates of the degree of property tax capitalization and are not used to estimate β. Nevertheless, as explained more fully below, these data proved to be helpful at several points in our analysis.

4. DERIVING AN ESTIMATING EQUATION

Our next task is to combine the basic theory of tax capitalization with the circumstances of revaluation in Massachusetts to derive an estimating equation.

4.1 Translating the Capitalization Equation into Change Form

As explained earlier, Equation (12) implies that a $1.00 increase in the discounted stream of taxes leads to a β decrease in house value. To be more precise, let Δ indicate a change, let a subscript "F" indicate a first sale and a subscript "S" indicate a second sale. With double-sales data, the change in a variable is its value at second sale minus its value at first sale; for example, $\Delta V = V_S - V_F$. Suppose for now that R, H, and i are constant across time and therefore require no time subscript. We will introduce time into these variables in later sections. The first and second sales prices can be represented as follows:

$$V_F = \frac{RH}{i + \beta t_F} \tag{16.1}$$

and

$$V_S = \frac{RH}{i + \beta t_S}. \tag{16.2}$$

In addition, the percentage change in V is

$$\frac{\Delta V}{V_F} = \frac{V_S - V_F}{V_F} = \frac{\dfrac{RH}{i + \beta t_S} - \dfrac{RH}{i + \beta t_F}}{\dfrac{RH}{i + \beta t_F}}$$

$$= \frac{(i + \beta t_F) - (i + \beta t_S)}{i + \beta t_S} = \frac{\beta(t_F - t_S)}{i + \beta t_S}$$

$$= \frac{-\beta(\Delta t)}{i + \beta t_S}. \tag{17}$$

For future reference, note that the second-sale tax rate appears in the denominator of Equation (17) — not the first-sale tax rate.[22]

By adding time subscripts to Equation (4) and subtracting the first sale from the second, one can derive an analogous expression for the change in T:

$$\Delta V = \frac{-\beta(\Delta T)}{i}. \tag{18}$$

Thus, the absolute change in V equals β multiplied by the change in the present value of tax payments. As explained earlier, the switch between tax rates and tax payments does not alter the interpretation of β; in both (17) and (18), β is the impact on V of a \$1 change in the present value of property taxes.

Our objective is to estimate β in (17). Because β enters this equation in a nonlinear fashion, we employ both a linear approximation and a nonlinear form, which are described in Chapter 5.

4.2 Deflating House Values: Removing Interjurisdictional Change

This study focuses on intrajurisdictional changes, that is, on changes in house values relative to other houses in the same jurisdiction. The observed change in a given house's sales price clearly includes both a change in the average value of houses in the town and the change in that house's value relative to the town average. Our first task is to remove from the data changes in town averages so that we can focus on changes relative to the average, that is, on intrajurisdictional changes.

Changes in town averages are not the same thing as interjurisdictional changes; a change in a town average need not represent a change relative to other towns. All towns could experience an increase in average house value, for example. Thus, removing changes in town averages removes interjuris-dictional change as well as change in the metropolitan average.

Interjurisdictional change involves growth in R and V. To analyze this change, and ultimately to remove it from our data, we must introduce the degree of capitalization, β, into Equation (5), which accounts for growth in R and V. After this step, the t in the denominator of (5) is multiplied by β, or equivalently, the R and i in Equation (12) are replaced with R_0 and r.

One further modification is necessary. The V_0 and R_0 in (5) are expressed in year-o dollars, where year o is the year of sale. This equation cannot be used, therefore, to compare house values for houses that sold in different years. To make this comparison, let y be the year of sale, so that the summation in (2a) goes from $(y + 1)$ to N, instead of from 1 to N, and add time subscripts to H, i, π, and t. Then adding β to (2a) and re-deriving (5) yields:

$$V_y = \frac{R_y H_y}{i_y - \pi_y + \beta t_y} = \frac{R_y H_y}{r_y + \beta t_y}, \tag{19}$$

where V_y and R_y are expressed in current dollars. Now suppose that I_y is an index of the average housing price in a given town in year y compared to a given base year. Then,

$$V_y = I_y V_y^*, \tag{20}$$

where V_y^* is V_y purged of all growth in the town average housing price between the base year and y. Note that V_y^* is not quite the same thing as V_y expressed in base-year dollars; an index of average housing price includes relative growth in housing prices as well as general inflation. This is entirely appropriate; in order to isolate intrajurisdictional variation in house values, we must "deflate" house values to remove both inflation and the town average appreciation above inflation.

The role of the price index on the right side of (19) is more compli-cated. Suppose R_y' is R_y purged of average rental growth between the base year and y. Then one cannot simply say that $R_y = I_y R_y'$, because I_y reflects changes in the town-wide average values of all elements on the right side of (19), including R_y, r, the average effective property tax rate, and the average size of housing as measured by H. To remove all town-wide changes in these variables, let us denote the real interest rate in the base year as r^* and define

$$R_y^* = R_y' - \overline{R_y'} \tag{21.1}$$

$$H_y^* = H_y - \overline{H}_y \tag{21.2}$$

and

$$t_y^* = t_y - \bar{t}_y, \tag{21.3}$$

where the bars indicate town averages. House value purged of changes in town averages, V_y^*, can now be determined by replacing the variables on the right side of (19) with these starred variables. Substituting the result into (20) yields

$$V_y = \frac{R_y H_y}{r_y + \beta t_y} = I_y \frac{R_y^* H_y^*}{r^* + \beta t_y^*}. \tag{22a}$$

The logarithm of (22a) is

$$\ln V_y = \ln I_y + \ln \frac{R_y^* H_y^*}{r^* + \beta t_y^*}. \tag{22b}$$

This equation clearly separates the town average price, $\ln I_y$, from the characteristics of an individual house, which are expressed as deviations from town averages. Furthermore, an average is not correlated with deviations around that average, so these two terms are not correlated. This lack of correlation implies that one can obtain unbiased estimates of a price index from (22b) even if one excludes all house-specific explanatory variables from the equation.

A method for estimating a price index with double-sales data has been developed by Baily, Muth and Nourse (1963). This method, which is based on a series of time dummy variables, leads to a price index in exactly the form our analysis requires. The details of this estimating procedure and of the resulting price indexes are presented in Appendix B.

Once a price index has been estimated for each town, we can deflate house values and state the capitalization equation in terms of V_y^*, instead of V_y. Dividing both sides of (22a) by I_y yields

$$V_y^* = \frac{R_y^* H_y^*}{r^* + \beta t_y^*}. \tag{23}$$

With sales in two years, S and F, the steps that lead from Equations (16) to Equation (17) allow us to express (23) in change form. These steps assume that R_y^* and H_y^* do not change. We eliminate this assumption in Section 4.5. The "deflated" capitalization equation in change form is

$$\frac{\Delta V^*}{V_F^*} = \frac{-\beta(\Delta t^*)}{r^* + \beta t_S^*} \tag{24}$$

As explained earlier, our study design takes advantage of the large changes in relative effective tax rates caused by revaluation; that is, it estimates tax capitalization in the sample of observations that straddle revaluation. The average house price, however, is determined by all sales, not just sales for observations that straddle revaluation. Hence, the price indexes are estimated using the sample of straddling as well as nonstraddling observations.

4.3 Mortgage Transactions and Federal Income Taxes

Virtually all houses are purchased with mortgages. In this section we explain our assumptions about mortgage transactions. In addition, the present value of a house is affected by federal income taxes in two ways. First, the real opportunity cost of investing in housing, r, reflects the income tax that must be paid on interest income. Second, homeowners can deduct property taxes and mortgage interest in calculating their federal income taxes. These deductions lower the burden of property taxes and interest payments on the homeowner. In this section, we explain how these deductions affect our analysis.

The present value of a mortgage transaction has three visible components: the mortgage itself, which is received by the household when the house is purchased; the stream of monthly payments by the household to the lender; and the stream of income tax deductions for the interest component of the mortgage payments. In addition, most mortgages have several less visible features that are valuable to a household. During our sample period, most mortgages were fixed-rate mortgages with prepayment clauses. These mortgages insured households to some degree against interest rate changes and house value declines. For homeowners who already hold a mortgage, interest rate increases do not lead to mortgage payment increases, whereas interest rate declines can, through prepayment, lead to mortgage payment declines. Similarly, a household whose house value drops below its mortgage amount can minimize its losses by defaulting on its mortgage. The market value of a house purchased with a mortgage reflects the present value of these hidden mortgage features as well as the present value of the visible ones.

During the sample period, mortgage rates in the Boston area ranged from 5.5% in 1965 to 9.0% in 1975. Nevertheless, the gap between this mortgage rate and the after-tax 10-year Treasury bond rate always fell between 2.1 and 2.6 percentage points.[23] A reasonable interpretation of this gap, but one we cannot prove, is that it reflects the value of prepayment and default options, insurance against interest rate increases, and interest deductions. On the basis of this interpretation, we assume that there is no net gain or cost from taking out a mortgage. In other words, the present value of a mortgage transaction, discounted at the after-tax 10-year Treasury bond rate, equals zero.[24] This assumption allows us to ignore mortgage rates and interest deductions in our capitalization equation.

Two other income tax effects must be considered. First, the real opportunity cost of investing in housing is the return one could earn after taxes on an alternative investment with similar characteristics. Let s stand for a household's marginal income tax rate. The r^* should be replaced by $r^*(1 - s)$ in the denominator of (24).

Second, a household can deduct its entire property tax payment, tV, from its federal taxable income. The value of this deduction is stV. Both property tax payments and their associated income tax deductions affect the market value of a house. In Equation (2b), therefore, the correct property tax expression is $(1 - s)tV$. If households do not expect their property taxes to remain constant, presumably they also do not expect their associated income tax deductions to remain constant.[25] It makes sense, therefore, to assume that the income tax deductions, like the tax payments themselves, are capitalized into house values at a rate β. In Equation (11), the correct property tax expression is $(1 - s)\beta tV$ and in Equation (24), βt must be multiplied by $(1 - s)$ in both the numerator and the denominator.

Combining these two tax effects yields

$$\frac{\Delta V^*}{V_F^*} = \frac{-\beta(1 - s)(\Delta t^*)}{r^*(1 - s) + \beta(1 - s)t_S^*} = \frac{-\beta(\Delta t^*)}{r^* + \beta t_S^*} \qquad (25)$$

Thus, the $(1 - s)$ term cancels out. Based on the assumptions presented here, which appear reasonable to us, mortgages and income taxes drop out of the capitalization equation.

4.4   Anticipation of Revaluation

As the case histories in Chapter 4 make clear, revaluation inevitably is accompanied by a great deal of publicity. Not only do house buyers know a year or two ahead of time that revaluation is going to take place, in most cases they also know their new assessed values several months before revaluation actually takes effect, that is, before the new tax bills are mailed out. To some degree, therefore, revaluation is likely to be anticipated and tax changes may be capitalized before they officially take effect.

At the time of revaluation, buyers know the difference between a given house's effective tax rate and the average tax rate in the jurisdiction. Since revaluation is supposed to bring all houses to the same effective tax rate, it is reasonable to suppose that buyers anticipate a shift to the average tax rate. When revaluation is fully anticipated, therefore, the first sale price reflects $\bar{t}_F$, not t_F; compared to Equation (23), in other words, anticipation raises a house's first-sale market value by

$$\frac{\beta(t_F - \bar{t}_F)}{r^* + \beta t_S^*} = \frac{\beta t_F^*}{r^* + \beta t_S^*}. \qquad (26)$$

Anticipation may not be complete, however, particularly after revaluation is announced but before the new tax bills are mailed out. Hence, let us
define two anticipation dummy variables:

DA0 = 1 if the first sale is after the new assessed values are announced but
before the new tax bills are sent out

= 0 otherwise

DA1 = 1 if the first sale is in the year before the new assessed values are
announced

= 0 otherwise.

To estimate the degree of anticipation in each of these time periods, we
interact each dummy variable with the impact of complete anticipation
given by Equation (26) to obtain

$$\frac{(DA0)(t_F^*)}{r^* + \beta t_S^*} \tag{27.1}$$

$$\frac{(DA1)(t_F^*)}{r^* + \beta t_S^*} \tag{27.2}$$

The coefficient of the first variable can be interpreted as $-\lambda_0 \beta$, where λ_0 is the
degree of anticipation in the period defined by DA0. The coefficient of the
second variable is $-\lambda_1 \beta$.

As explained in Section 2.3, a similar anticipation process could
operate even before revaluation is announced, and, as expressed in Equation
(15), could lead to capitalization below 100%. We cannot estimate the impact of this earlier anticipation on the degree of capitalization, however,
because we cannot separate its impact from the impacts of imperfect information and high search costs. Nevertheless, the results for the above anticipation variables may indicate whether earlier anticipation is likely. If tax
changes are anticipated once revaluation is announced, then it is plausible to
argue that they are anticipated to some degree when revaluation is simply
under discussion.

4.5 Changes in Relative Housing Prices and in Housing Characteristics

So far we have focused on changes in the effective tax rate. We also have
accounted for changes in other variables that affect all houses equally. It is
clear, however, that the housing and neighborhood characteristics of a single
house or the market valuation of these characteristics can also change rela-

tive to other houses. If these changes are not correlated with changes in the tax variables, then leaving them out of our regressions will not bias our results. Even in this case, however, accounting for intrajurisdictional changes in R^* and H^* will increase the explanatory power of our regressions and thereby increase the precision of our estimates of tax capitalization. As explained earlier, our study design minimizes the correlation between housing characteristics and property taxes, but we cannot be certain that changes in R^* and H^* are not correlated with changes in effective tax rates. Including these changes will therefore provide insurance against left-out-variable bias.

The numerator of (23) can change in three ways. Over time, houses in certain locations may become relatively more valuable; that is, their relative rent per unit of housing services, R^*, may rise. Second, the relative market valuation of certain housing characteristics may change over time; that is, the housing services, H^*, in a particular house (as measured by the market) may change. Finally, houses may be renovated or receive additions and thereby undergo a direct change in their quantity of housing services.

To account for these factors, let us add S and F subscripts to R and H. Deflated house values in the first and second years are now:

$$V_F^* = \frac{R_F^* H_F^*}{r^* + \beta t_F^*} = \frac{R_F^* H_F^*}{D_F} \tag{28.1}$$

$$V_S^* = \frac{R_S^* H_S^*}{r^* + \beta t_S^*} = \frac{R_S^* H_S^*}{D_S}, \tag{28.2}$$

and the percentage change in deflated house value is:

$$\frac{V_S^* - V_F^*}{V_F^*} = \frac{\dfrac{(R_S^* H_S^*)(D_F) - (R_F^* H_F^*)(D_S)}{(D_S)(D_F)}}{\dfrac{R_F^* H_F^*}{D_F}}$$

$$= \frac{(R_S^* H_S^*/R_F^* H_F^*)D_F - D_S}{D_S} = \frac{R_S^* H_S^*}{R_F^* H_F^*}\frac{D_F}{D_S} - 1$$

$$= \left(1 + \frac{d(R^* H^*)}{R_F H_F}\right)\left(\frac{D_F}{D_S}\right) - 1$$

$$= \left(1 + \frac{dR^*}{R_F^*} + \frac{dH^*}{H_F^*}\right)\left(\frac{D_F}{D_S}\right) - 1. \tag{29}$$

We do not observe R^* and H^* directly, so we approximate their role in (29) using housing and neighborhood characteristics. The rental price of housing services is a function of neighborhood characteristics, L, and housing services are a function of housing characteristics, Q. The functions R and H may change over time. Let y indicate year and dy indicate a change in time. For a change from the first-sale year to the second-sale year, $dy = S - F$. Now assuming that relative to town-wide averages the rental values of houses in certain neighborhoods change at a steady annual rate, $\partial R^*/\partial y$, and that the housing services index for houses with certain structural characteristics changes at a steady annual rate, $\partial H^*/\partial y$, then we can write:

$$\frac{dR^*}{R_F^*} = \frac{\partial R^*}{\partial y} \frac{dy}{R_F^*} \qquad (30.1)$$

and

$$\frac{dH^*}{H_F^*} = \frac{\partial H^*}{\partial y} \frac{dy}{H_F^*} + \frac{\partial H^*}{\partial Q} \frac{dQ}{H_F^*} \qquad (30.2)$$

Now $dy = (S - F)$; $\partial R^*/\partial y$ is a function of L; $\partial H^*/\partial y$ is a function of Q; and dQ reflects additions of renovations. Let ADD_k be a dummy variable for an addition or renovation of type k. Then with simple linear forms we can write

$$\frac{dR^*}{R_F^*} = \sum_i \delta_i(S - F)L_i \qquad (31.1)$$

$$\frac{\partial H^*}{\partial y} \frac{dy}{H_F^*} = \sum_j \zeta_j(S - F)Q_j \qquad (31.2)$$

$$\frac{\partial H^*}{\partial X} \frac{dX}{H_F^*} = \sum_k \xi_k \text{ADD}_k. \qquad (31.3)$$

Equations $(31.1) - (31.3)$ specify changes in R^* and H^* as a function of observable variables. Substituting these equations into (29), through (30), yields an equation for $\Delta V^*/V_F^*$ that accounts for changes in R^* and H^* and that can be estimated.

4.6   Correcting for Simultaneity

As many of the studies reviewed in Chapter 2 pointed out, house values and property tax rates are simultaneously determined. Within a jurisdiction this simultaneity takes two forms. First, assessors consider house values in setting assessed values and hence property taxes. Second, house value is the denominator of the effective tax rate and thereby influences t by definition. Estimates of β that do not recognize this simultaneity may be subject to severe simultaneous equations bias.

If the tax variable is based on tax payments, as in Equation (15), then the positive behavioral link between T and V adds a positive bias to $-\beta$ and could make it positive. If the tax variable is based on the tax rate, on the other hand, the positive behavioral link between T and V and the negative definitional link between V and t work in opposite directions, and the simultaneity bias is not likely to be as severe. Nevertheless, we suspect that the negative definitional link probably dominates, thereby biasing $-\beta$ downward, that is, biasing upward the estimated degree of capitalization.

In a model of house value and tax rate changes, these two types of simultaneity are present in a particular form. Relative changes in house values may be reflected in assessors' new assessments and these changes automatically alter the denominator of the effective tax rate expression. Note, however, that a random error in $\Delta V^*/V_F^*$ cannot alter a house's starting point, that is, its characteristics at first sale. In other words, the first-sale effective tax rate is not endogenous. To eliminate simultaneity, therefore, we need only consider the link between $\Delta V^*/V_F^*$ and the second-sale tax rate, t_S, which is one element of t_S^* and dt^*.

Our ability to model the determinants of the second-sale tax rate is greatly aided by the context of this study, namely revaluation. The basic point of revaluation is for the assessor to bring all houses to the same assessment-sales ratio and hence to the same effective tax rate. Suppose that the target ratio is K and that the assessor meets this target for all houses in the revaluation year. (We will relax the latter assumption shortly.) Then we can write

$$\frac{A_{Re}}{V_{Re}} = K \tag{32}$$

for all houses, where the subscript "Re" stands for the year in which revaluation was carried out. Furthermore, in the communities we are examining, assessed values are set at revaluation and not updated, unless the house either undergoes a major renovation or receives an addition; both of these possibilities have been accounted for in the previous section.

Thus, second-sale assessments equal assessments at revaluations, or

$$A_S = KV_{Re}. \tag{33}$$

To find the second-sale effective tax rate, one must also know the second-sale price, which is defined as

$$V_S = V_F \frac{I_S}{I_F} \frac{V_S^*}{V_F^*}. \tag{34}$$

Thus,

$$t_S = m_S \frac{A_S}{V_S} = \frac{m_S K V_{Re}}{V_F \dfrac{I_S}{I_F} \dfrac{V_S^*}{V_F^*}}, \tag{35}$$

where m_S is the nominal tax rate at second sale.

The problem here is that V_{Re} is not observed. In order to estimate V_{Re}, let us assume that the annual relative growth rate in house value is constant for each house. In symbols,

$$V_S^* = V_F^* (1 + g)^{S-F}. \tag{36}$$

Hence, the annual growth rate is a function of observed sales prices; that is,

$$g = \left(\frac{V_S^*}{V_F^*}\right)^{1/(S-F)} - 1. \tag{37}$$

From this expression, it follows that

$$V_{Re} = V_F \frac{I_{Re}}{I_F} (1 + g)^{Re-F}$$

$$= V_F \frac{I_{Re}}{I_F} \left(\frac{V_S^*}{V_F^*}\right)^{(Re-F)/(S-F)}. \tag{38}$$

Substituting this expression into (37) yields

$$t_S = K m_S \frac{I_{Re}}{I_S} \left(\frac{V_S^*}{V_F^*}\right)^{-(S-Re)/(S-F)}$$

$$= K m_S \frac{I_{Re}}{I_S} \left(1 + \frac{dV^*}{V_F^*}\right)^{-(S-Re)/(S-F)}. \tag{39}$$

Equation (39) explains the second-sale effective tax rate based on assessor behavior. Furthermore, it identifies the key exogenous factors that influence t_S, namely m_S and I_{Re}/I_S. These two factors affect t_S in a multiplicative fashion. To correct for simultaneity, therefore, the product of m_S and I_{Re}/I_S is an essential instrument for estimating a linear or nonlinear simultaneous equations procedure.

The assumption that the assessor succeeds in setting a constant K is a strong one. In fact, of course, assessors are not so accurate. To the extent that variation in K is systematically related to observable housing characteristics, we can identify additional instruments to improve the performance of our simultaneous equations procedure.[26]

In the jurisdictions in our sample, assessors relied heavily on the replacement-cost method. This method is best at measuring the value of easily reproduced housing characteristics, such as rooms or square feet, but is not likely to be so good at estimating those characteristics associated with style or location. For example, the market value of old houses may bear little relation to their replacement cost. Furthermore, changes in the relative cost of energy may have altered the value of energy-related housing characteristics.

We determine the systematic component of variation in K by drawing on the sample of nonstraddling double sales. In particular, the first sales of post-revaluation nonstraddling double sales occur soon after revaluation and reflect the assessor's attempts to set K. Because these sales are not included in our tax-capitalization regressions, we can employ them to examine the determinants of K without contaminating our estimates of capitalization. Thus, our approach is to use this subsample to search for the systematic component of variation in K, with guidance from the above theory. This is, we regress actual assessment – sales ratios (with the denominator deflated back to the revaluation year) on housing characteristics. Any significant variables are included in a final vector, Z, of variables that influence K. Because not all the sales are exactly at revaluation and because housing characteristics tend to be highly collinear, we use a fairly weak test of significance, namely a t-statistic greater than unity.

In symbols, let Z be the vector of housing and neighborhood characteristics that influences K and let δ be the vector of their coefficients. Then the above procedure yields:

$$K = K' + \delta Z \qquad (40)$$

Substituting this equation into (39) yields:

$$t_S = (K' + \delta Z)\left(m_S \frac{I_{Re}}{I_S}\right)\left(\frac{V_S^*}{V_F^*}\right)^{-(S-Re)/(S-F)} \qquad (41)$$

Thus, all the housing and neighborhood characteristics in Z, interacted with $m_S(I_{Re}/I_S)$, also appear as instruments in our simultaneous equations procedures.

5. SUMMARY

Because assessed values had not been updated for so long, the town-wide reassessments in Massachusetts in the early 1970s led to large and varied changes in effective tax rates within towns. Our study takes advantage of these circumstances to obtain a precise estimate of the degree of property tax capitalization. We collect data on houses that sold twice, once before and once after revaluation. Then we determine the extent to which changes in effective tax rates, relative to the town average, lead to changes in house values, relative to the town average.

Our estimating equation carefully accounts for many factors that have proved troublesome in previous studies. We account for the simultaneity between house values and property tax rates by employing a model of assessor behavior to identify the instruments for a simultaneous equations procedure. We avoid left-out-variable bias by using the effective property tax rate as our tax variable and by making use of an extensive set of controls for housing and neighborhood characteristics. We avoid misspecification in our functional form by basing our estimating equation on well-known models of asset-pricing. And we minimize the arbitrariness of our discount-rate assumption by bringing in an outside estimate of households' expected rate of inflation.

We also deal with several methodological problems that are unique to our approach. To focus on intrajurisdictional property tax capitalization, we estimate town-specific housing price indexes and use them to remove all changes in town average house values. We model the effect on house values of mortgage contracts and of federal income tax deductions for property taxes and mortgage interest. And we incorporate into our analysis the possibility that revaluation is anticipated.

The result of all these steps is an estimating equation that can provide an accurate and precise estimate of the degree of intrajurisdictional property tax capitalization in Massachusetts.

NOTES

[1] These data also provide an immediate improvement upon the approach of Wicks, Little and Beck (1968) and of Smith (1970), who must estimate post-revaluation sales prices.

[2] The asset-pricing model is discussed in any finance text. See for example, Copeland and Weston (1983). The income method of property assessment is discussed in appraisal texts. See for example Hines (1981).

[3] Please note the change in notation from Chapter 2; R now denotes rental value per unit of housing services.

[4] A more general assumption would be to say that total rental value is a function of both structural and neighborhood characteristics. Our analysis could be carried out with this assumption and with no change in our results; our assumption is intended to highlight the distinct roles played by structural and neighborhood characteristics.

[5] A household receives rental services until the year of resale and is paid by the next buyer for the rental services in all the years after resale. As long as buyer and seller have the same discount rate, resale therefore has no effect on Equation (2b). As we will see in the derivation of Equation (5), one can incorporate steady rent and value growth into Equation (2b). Such growth does not alter this result. This result would change if a household had to pay a capital gains tax

on housing appreciation, but as long as capital gains are reinvested in housing, no such tax is due.

[6] The closeness of the approximation depends on i and on N. Here are some examples (with i and i' in percent):

i	N	i'
3.0	40	4.3262
3.0	100	3.1647
6.0	40	6.6462
6.0	100	6.0177

[7] Equation (3) can be used to introduce a finite expected lifetime into Equation (5); simply replace r with r'. Regardless of the expected lifetime, the real interest rate must be positive, that is i must be greater than π, for Equation (5) to apply.

[8] Formally, $\pi = p + a$, where p is general price inflation and a is the rate of change in housing prices above inflation. In addition, uV_y must be added, where u is expected housing upkeep or maintenance expenditure as a fraction of V_y to the model. Thus, $r - (p + a - u)$ appears in denominator of (5). We assume that $a = u$.

[9] In deriving Equation (5), we assume that investors expect the effective property tax rate to remain constant. We weaken this assumption in the next section. In order to make Equation (2b) equivalent to Equation (5), we assume that investors expect their tax payment to grow at the same rate as their rent (and their house value). A different assumption, such as no expected growth in tax payment, would lead to a different result.

[10] Because the household does not literally determine E and t, a community budget constraint does not belong in this problem. Voters' decisions about E and t are influenced by wealth and cost considerations, but households searching for housing care only about the outcome of voting, as indicated by E and t. See Yinger (1982).

[11] The bid function that satisfies (7) is analogous to the "price-distance" function in a mathematical urban model (Mills (1967), Muth (1969), and Mills and Hamilton (1984)), which shows that households bid more per unit of housing in locations that are close to employment centers. Several authors (Polinsky and Shavell (1974), Yinger (1976), Polinsky and Rubinfeld (1977)) have extended this analysis to neighborhood amenities, such as clean air. The unifying point in this work is that households have an incentive to move unless housing prices exactly reflect household valuations of the characteristics of different locations. Note, however, that the effect of property taxes on bid functions, unlike the effect of amenities or distance to employment, does not depend on the form of household utility functions; property taxes are already in dollars and affect every household's bids in the same way.

[12] The capitalization of E and L into house values could also be derived. This derivation, unlike the derivation of (9), requires an assumption about the form of the household utility function. See Yinger (1982).

[13] Although the bid for a given house is the same whether a household looks at tax rates or tax payments, the demand for housing services is different for these two alternatives. If a household focuses on tax payments, then property taxes simply have an income effect; they lower the consumption of housing services as much as an equal drop in income. If the household focuses on tax rates, on the other hand, property taxes have a price effect as well. As the budget constraint in (6) makes clear, they raise the price per unit of housing services and therefore cause substitution away from housing. Our estimating procedure is valid whether or not taxes

have price effects, but as discussed in Chapter 7, this issue could be important in analyzing the efficiency consequences of the property tax.

[14] These three reasons are not new. Indeed, they are all expressed, in one form or another, in Seligman (1932). A fourth reason, the federal income tax deduction for property tax payments, might apply to many studies but, as shown in Section 4.3, is not relevant for our study.

[15] The standard errors-in-variables result carries over to a multivariate linear problem if the other variables are not measured with error, but the direction of the effect is not known if more than one explanatory variable has measurement error. See Fomby et al. (1984), p. 276.

[16] A similar argument, based on somewhat stronger assumptions, can be found in Ihlanfeldt and Jackson (1982). Suppose the housing market is divided into submarkets which are imperfect substitutes for each other and suppose that the property tax rate varies systematically by submarket. In this case, the logic of the property tax is just like the logic of a selective sales tax. An increase in the tax rate in a submarket leads to a downward shift in the demand curve for housing there, but unless the supply of housing is fixed, the drop in the market price of housing is less than the drop in the demand curve. We regard these assumptions as too strong for the Massachusetts case because the assessment errors are essentially random; even if there were housing submarkets, the average effective property tax rate would be approximately the same in all of them.

[17] Edel and Sclar (1974) and Hamilton (1976b) have gone so far as to argue that supply responses will eliminate the capitalization of property tax differences across communities in the long run. As Yinger (1982) explains, however, this argument ignores the fact that a community has fixed boundaries, so the supply curve within a community cannot be horizontal. Once all available land is used up, tax capitalization, which is a condition for equilibrium in household location, will once again arise.

[18] More formally, house buyers are uncertain how long tax differentials will persist. The assumption that they expect differentials to persist N' years is equivalent to the assumptions that they are risk neutral and that N' is the expected value of possible outcomes for tax-differential persistence.

[19] For more on the court cases, see Paul (1975). The City of Boston was exceptionally slow to revalue. As documented by several studies (Oldman and Aaron (1965), Engle (1975), Avault et al. (1979)), the effective tax rate in Boston was much higher on commercial and industrial property than on residential property. Any shift to full value assessment, therefore, would have yielded the politically unacceptable result of a large increase in taxes on voters. Boston was finally moved to revalue its property with the carrot of tax classification and the stick of Proposition 2 1/2. Tax classification was a carrot because it allowed the city to set higher nominal tax rates on commercial and industrial property and therefore to avoid large increases in residential taxes. Proposition 2 1/2 was a stick because, after a few years of transition, it limited the City's property tax revenue to 2 1/2% of the market value of its property. Without a revaluation, any estimate of the market value of property would have been based on poor information and would undoubtedly have been too low, thereby directly limiting the City's revenue. So in 1983, Boston finally revalued its property. For more on this history, see Avault et al. (1979).

[20] The most common assessment method used by these firms was the replacement-cost method. In a town with many house sales, this method is not as accurate as a regression-based approach, and sometimes yielded marginally acceptable results. Schafer (1977) studied the 1974 revaluation in Newton, a large suburb of Boston which is similar to some of the towns in our sample. The firm that did this revaluation relied on the replacement-cost method. Schafer found that the average assessment-sales ratio was 94%, with a standard deviation of 7.6 percentage points. Thus, the coefficient of dispersion, a standard measure of assessment accuracy, was

7.6/94 = 8.1%, which is somewhat above the 5% target usually considered acceptable for residential assessments.

[21] Community populations and sample sizes, for both straddling and nonstraddling double sales, are provided in Chapter 4.

[22] The most natural alternative to our derivation is to differentiate Equation (16.1) and substitute the first-sale tax rate into the resulting derivative. This approach corresponds to a Taylor series expansion evaluated at the first-sale values. The result is the same as Equation (17) except that the first-sale tax rate is in the denominator. Although this approach appears natural, the first- and second-sale tax rates may differ substantially, so it may provide a very poor approximation to the exact result, Equation (17).

[23] Mortgage rate information was obtained from the Federal Home Loan Bank Board. A typical marginal income tax rate over the sample period was 20%, so after-tax returns were estimated by multiplying the 10-year Treasury bond rate by 0.8. A similar result is obtained using the rate of return on high-grade municipals, which is already an after-tax rate.

[24] A similar assumption is discussed by Hendershott and Ling (1986). With the mortgage rate assumed to be equal to r, the mortgage involves an initial payment to the household, $(1 - q)V$, where q is the down payment percentage. The annual payment is $r(1 - q)V/[1 - (1 + r)^{-N}]$, where N is the length of the mortgage. The present value of this payment stream equals $(1 - q)V$ and therefore exactly offsets the original payment.

[25] In addition, poor information about relative property tax rates can reasonably be assumed to imply poor information about relative property tax deductions.

[26] Remember the study of Newton cited in footnote 20. Schafer found that the post-revaluation assessment-sales ratio had a standard deviation of 7.6 percentage points, which indicates a fair amount of divergence from a constant K.

4

Sample Communities, Data Sources, and Revaluation Histories

To take advantage of the quasi-experiment generated by revaluation, we collected data on paired sales of single-family houses, one sale before and one sale after revaluation, in seven Massachusetts communities. In this chapter, we explain our criteria for selecting communities, describe the seven communities in our sample, list the sources of our double-sales data, and recount assessment procedures and revaluation histories in the sample communities.

1. COMMUNITY SELECTION

As explained in Chapter 3, the degree of property tax capitalization need not be the same in all communities. Our general sample-selection objective, therefore, is to obtain a diverse set of communities that allows us to determine whether or not the degree of capitalization varies with community characteristics. Our specific sample-selection criteria combine this general objective with the requirements of our study design and the availability of data.

Our selection was based on five criteria. First, the community obviously must have revalued. Second, to assure that a sufficient number of house sales could be observed after revaluation, the community must have revalued before 1975. In combination, these two criteria rule out most large cities in Massachusetts. Brockton, with a 1975 population of 95,688, was the largest city to revalue before 1980. Third, data on house sales in the community must be available. As explained below, we had access to three main data sources: the Metropolitan Mortgage Bureau (MMB), the Massachusetts Department of Revenue, and a computer tape based on data obtained from the MMB by Professor Jerome Rothenberg of M.I.T. These data sources covered different jurisdictions for different periods, thereby limiting our options considerably. Fourth, the community must have sufficient turnover of single-family houses to yield an adequate sample of double sales. Finally, the sample of communities should be as diverse as possible given the other four criteria.

On the basis of these criteria, we selected seven Massachusetts communities: Arlington, Barnstable, Belmont, Brookline, Brockton, Waltham, and Wellesley.

2. DESCRIPTION OF THE SAMPLE COMMUNITIES

The communities range from the high-income suburban town of Wellesley to the industrial cities of Waltham and Brockton and the Cape Cod resort town of Barnstable. Table 4-1 shows the variation across the seven commu-

Table 4-1
Characteristics of the Sample Communities

Town	Year of Revaluation	Population[a]	Median Income[b] Families & Individuals	Families	Equalized Tax Rate[c]	No. of Single Family Houses[d]	Rental Units/ Total Units[e]
Arlington	1969	50,223	$10,767	$12,247	48.40	7,904	.42
Barnstable	1973	26,699	7,609	9,738	16.64[f]	11,024	.22
Belmont	1968	27,660	11,578	13,559	36.00	4,443	.36
Brockton	1974	95,688	8,764	10,377	59.10	15,584	.43
Brookline	1968	53,150	7,674	13,701	56.10	4,984	.73
Waltham	1971	56,757	8,544	11,523	42.00	7,552	.52
Wellesley	1967	26,593	11,794	19,401	35.00	7,108	.19

[a] 1975 State Census.
[b] U.S. Census of Population 1970, *General Social and Economic Characteristics*.
[c] Dollars per thousand dollars of estimated market value, 1977.
[d] Single family tax parcels as of January 1, 1975 reported in the Commonwealth of Massachusetts, Department of Corporations and Taxation, *1976 Equalized Valuations of Massachusetts Cities and Towns*.
[e] U.S. Census of Housing 1970, *General Housing Characteristics*.
[f] Excludes fire district rates.

nities in population, income, property-tax rate, number of single-family houses, and proportion of renter households. All of the communities except Barnstable and Brockton are in the Boston metropolitan area.

Wellesley, with a 1969 median family income of $19,401, is one of the wealthiest communities in the state. Belmont, which also has a relatively high income, differs from Wellesley in that it is closer to Boston, has a higher proportion of rental housing units, and an older housing stock. Brookline, another old inner suburb of Boston, has an unusual mixture of large, expensive houses and a high proportion of rental property. Its high equalized tax rate reflects both its housing mix and its high level of public services. Arlington, a middle-income, working-class community with moderately priced houses, has about the same population as Brookline but many more single-family houses and less rental property.

Waltham, which is located 9 miles from Boston and close to Boston's circumferential highway, Route 128, is an industrial city. Its population mix and housing stock are typical of a manufacturing city with a relatively stable population. Brockton, the central city of its own metropolitan area has been described as a dying mill town. In spite of this image, however, Brockton was one of the fastest growing cities in New England during the 1960s; its relatively cheap housing attracted both workers in southeastern Massachusetts and commuters to Boston.

The Cape Cod town of Barnstable is primarily a summer resort. One of its seven villages, Hyannis, is the business center for the entire Cape. Barnstable's booming housing market, relatively low effective tax rate, and non-Boston area location place it in sharp contrast to the other communities in this study.

3. DATA SOURCES

Our three major data sources for sales and assessment information are (1) monthly reports submitted by local assessors to the Massachusetts Department of Revenue (formerly, Massachusetts Department of Corporations and Taxation) for the purposes of its biennial equalization study, (2) property transaction records from 1946 to the present in 45 Boston area communities kept by the Metropolitan Mortgage Bureau (MMB), and (3) the Rothenberg tape. This tape includes information on all double sales from 1946 to 1970 for the 45 communities in the MMB region. Because M.I.T. researchers gathered this data directly from the MMB in the early 1970s, the availability of the tape significantly reduced our direct data-gathering effort. These sources were supplemented where necessary with data from the Real Estate Transfer Directory, which includes sales data but no assessed values, and

Table 4-2
Data Sources: Year and Purposes for Which Each Source Was Used by Community

Town	Massachusetts Department of Revenue	Metropolitan Mortgage Bureau	Rothenberg Tape	Local Assessor	Real Estate Transfer Directory
Arlington	All Sales 1971–1974 (except July–Dec. 1973)	First sale of double sales straddling 1970	Double sales 1960–1970	Sales, assessed values, July–Dec., 1973	—
Barnstable	All Sales 1969–1977 (except April–Dec. 1973)	—	—	Some assessed values	All sales April–Dec. 1973
Belmont	All Sales 1971–1973	First sale of double sales straddling 1970	Double sales 1960–1970	Some assessed values	—
Brockton	All Sales* 1969 1972–1977	—	—	Assessed values 1971	All sales 1971
Brookline	—	Double sales ending in 1971–1973	Double sales 1960–1970	Some assessed values	—
Waltham	All Sales 1971–1976 (except Nov.–Dec. 1972 and Sept.–Dec. 1973	First sale of double sales straddling 1970	Double sales 1960–1970	Some assessed values	Sales, Nov.–Dec. 1972 and Sept.–Dec. 1973
Wellesley	—	Double sales ending in 1971–1972	Double sales 1960–1970	—	—

* 1970 data for Brockton are unavailable.

with information from local assessors. A more detailed discussion of these data sources is provided in Appendix A.

Table 4-2 lists the data sources we used for each sample community. We decided to minimize our data collection at the Metropolitan Mortgage Bureau because of the daily charge, restrictions placed on the time we could spend there, and reports that the quality of MMB data declined after 1973.[1] Consequently, we relied heavily on the Massachusetts Department of Revenue for data after 1973, on the Metropolitan Mortgage Bureau for data in intermediate years, and on the Rothenberg tape for the data in the 1960s.

Although we have merged data from many sources, it should be noted that all sales information ultimately came from the same source, namely, the Registry of Deeds. In addition, all assessed values ultimately came from local assessors. As elaborated in Appendix A, we carefully checked the data and made every possible effort to cross-check data sources against each other.

The final sample sizes for each community are summarized in Table 4-3. The differences between the sample sizes for the price index and capitalization equations reflect deletion from the capitalization equations of double sales with incomplete assessment informaion or double sales that did not straddle revaluation. Based on sample sizes alone, our results for Arlington, Brockton, and Waltham should be the most reliable.

For two communities, Waltham and Brockton, we also gathered detailed data on housing and neighborhood characteristics. With cooperation from the Waltham assessors, we determined the characteristics of all the houses in our Waltham sample. In Brockton, we identified the characteristics of houses with double sales that straddled revaluation.

In addition, we obtained some information on the location of houses in our Barnstable sample, largely because tax rates in Barnstable vary by fire district. These housing and neighborhood characteristics are listed in Table 4-4 and described more fully in Appendix A.

Table 4-3
Sample Sizes by Community and Model

Town	Price Index Equation	Capitalization Equations
Arlington	483	313
Barnstable	202	103
Belmont	192	111
Brockton	545	282[a]
Brookline	264	142
Waltham	599	353
Wellesley	424	175

[a] The sample size with complete housing characteristics is 196.

Table 4-4
Housing and Neighborhood Characteristics

	Available In		
Housing Characteristics	Waltham	Brockton	Barnstable
Age	x	x	
Floor area	x	x	
Rooms	x	x	
Bedrooms	x	x	
Type of exterior	x	x	
Hardwood floors	x	x	
Number of fireplaces	x	x	
Number of baths	x	x	
Area of garage	x	x	
Lot size	x	x	
Assessor's quality rating		x	
Additions and Renovations			
Major additions	x		
Bath or kitchen renovation	x		
New garage	x		
Minor additions or renovations	x		
Land purchase	x		
New pool	x		
Neighborhood Characteristics			
Median years of school completed in census tract	x	x	
Percent of persons in same house in 1965 and 1970 in census tract	x	x	
School district	x	x	
Fire district			x

4. REVALUATION HISTORIES

In addition to collecting double sales data, we inquired about assessment procedures and the revaluation process in each sample community. We paid particular attention to timing: When did residents first become aware that 100% assessment was to be implemented? When were the new valuation notices first made public? When were the first post-revaluation tax bills mailed to taxpayers? In two communities, Waltham and Brockton, we investigated assessment procedures and the history of revaluation in some detail.

4.1 Overview

For communities other than Brockton, the new valuation notices were mailed in late spring or early summer and the new tax bills were mailed in late summer or early fall. This timing, which gave residents three to four months to appeal their new valuations, reflects Massachusetts communities' calendar-year budgetary period prior to 1974. The late-summer tax bills were based on property assessments for January 1 and on a state-certified property tax rate for the calendar year. In Waltham, the new assessments were publicized somewhat earlier than in the other communities, namely in February of the revaluation year.

Brockton's 1974 revaluation occurred during the switch by all Massachusetts communities to a new fiscal year, July 1 to June 30. This switch necessitated a six-month budgetary and tax period covering January to June 1974. Notices for the new property valuations in Brockton were mailed in January 1974. The first post-revaluation tax bills covered the six-month transitional period and were mailed in July 1974. Taxpayers received a second tax bill in December 1974 for the 1975 fiscal year. In their records, the Brockton assessors listed the new rather than the old assessments for all sales during the six-month transitional period. This practice contrasts with the record keeping in other communities, in which new assessments were not listed until the new tax bills were sent out.

The standard assessment procedures in our sample communities involve relatively little updating of assessments between jurisdiction-wide revaluations. In most cases, reassessment occurs only after major renovations, such as additions, new bathrooms, or kitchen remodeling. As a rule, communities do not reassess property upon sale, although some communities reassess parcels selling at prices substantially in excess of their assessed values. Because none of the sample communities had revalued in more than ten years, assessment – sales ratios before revaluation were low and were characterized by substantial variation across parcels. The effect of revaluation was to raise all assessments and to greatly diminish the variation in assessment-sales ratios within a community. After revaluation, assessment procedures reverted to their historical standard. None of the communities in our sample devoted the resources necessary to maintain market-value assessments after revaluation.[2]

4.2 Revaluation in Waltham[3]

The 1971 revaluation does not appear to have altered assessment procedures in Waltham. Both before and after revaluation, only a few events triggered the reassessment of residential property. Houses are reassessed on sale only when the sale price substantially exceeds the assessed value. The major causes of reassessment are renovations requiring building permits. At the time of our interviews, additions and new structures were assessed at 90% of their 1970 costs. Every few years, the assessors go on a "pool search" to locate swimming pools or additions that have been installed without permits. Previously unrecorded pools or additions are assessed when discovered and are reflected in the homeowner's next tax bill. Owners are not liable for past taxes on these pools or additions. Reassessments also occur when abatements are granted. Abatements are relatively infrequent, however, largely because the abatement procedure must be initiated by the homeowner.

Waltham's previous jurisdiction-wide revaluation took place in 1956. By 1965, residents were aware of substantial assessment imbalances between new and old houses, declining and growing neighborhoods, and residential property and the new industrial firms locating along Route 128, the Boston area's circumferential highway. The October 25, 1965 edition of the *News Tribune,* Waltham's newspaper, reported that Waltham residents were angry about the tax advantages apparently granted some firms on Route 128. During his November campaign, the successful mayoral candidate, Richard Dacey, responded to this concern with a call for property tax revaluation. Editorials in the *News Tribune* supported this position.[4] Nevertheless, no action on reassessment was taken for several years. Pressure for revaluation came to a climax in 1968 when a Waltham watch factory contested its assessment in court. Recognizing that the City might not win this case and that it might lead to abatement requests from other firms, the Mayor asked the City Council in December 1968 to fund revaluation.[5]

With only one full-time and two part-time assessors, the Waltham Assessors Office needed outside help. So the City Council, with attendant publicity in the *News Tribune,* debated a revaluation budget, solicited bids from outside firms, and, in August 1969, selected a firm to carry out the revaluation. The revaluation schedule, which was announced on the front page of the *News Tribune,* was to begin in September 1969 and end in January 1971. In fact, revaluation was completed in late 1970. The new assessments were printed in the *News Tribune* between February 15 and February 20, 1971. A public meeting was held to answer questions about the revaluation and the assessor's office received many inquiries, mostly by telephone, through the middle of March. It appears that both the Waltham assessors and homeowners believed that the assessing firm did a good job.[6] The new tax bills were mailed in late September 1971.

The publicity for revaluation was complicated by a large increase in the effective property tax rate that occurred at the same time as revaluation.[7] This increase, which was originally approved by the City Council in July 1970, was reflected in the first post-revaluation tax bills. As explained in the *News Tribune,* the nominal tax rate declined from $110.70 per $1000 of assessed value in 1970 to $42.50 per $1000 in 1971, but the impact of this decline on property tax bills was more than offset by the large increases in assessed values from revaluation.

4.3 Revaluation in Brockton[8]

Brockton's assessment procedures are similar to Waltham's. Parcels are not automatically reassessed upon resale. At the time of our interviews, Brockton's official policy was to reassess only if a house sold for more than 175% of its assessed value; in practice, however, even this rule was rarely applied. Moreover, the assessors did not automatically reassess when the selling price was below the assessed value; instead, they waited for the homeowner to apply for an abatement. Renovations receiving building permits, such as additions and new structures, were assessed at 100% of their 1974 costs. Renovations without building permits often escaped the assessor's notice for substantial periods of time. Unlike the Waltham assessors, the Brockton assessors did not engage in periodic searches for pools or additions; instead, their main source of information for this type of renovation appears to have been complaints from neighbors. Previously unrecorded renovations were taxed from the date of discovery.

Property in Brockton was reassessed in the 1930s. By the 1960s, many houses had maintained the same assessed value for decades and large and growing assessment imbalances existed between old and new houses. In 1968, some new houses in the Southfield area of Brockton were purchased by low-income households who were subsidized through the federal 235 housing program. Because these were new houses, their effective property tax rate was high relative to the average rate in the city. The combination of low incomes and a high effective tax rate induced these households to organize the Southfield Residents' Association Tax Committee and to file for property tax abatements. The Brockton Board of Assessors denied the abatement requests and the residents appealed the decision to the State Appellate Tax Board. The State Board recommended granting the abatements, but the Board of Assessors still refused to grant them. As a final step, the residents sued the City of Brockton and won. The State Superior Court ordered Brockton to revalue all property by January 1, 1971.

Despite the Court Order, the Brockton City Council dragged its feet, apparently reluctant to impose large tax increases on long-time city residents. The Superior Court threatened the city councilors with contempt and in March 1971 the Council finally appropriated money for the first stage of a three-year revaluation program. With only three full-time assessors and 26,000 parcels, Brockton hired an outside firm to carry out the revaluation. The new assessments were made public in January 1974 and the first tax bills based on them were mailed in July 1974. As noted earlier, these bills covered the six-month period from January to June. Because of the active resistance to revaluation, which continued throughout the process, the consequences of revaluation were widely understood well before these bills took effect.

5. CONCLUSIONS

Revaluation was big news in both Waltham and Brockton. Because assessed values were rarely updated and because decades had passed since the previous revaluation, effective property tax rates varied widely from one house to another. Revaluation, which is a movement to equal effective tax rates, therefore involved large tax increases for some residents and large tax decreases for others. Such large tax changes are bound to attract the attention of homeowners, city councilors, and newspaper editors. In both cities, homeowners knew that revaluation was likely several years before it actually took place. On the other hand, precise understanding of revaluation may have been hampered by the accompanying effective tax rate increase in Waltham and by the acrimonious debate in Brockton.

NOTES

[1] We received these reports from John Avault of the Boston Redevelopment Authority.

[2] At the time of our study, Brookline had plans to revalue again in the near future and to develop a regression-based technique for providing biannual revaluations. In principle, all communities were supposed to revalue every three years.

[3] The material in this section is based primarily on interviews during August 1979 with Philip Berquist, Chairman of the Waltham Board of Assessors; Frank Reed, Waltham Assessor; Lawrence Duffy, Previous Chairman of the Waltham Board of Assessors; Thomas Murphy, Editor, Waltham *News Tribune;* and real estate agents Nick Satielli and Don Bowles, and on articles in the *News Tribune* between 1965 and 1971. We are grateful to Peter Miller for gathering this information and drafting this section.

[4] One such editorial was on July 26, 1966.

[5] This request was reported in the *News Tribune* on December 4, 1968.

[6] The Chairman of The Board of Assessors expressed his approval of the assessment firm by becoming its New England Representative when he retired shortly after the revaluation was completed. Homeowners expressed their approval by not reelecting a city councillor who tried to make an issue of alleged inequities in the revaluation process.

[7] Many Massachusetts communities raised their effective property tax rates when they revalued. According to a study by Bloom and Ladd (1982), however, these tax rate increases disappeared in the few years after revaluation.

[8] The material in this section is based on interviews in the Spring of 1980 with Richard O'Flaherty, Chairman of the Brockton Board of Assessors; Melvin Pauze, Brockton Assessor; Patrick Piscatelli, a Brockton lawyer; Julia Yakavonis, previous Chairperson, Brockton Board of Assessors; and several local real estate agents; and on the Fact Sheet of the Tax Committee of the Southfield Residents' Association. The local newspaper was of limited usefulness because it lacked an index. We are grateful to Peter Miller for gathering this information and drafting this section.

5
Econometric Methodology

As the discussion in Chapter 3 makes clear, the degree of property tax capitalization cannot be estimated with ordinary least squares; the basic capitalization equation is nonlinear and the tax variable and the dependent variable are determined simultaneously. In this chapter, we describe our econometric methodology and in particular explain how we account for the nonlinearity and simultaneity in the capitalization equation. We present our results in Chapter 6.

In the three following sections, we address the question of identification in our simultaneous equations system, provide a technical discussion of Amemiya's (1974) nonlinear two-stage least squares estimating procedure, and derive a simple linear approximation for our capitalization equation. Along the way, we explain how other features of our analysis, such as anticipation of tax changes and controls for housing and neighborhood characteristics, can be incorporated into our econometric procedure.

1. IDENTIFICATION OF THE BASIC MODEL AND THE FULL MODEL

In Chapter 3, we derived a system of two simultaneous equations, Equations (3-24) and (3-39) or (3-29) and (3-41), which describe the capitalization of property taxes and the determination of the effective tax rate. In the simplest case, in which housing and neighborhood characteristics do not change between first and second sale, these equations are

$$\frac{\Delta V^*}{V_F^*} = -\frac{\beta(t_S^* - t_F^*)}{r^* + \beta t_S^*} \tag{1}$$

and

$$t_S = m_S \cdot \frac{A_S}{V_S} = n_S \cdot \frac{I_{re}}{I_S} \cdot \frac{A_{re}}{V_S} = n_S \cdot \frac{I_{re}}{I_S} \cdot Z_1 \gamma. \tag{2}$$

We call these two equations our basic model.

In the more complicated case, in which housing and neighborhood characteristics or their market values change between first and second sale, the capitalization equation (1), is replaced by

$$\frac{\Delta V^*}{V_F^*} = \left(1 + \frac{R_S H_S - R_F H_F}{R_F H_F}\right) \cdot \left(\frac{r^* + \beta t_F^*}{r^* + \beta t_S^*}\right) - 1$$

$$= (1 + Z_2(S - F)\theta) \cdot \left(\frac{r^* + \beta t_F^*}{r^* + \beta t_S^*}\right) - 1. \tag{3}$$

Equations (3) and (2) constitute our full model. In addition to the symbols introduced in Chapter 3, Z_i denotes a vector of housing and neighborhood characteristics, γ and θ are parameter vectors, and $(S - F)$ denotes the time elapsed between first and second sale. For notational simplicity, we omit the asterisks denoting the deviation from the town average in rental price, R, and housing services, H.

Both models are two-equation systems in two endogenous variables: the relative change in house values, $\Delta V^*/V_F^*$; and the relative effective tax rate at the second sale, t_S^*. Only two exogenous variables enter the capitalization equation of the basic model: the effective tax rate at the first sale, t_F^*, and the time invariant real discount rate, r^*. In the full model, interactions of housing and neighborhood characteristics and the elapsed time between first and second sale, $Z_2(S - F)$, are added to the capitalization equation as exogenous variables. Equation (2) closes both simultaneous equation systems. This equation is auxiliary because our main goal is to estimate the tax capitalization rate β in Equations (1) and (3).

A key question in both the basic and full models is whether the capitalization equation is identified, that is, whether all the parameters of the equation can be estimated with available data. The essential identification condition for any linear or nonlinear regression equation is as follows: the number of exogenous variables in the regression plus the number of additional exogenous variables that appear in other equations of the simultaneous equation system must be at least as large as the number of parameters to be estimated.[1]

In our model, the auxiliary regression, (2), contains at least one additional exogenous variable, namely m_s interacted with I_{Re}/I_S, even without housing or neighborhood variables. As a result, the basic capitalization equation, (1), which contains one parameter, is exactly identified.[2] Adding housing and neighborhood characteristics to the auxiliary regression, but not to the capitalization equation, simply strengthens this identification result. The full model also is identified. In this model, housing and neighborhood characteristics appear in the auxiliary regression and in the capitalization equation, but they are interacted with $m_s(I_{Re}/I_S)$ in the former and with $(S - F)$ in the latter. Even if the same characteristics appear in both regressions, therefore, the actual exogenous variables in the two equations are different and the capitalization equation is identified. In fact, the interaction term is not the only thing that distinguishes the housing and neighborhood variables in the two equations; as explained in Section 3-4.6, we employ a different set of housing and neighborhood characteristics in (2), which describes assessor behavior, and in (3), which describes house-value changes. These differences strengthen the identification result in the full model.

A further identification issue, which was mentioned in Chapter 2, arises in connection with the real discount rate, r^*. Because r^* is a constant, one would like to be able to estimate it, but this approach is not feasible. In the basic model,

$$\frac{\Delta V^*}{V_F^*} = -\frac{\beta(\Delta t^*)}{r^* + \beta t_S^*} = -\frac{\frac{\beta}{r^*}(\Delta t^*)}{1 + \frac{\beta}{r^*}t_S^*}. \tag{4}$$

This equation reveals that one cannot estimate β and r^* separately. The discount rate and the rate of capitalization also are confounded in the full model:

$$\frac{\Delta V^*}{V_F^*} = (1 + Z_2(S - F)\theta) \cdot \frac{r^* + \beta t_F^*}{r^* + \beta t_S^*} - 1$$

$$= (1 + Z_2(S - F)\theta) \cdot \frac{1 + \frac{\beta}{r^*}t_F^*}{1 + \frac{\beta}{r^*}t_S^*} - 1. \tag{5}$$

Hence, any estimate of the rate of tax capitalization must be conditional on a choice of the discount rate.

As explained in Chapter 3, the appropriate discount rate is the real discount rate in the base year of our housing price index, and the real discount rate is the nominal discount rate minus anticipated inflation. Because long-term Treasury bonds were a reasonable alternative to investment in housing during the sample period, we use the 10-year Treasury bond rate as a measure of the nominal discount rate. The study by Gramlich (1983) explains households' expectations about future inflation as a function of past inflation and several other variables. We employ Gramlich's equations to obtain an exogenous estimate of expected inflation in the base year of our housing price index. Our assumed value for r^* is 3%, which is the Treasury bond rate minus the estimated inflation expectation in the base year.[3]

2. THE NONLINEAR TWO-STAGE LEAST SQUARES ESTIMATOR

The main regression equations, (1) in the basic model and (3) in the full model, are nonlinear in the crucial parameter, β, as well as in the right-side variables t_S^*, t_F^*, r^*, and $Z_2(S - F)$. The combination of a nonlinear functional form and the endogeneity of t_S^* in both equations requires an elaborate estimation procedure.

If Equations (1) and (3) were linear, Equation (2) would provide the additional exogenous variables that should be included in the first stage of a standard two-stage least square (2SLS) estimation procedure to yield a prediction of t_S^*. If Equations (1) and (3) were linear in at least the parameters *or* the variables, a transformation described in Theil (1971) or the Goldfeld and Quandt (1972) method could be employed to preserve the two-stage regression procedure. Because our capitalization equations are nonlinear in the parameters *and* the variables, however, neither of these approaches is feasible.

We employ Amemiya's (1974) generalization of the two-stage least squares procedure to a nonlinear minimization problem. Some intuition may help to motivate this approach. Any two-stage least squares technique can be interpreted as the minimization of the sum of the squared residuals in the main regression equation after the endogenous right-side variables of this equation have been purged of their endogenous components. In the linear case, this purging is achieved by replacing the endogenous right-side variables by their predictions from a first-stage regression. The minimization of the sum of the squared residuals of the purged regression equation then corresponds simply to the second-stage regression. Geometrically speaking, the predicted values are the orthogonal projections of the endogenous right-side variables on the space of all first-stage predictors. In effect, this step approximates the endogenous variables by a linear combination of all exogenous predictors. These predictors, or instruments, include all exogenous variables in the main regression equation plus a selection (full or partial) of the exogenous variables that are included in the other equations of the simultaneous equation system but excluded from the main regression equation.

Algebraically, Amemiya's generalized nonlinear two-stage least squares (NL2SLS) estimation approach chooses the parameters, α, in the main regression equation $\mathbf{y} = f(\mathbf{X}, \alpha)$ to minimize

$$\text{WSSR}(\alpha) = (\mathbf{y} - f(\mathbf{X}, \alpha))'\mathbf{W} \cdot (\mathbf{W}'\mathbf{W})^{-1} \cdot \mathbf{W}'(y - f(X, \alpha)). \quad (6)$$

Note, that the name "two-stage" least squares is misleading insofar as it is generally impossible to decompose this minimization into two separate regression stages.

In our case, the dependent variable for the main regression equation, $\mathbf{y} = f(\mathbf{X}, \alpha)$, is the vector of observations for $\Delta V^*/V_F^*$. All exogenous *and* endogenous right-side variables of the regression equation are contained in $\mathbf{X}$, and all parameters that have to be estimated in the main regression equation are arranged in the parameter vector α. In the basic model, $f(\mathbf{X}, \alpha)$ represents Equation (1) with $\mathbf{X} = (t_S^*, t_F^*, r^*)$ and $\alpha = \beta$. In the full model, $f(\mathbf{X}, \alpha)$ represents Equation (3) with $\mathbf{X} = (t_S^*, t_F^*, r^*, Z_2(S - F))$ and $\alpha = (\beta, \theta)$.

$\mathbf{W} \cdot (\mathbf{W}'\mathbf{W})^{-1} \cdot \mathbf{W}'$ is the projection matrix on the linear space spanned by the predictors or instruments. The instruments are denoted by $\mathbf{W}$ and contain all variables that would be included in the first-stage regression of a conventional linear two-stage least squares procedure. As noted above, these variables are all exogenous variables included in $\mathbf{X}$, plus exogenous variables that are included in Equation (2) but not in $\mathbf{X}$. As we explain below, powers and multiplicative combinations of these original instruments also are valid instruments.

Following the intuition presented above, one can interpret (6) as follows: the residuals of the main regression equation, $u = \mathbf{y} - f(\mathbf{X}, \alpha)$, are purged of the endogenous components in $\mathbf{X}$ by projecting them on the space spanned by the instruments, $\mathbf{W}$; then, the parameters, α, are selected to minimize the sum of squares of these purged residuals. The first-order conditions for this minimization are

$$\frac{\partial \text{WSSR}(\alpha)}{\partial \alpha_k} = \left(\frac{\partial f(\mathbf{X}, \alpha)}{\partial \alpha_k}\right)' \mathbf{W} \cdot (\mathbf{W}'\mathbf{W})^{-1} \cdot \mathbf{W}'(\mathbf{y} - f(\mathbf{X}, \alpha)) = 0, \quad (7)$$

where $k = 1, \ldots, K$, for the K parameters in α. At the optimal values α^*, an estimate of the variance-covariance matrix is

$$\sigma^2 \cdot \left\{ \left(\frac{\partial f(\mathbf{X}, \boldsymbol{\alpha}^*)}{\partial \boldsymbol{\alpha}} \right)' \mathbf{W} \cdot (\mathbf{W}'\mathbf{W})^{-1} \cdot \mathbf{W}' \left(\frac{\partial f(\mathbf{X}, \boldsymbol{\alpha}^*)}{\partial \boldsymbol{\alpha}} \right) \right\}^{-1} \geqq 0 \qquad (8)$$

with

$$\sigma^2 = \frac{1}{T - K} \cdot (\mathbf{y} - f(\mathbf{X}, \boldsymbol{\alpha}))'(\mathbf{y} - f(\mathbf{X}, \boldsymbol{\alpha})).$$

These equations reduce to the estimating equation and the variance-covariance matrix of the 2SLS estimator when f is linear, that is, $f(\mathbf{X}, \boldsymbol{\alpha}) = \mathbf{X}'\boldsymbol{\alpha}$. In this case, $\partial f(\mathbf{X}, \boldsymbol{\alpha})/\partial \boldsymbol{\alpha} = \mathbf{X}$ and the first stage predicted values of the endogenous variables are $\mathbf{W} \cdot (\mathbf{W}'\mathbf{W})^{-1} \cdot \mathbf{W}'\mathbf{X}$. In the fully nonlinear case, the minimization of (6) cannot be done in two stages but rather requires an iterative algorithm that solves Equation (7) directly. We employ a modified version of the quadratic hill-climbing method developed by Goldfeld, Quandt and Trotter (1966), in which the hessian matrix is based on the variance-covariance matrix (8) evaluated at the values of the parameter vector, $\boldsymbol{\alpha}$, from the previous iteration.

Finally, the nonlinear approach suggests a method for expanding the set of instruments, $\mathbf{W}$. Equation (8) implies that the best choice of instruments would be the expected value of $\partial f(\mathbf{X}, \boldsymbol{\alpha}^*)/\partial \boldsymbol{\alpha}$, which would minimize the variance-covariance matrix and lead to estimators with the smallest possible standard errors. This choice is impractical, however, because $E[\partial f(\mathbf{X}, \boldsymbol{\alpha}^*)/\partial \boldsymbol{\alpha}]$ is difficult to evaluate explicitly and depends on the unknown parameters, $\boldsymbol{\alpha}^*$. One possible approximation proposed by Amemiya (1974) is a linear combination of all available original instruments, their powers, and their combinations. As long as the original instruments exhibit sufficient variation in the sample, their powers and combinations will also be linearly independent and can serve as separate instruments. Thus, the nonlinearity of the full model leads to an improvement on the weak identification in the linear case. In practice, only a small set of powers (squares and cubes) can be included without introducing near-singularity into the matrix $\mathbf{W}'\mathbf{W}$.

3. A LINEAR APPROXIMATION

Although Equation (1) is nonlinear, the circumstances of revaluation make possible a close linear approximation. As shown in the preceding section, nonlinearity adds considerable technical complexity to the estimation procedure. If a linear approximation is sufficiently accurate, therefore, it may be preferable to the nonlinear estimation technique. In addition, the linear estimates provide a point of reference to previous studies, most of which estimate linear regressions.

The estimating equation is nonlinear because β appears in both the numerator and the denominator. In the numerator, β is multiplied by Δt^*; in the denominator, it is multiplied by t_S^*, which is the difference between the actual second-sale effective tax rate and the town average effective tax rate that year. The value of Δt^* obviously varies widely across houses; indeed, this fact is the key to our study design. On the other hand, revaluation is an attempt to make t_S constant across houses. If this attempt is successful, that is, if every house has the same effective tax rate, then t_S^* equals zero for every house and drops out of the denominator. Furthermore, r^*, the base year real interest rate, is the same for every house, regardless of the year in which it is sold. To the extent that revaluation succeeds in its primary goal, therefore, the capitalization equation simplifies to

$$\frac{\Delta V^*}{V_F^*} = \frac{\beta(\Delta t^*)}{r^*} = \beta\left(\frac{\Delta t^*}{r^*}\right), \qquad (9)$$

where β is the coefficient of the tax rate change, Δt^*, divided by an outside estimate of r^*.

Equation (9) provides a simple linear approximation to the basic capitalization equation. As explained in Chapter 3, a complete analysis also must recognize anticipation, housing and neighborhood controls, and the simultaneity between tax rates and house values. All these factors are easily incorporated into this linear framework.

The anticipation variables described in Chapter 3 have the same denominator as the tax-rate-change variable, so the above approximation can be applied directly to them. See Equations (3-27.1) and (3-27.2).

The housing and neighborhood characteristics enter the analysis in a nonlinear way, but calculus provides a simple linear approximation. To be specific, let us differentiate Equation (3-23) with respect to y (for changes over time) and Q (for additions or renovations) and divide the result by V_F^*.[4] These steps lead to

$$\frac{dV^*}{V_F^*} = \frac{\partial R^*}{\partial y}\frac{dy}{R^*} + \frac{\partial H^*}{\partial y}\frac{dy}{H^*} + \frac{\partial H^*}{\partial Q}\frac{dQ}{H^*}, \qquad (10)$$

where d indicates a differential. The terms on the right side of (10) are the same terms that appear in Equations (3-30) and that can be operationalized with Equations (3-31). Hence, adding housing characteristics and neighborhood variables, interacted with $(S - F)$, plus additions dummies to the above linear approximation controls for possible changes in R^* and H^*.

Finally, we have to account for the simultaneity between $\Delta V^*/V_F^*$

and t_S^*. Unlike its nonlinear counterpart, this linear approximation can be estimated using conventional 2SLS. The instruments added to the first-stage regression are the same ones identified in the section on the nonlinear model, namely m_S multiplied by I_{Re}/I_S plus the housing characteristics that influence K in Equation (3-40) interacted with this product.

4. SUMMARY

A variety of technical problems confront anyone who tries to estimate the degree of property tax capitalization. These problems include recognizing the nonlinearity of the basic capitalization equation, accounting for the simultaneity between house values and property tax rates, and controlling for the effect on house values of nontax variables. In this chapter we described our solutions to these problems. Our final nonlinear simultaneous equations system is fully identified and our nonlinear two-stage least squares procedure will yield consistent estimates of the degree of tax capitalization.

NOTES

[1] In addition, functional singularities have to be excluded. For formal identification conditions, see Amemiya (1983).

[2] Strictly speaking, the capitalization equation in our basic model also includes two parameters for the anticipation variables, but both of these variables are exogenous and therefore do not affect identification of the equation.

[3] For most of the communities, the base year of the price index was 1960; for Barnstable and Brockton, it was 1969. Using the coefficients from the 1956–1970 regression in Gramlich's Table 5 and data from the Annual Report of the Council of Economic Advisers, we calculate that households' expected rate of inflation was 1.3% in 1960 and 3.8% in 1969. The corresponding 10-year Treasury Bill rates were 4.1% and 6.7%. According to these calculations, therefore, the real rate of interest was $(4.1 - 1.3) = 2.8\%$ in 1960 and $(6.7 - 3.8) = 2.9\%$ in 1969. We round both of these rates to 3%.

[4] Please note that in this section y stands for time, not for the dependant variable, as it did in Section 2.

6

Estimates of Intrajurisdictional Property Tax Capitalization in Massachusetts

The data described in Chapter 4 and the econometric techniques described in Chapter 5 allow us to estimate the degree of property tax capitalization in seven Massachusetts communities. In this chapter we present our results. The focus of the chapter, of course, is on our estimates of the degree of property tax capitalization. In addition, we present our estimates of the other coefficients in our model and examine the impact on estimated capitalization rates of various features of our approach, such as accounting for simultaneity and controlling for housing and neighborhood characteristics. We provide a detailed interpretation of our capitalization results in the first section of Chapter 7.

We begin with a discussion of our estimated capitalization rates. We present the rates obtained from our linear approximation in Section 1, and the rates obtained from the full nonlinear estimation technique in Section 2. In Sections 3 and 4, we report on our results for the other variables in the model, including anticipation, additions, and housing and neighborhood characteristics. In Section 5 we test the consequences of the linear restrictions implicit in our tax capitalization equation. We finish this chapter with a summary of our main results. Detailed regression results are presented in Appendix C.

In a nutshell, we find significant but fairly low capitalization rates, falling between 15% and 30%. Our methodology enables us to estimate these rates very precisely in most communities. Solutions to all the technical complications (simultaneity, nonlinearity, control variables) are necessary to achieve these results.

1. LINEAR ESTIMATION RESULTS

A synopsis of our estimates of tax capitalization obtained from the nonlinear model and our linear approximations is presented in Table 6-1. The ten columns of this table refer to alternative estimation techniques, and the seven rows refer to the seven Massachusetts communities in our sample. The table contains ten results for Waltham, Brockton, and Barnstable, and four results for the remaining communities. As explained in Chapter 4, the data contain housing controls for only two cities, Waltham and Brockton, neighborhood controls for only three cities, Waltham, Brockton, and Barnstable, and additions dummies for only one city, Waltham. A lack of controls in the other cities weakens our ability to capture assessor behavior in Equation (5-2) and leaves open the possibility of left-out-variable bias in the main regression equation. To determine the magnitude of these problems, we estimate our equations with and without controls in those cities where controls are available.

1.1 Estimates of the Degree of Property Tax Capitalization

The nonlinear results, which are discussed in Section 2, are in the first five columns of Table 6-1 and the linear results are in the second five columns. Column (L1) contains our preferred linear estimates, which employ the full set of controls and are estimated with 2SLS using the complete set of instruments, namely the housing and neighborhood characteristics identified in Equation (3-40). The results in column (L2) disregard the simultaneity in t_S^* and are estimated by OLS. The remaining columns refer to the basic model without controls for changes in housing and neighborhood characteristics. Columns (L3) and (L4) represent estimates based on 2SLS using all available instruments ((L3)) and on 2SLS using only m_S, I_{Re}/I_S, and their combinations and powers ((L4)). Finally, (L5) refers to a simple model without controls and estimated by OLS. All estimated capitalization rates are measured as percentages and their asymptotic t-statistics are in parentheses.

Our preferred linear results, in column (L1), are available only for cities with housing and neighborhood controls. In Waltham, the community

Table 6-1
Synopsis of Estimated Tax Capitalization Rates
(in percent; asymptotic *t*-statistics in parentheses)

Functional Form	Nonlinear					Linear				
Controls	Full Model		Basic Model			Full Model		Basic Model		
Estimation	NL2SLS	NLLS	NL2SLS		NLLS	2SLS	OLS	2SLS		OLS
Instruments	Full	None	Full	Small	None	Full	None	Full	Small	None
Column	(N1)	(N2)	(N3)	(N4)	(N5)	(L1)	(L2)	(L3)	(L4)	(L5)
Waltham	21.1%	44.8%	20.1%	15.5%	41.8%	22.2%	36.6%	18.5%	14.6%	34.6%
	(5.0)	(17.0)	(5.2)	(3.4)	(16.0)	(5.6)	(18.0)	(5.3)	(3.5)	(17.0)
Brockton	15.8%	23.4%	12.0%	12.6%	20.3%	15.8%	24.0%	11.9%	12.7%	19.4%
	(9.6)	(12.0)	(7.0)	(5.5)	(11.0)	(8.2)	(12.0)	(6.8)	(5.5)	(10.0)
Barnstable	33.1%	50.3%	16.4%	26.0%	47.3%	43.9%	41.6%	15.0%	34.1%	35.7%
	(2.9)	(6.0)	(1.2)	(2.1)	(5.5)	(3.6)	(7.8)	(1.3)	(2.6)	(7.0)
Arlington				3.9%	20.6%				3.8%	19.2%
				(1.4)	(9.4)				(1.4)	(9.4)
Belmont				73.6%	73.8%				52.6%	69.5%
				(7.5)	(17.0)				(5.0)	(13.0)
Brookline				40.7%	44.9%				44.7%	37.1%
				(6.3)	(15.0)				(4.5)	(11.0)
Wellesley				6.9%	20.2%				6.9%	19.7%
				(1.8)	(6.4)				(1.7)	(6.2)

Notes: The entries represent the percentage at which property tax changes are capitalized into changes in sales price. See Tables 6-2–6-4 for additional details.

with the best data, we find 22.2% capitalization. This estimate is precisely measured, with a t-statistic above 5.0, and is significantly larger than zero and significantly smaller than one at the 1% level. In short, we find positive but incomplete property tax capitalization. This result indicates that about one fifth of the relative change in a house's effective tax rate appears in the change in its market value. To put it another way, a $1.00 increase in the present value of a house's property tax payment relative to the community average leads to a $0.22 decline in its house value relative to the town average. In Brockton, the community with the second-best data, we find a similar result: 15.8% capitalization, even more precisely estimated than in Waltham, and significantly different from zero and one at the 1% level. In Barnstable, which has an incomplete set of control variables, we find that capitalization is about twice as large. The 43.9% capitalization result can statistically be distinguished from zero and one at the 1% level of significance.

As shown in column (L4), the 2SLS results for communities without housing and neighborhood controls are more varied and statistically less precise. The estimated degree of capitalization ranges from a low 3.8% in Arlington and 6.9% in Wellesley, to a high 44.7% in Brookline and 52.6% in Belmont. All estimates indicate incomplete capitalization. Except for Arlington and Wellesley, the estimated capitalization ratios are also significantly larger than zero at the 1% confidence level.

1.2 The Importance of Methodology

The results in Table 6-1 provide some insight into the importance of key aspects of our methodology. First, consider the importance of the housing and neighborhood control variables. Column (L3) presents estimates of capitalization in Waltham, Brockton, and Barnstable with housing and neighborhood characteristics as instruments in the simultaneous equations procedure, but without direct housing and neighborhood controls. A comparison of this panel with column (L1) reveals the magnitude of the left-out-variable bias from excluding housing and neighborhood controls. In all three communities, omitting controls lowers the estimated capitalization rate and reduces its precision. In Waltham and Brockton, the left-out-variable bias is about 4 percentage points; in Barnstable, it is almost 30 percentage points and is accompanied by a large loss in statistical precision. These results indicate that left-out-variable bias can be a serious problem; omitting housing and neighborhood variables can lead to a severe underestimate of capitalization and of its statistical significance.

The lack of data on housing and neighborhood characteristics also precludes us from using them as components of the instruments in some

communities.[1] As explained in Chapter 3, these variables account for systematic variation in assessment – sales ratios across houses after revaluation.
Column (L4) presents estimates of capitalization in Waltham, Brockton,
and Barnstable with only a small set of instruments for the simultaneous
equations procedure. These instruments include the nominal property tax
rate, m_S, the housing price index variable, (I_{Re}/I_S), their product, and squares
of these three variables. A comparison of this column with column (L3)
reveals the importance of housing and neighborhood variables in the correction for simultaneity. In all three communities, adding the full set of instruments alters the estimate of capitalization and, in all the communities except
Waltham, raises the precision of the estimate.

A comparison of columns (L1) and (L4) reveals the combined effect
of omitting housing and neighborhood variables both as regressors and as
instruments. In all cases, this combined effect is to lower the estimate of
capitalization and to reduce its precision. Thus, both adequate instruments
and full controls in the second stage appear to be necessary for the precise
estimation of β. This finding implies that the results for the four communities without housing and neighborhood variables, and perhaps even for
Barnstable with its partial information, may not be accurate estimates of
capitalization.

Table 6-1 also reveals the importance of correcting for simultaneity.
A comparison of the OLS results in column (L2) and the 2SLS results in
column (L1) reveals that in Waltham and Brockton, OLS leads to a substantial overstatement of the degree of capitalization and of its statistical significance. OLS also leads to an overstatement of statistical significance in Barnstable but has little effect on the estimate of β.

The difference between the results in columns (L1) and (L4) for
Waltham, Brockton, and Barnstable, can be interpreted as the overall impact
of control variables on an estimate of capitalization. This difference can be
used, therefore, to estimate what the degree of capitalization would be in the
other communities if these controls were available there. This difference
ranges from 7.6 percentage points in Waltham to 9.8 percentage points in
Barnstable and averages 8.6 percentage points. Adding 8.6 to the estimates
for the other four communities yields the following estimates of capitalization: 12.4% in Arlington, 61.2% in Belmont, 53.3% in Brookline, and 15.5%
in Wellesley.

1.3 Summary

In summary, one cannot obtain an unbiased, precise estimate of the degree
of capitalization without (a) extensive controls for housing and neighborhood controls, (b) a simultaneous equations procedure, and (c) extensive

Table 6-2
Goodness of Fit
(r-squared)[a]

Functional Form	Nonlinear					Linear				
Controls	Full Model		Basic Model			Full Model		Basic Model		
Estimation	NL2SLS	NLLS	NL2SLS		NLLS	2SLS	OLS	2SLS		OLS
Instruments	Full	None	Full	Small	None	Full	None	Full	Small	None
Column	(N1)	(N2)	(N3)	(N4)	(N5)	(L1)	(L2)	(L3)	(L4)	(L5)
Waltham	.394	.449	.307	.298	.311	.411	.437	.301	.294	.307
Brockton	.386	.308	.243[b]	.171	.176	.364	.332	.226[b]	.166	.168
Barnstable	.373	.385	.234	.265	.280	.409	.409	.249	.297	.297
Arlington				.081	.148				.079	.144
Belmont				.486	.487				.431	.431
Brookline				.385	.387				.316	.316
Wellesley				.101	.104				.101	.102

[a] R-squared is calculated as the correlation between the actual dependent variable (the relative change in house value) and its prediction.
[b] Value not comparable to two values to the right because it is based on the subsample with housing and neighborhood characteristics.

instruments to account for assessor behavior. Following these three steps in the community with the best data, Waltham, leads to an estimate of 22.2% capitalization. In Brockton, for which the data are almost as good, the estimate is similar, 15.8%. In Barnstable, for which we have some neighborhood variables but no housing characteristics, we estimate a capitalization rate of 43.9%. As shown in Table 6-2, the goodness of fit in this cross-sectional study is reasonably high in all three communities.

2. NONLINEAR ESTIMATION RESULTS

The five leftmost columns in Table 6-1 present estimates of the degree of property tax capitalization based on the correct nonlinear functional forms in Equations (5-1) and (5-3). The arrangement of these results corresponds to the arrangement of the linear estimates and carries an analogous notation. The basic model is estimated with nonlinear least squares (column (N5)), nonlinear two-stage least squares with a limited set of instruments (column (N4)), and nonlinear two-stage least squares with the full set of instruments (column (N3)). The full model is estimated with nonlinear least squares (column (N2)), and with nonlinear two-stage least squares with the full set of instruments (column (N1)).

Our preferred estimates of the property tax capitalization rates are the leftmost entries for each community. All features of our methodology could be implemented only for two communities, Waltham and Brockton. As a result, we consider the results for these two communities to provide the most reliable estimates of the rate at which tax changes are capitalized into house value changes. The results in column (N1) are obtained from the full model with extensive housing and neighborhood characteristics; they have the correct functional form, including the nonlinearity suggested by economic theory, and they are estimated by nonlinear two-stage least squares, to correct for the endogeneity of the second-sale tax rate.

2.1 Estimates of the Degree of Property Tax Capitalization

Our preferred estimate of the capitalization rate is 21.1% in Waltham and 15.8% in Brockton. These rates are measured consistently and precisely; in these two Massachusetts communities there is positive but incomplete capitalization of property tax changes into the sales prices of single-family houses. The two-standard-deviation confidence intervals are 12.7 to 29.5% in Waltham, and 12.5 to 19.1% in Brockton, thereby rejecting the hypotheses of zero as well as full capitalization.

Because of the data limitations described above, it is more difficult to obtain satisfactory estimates of the degree of property tax capitalization in the other five communities. In Barnstable, the best achievable estimate of the degree of capitalization is 33.1%, with a two-standard-deviation confidence interval from 10.3% to 55.9%. This estimate is higher and less precise than the estimates in Waltham and Brockton. For all other communities, the best estimation method that can be employed with the available data is the nonlinear two-stage least squares procedure applied to the basic model, with the nominal tax rate as the main identifying instrument (Table 6-1, column (N4)). It appears that Arlington and Wellesley have low tax capitalization rates, 3.9% and 6.9%, whereas Belmont and Brookline have very high capitalization rates, 73.6% and 40.7%.

2.2   The Importance of Methodology

The results in Table 6-1 allow us to examine the importance of three features of our specification: (1) treating the second-sale effective tax rate as endogenous, (2) including housing and neighborhood characteristics in the capitalization equation, and (3) employing a nonlinear functional specification. In the following paragraphs, we determine the biases that are produced (at least on average) by ignoring each of these features.

Ignoring the endogeneity of the second-sale effective tax rate leads to a considerable overestimation of the true tax capitalization rate. This upward bias is expected, because the effective tax rate t_s is by definition negatively linked to market value. This result can be seen by comparing column (N1) and column (N2) and by comparing columns (N3) and (N4) with column (N5). Furthermore, the least squares estimates in columns (N2) and (N5) appear to be very precise because of large estimated t-ratios. The negative feedback from house value to second-sale tax rate also appears to improve the goodness of fit; in the case of the full nonlinear model in Waltham, least squares overestimates β by about 90%, and the t-statistic is more than three times as large as in the correct simultaneous model. For the towns with data on housing and/or neighborhood characteristics (Waltham, Brockton, and Barnstable), this pattern of severe overestimation holds in the linear specification as well as the nonlinear functional form, and in the basic model as well as the full model. The only exception is the linear version of the model in Barnstable.

Omitting the controls for housing and neighborhood characteristics consistently biases estimated capitalization toward zero. This result can be seen by comparing column (N1) with column (N3) or (N4). In addition, the capitalization rates usually are more precisely estimated when these controls are included. A comparison of columns (N1) and (N4) in Waltham and Brockton shows that the omission of housing and neighborhood characteristics leads to an underestimation of the true capitalization rate by about 25% or about 4 to 7 percentage points. Left-out-variable bias equals the true coefficient of the left-out variable multiplied by the partial correlation between the left-out variable and the included variable, which in this case is the property tax rate. As we show in Section 6.3, the additions variables and some of the housing and neighborhood characteristics have high t-statistics, which indicate significant true effects on house value changes. These variables are correlated with the tax rate change because of assessor behavior. Variables with positive (negative) coefficients, such as additions, are positively (negatively) correlated with the tax rate changes, so the left-out-variable bias is positive (negative). Because the coefficient of the tax change variable is negative, a positive bias pushes the estimated coefficient toward zero.[2] This underestimation also holds in the simple least squares estimation results uncorrected for simultaneity.

Ignoring the relationship between housing and neighborhood characteristics and the post-revaluation assessment – sales ratio also affects estimated capitalization rates. This result can be seen by comparing column (N3) with column (N4) in Waltham, Brockton and Barnstable. Comparing columns (N1) and (N4) reveals the impact of omitting housing and neighborhood characteristics both as control variables and as instruments in the simultaneous equations procedure. In all three cases, the downward bias in β is between 20 and 27%.

Employing the linear approximation appears to lead to a slight overestimate of the capitalization rate in the full model. This result can be seen by comparing columns (N1) and (L1) in Table 6-1. In two of the three communities, the linear functional form also produces somewhat higher standard errors than the nonlinear specification. In the full model, the linear approximation raises the estimated capitalization rate from 21.1 to 22.2% in Waltham and from 33.1 to 43.9% in Barnstable. It has no effect on the estimate in Brockton. At the same time, the linear approximation raises the associated standard errors from 1.65 to 1.93 in Brockton and from 11.4 to 12.2 in Barnstable. This pattern is not consistent, however; in Waltham, the approximation lowers the standard error of estimated capitalization slightly from 4.24 to 4.00.

Overall, the correct nonlinear functional form tends to increase estimating efficiency, but the differences between linear and nonlinear models are relatively small. The nonlinear model insures consistent estimates when t_g^* is not constant. In fact, however, the variation in t_g^* is small, providing a good rationale for the linear approximation.

2.3 Summary

By comparing the results of different estimation methods for the communities with satisfactory data, we can obtain more realistic estimates of property tax capitalization rates in communities with insufficient data. The difference between the results in columns (N1) and (N4), which indicates the overall impact of control variables, averages 5.3 percentage points for Waltham, Brockton, and Barnstable. Adding this difference to the other communities yields corrected estimates of capitalization equal to 9.2% in Arlington, 78.9% in Belmont, 46.0% in Brookline, and 12.2% in Wellesley. In every community except Belmont, these corrected nonlinear estimates are similar to the corrected linear estimates.

These empirical results confirm the theoretical arguments in Chapter 3 that a consistent estimation of the rate at which property taxes are capitalized needs to account for the endogeneity of the second-sale effective tax rate and for the impact of housing and neighborhood characteristics on both house values and post-revaluation assessment – sales ratios. In addition, the nonlinear functional relationship generally increases the precision of the estimates and insures consistency even if variation in effective tax rates persists after revaluation.

Our preferred nonlinear estimates, corrected for the lack of controls if necessary, vary across the seven communities. The degree of capitalization is low in Waltham and Brockton, 16% and 21%, and even lower in Arlington and Wellesley, 9% and 12%. In contrast, the degree of capitalization takes intermediate values in Barnstable and Brookline, 33% and 46%, and a high value in Belmont, 79%. For all communities, however, the data indicate that there is indeed capitalization of property tax changes and that it is incomplete.

3. ANTICIPATION OF PROPERTY TAX CHANGES

In the following sections, we discuss results for the auxiliary variables involved in estimating property tax capitalization. Table 6-3 presents our notation and definitions. Complete estimation results are given in the Appendix C.

The first auxiliary variables are the two anticipation dummies. DA0 equals one whenever the first sale took place after revaluation was announced but before the new tax bills were actually sent out; DA1 equals one whenever the first sale took place in the year preceding the announcement of revaluation. The coefficients of these variables indicate whether the revaluation could already have been anticipated at the time of the first sale. For notational clarity, we omitted these variables in the capitalization equations

Table 6-3
Variable Names, Models, and Estimation Procedures

(1) Tax Rates, Anticipation Effects, Objective Function

ETAXS	Second sale effective tax rate (in percent),
ETAXF	First sale effective tax rate (in percent),
ETBARS	Average effective tax rate in town, at second sale (in percent),
ETBARF	Average effective tax rate in town, at first sale (in percent),
DA0	Anticipation dummy (1 if first sale while new tax rates announced),
DA1	Anticipation dummy (1 if first sale in year before announcement),
WSSR	Minimal weighted sum of squared residuals from Equation (5.6).

(2) Housing and Neighborhood Attributes Times Months Between First and Second Sale

AGE	Age of structure (years),
HAREA	Area of house (1000 sq.ft.),
ROOMS	Number of rooms,
STUCCO	Wall material (1 if stucco exterior),
BRICKS	Wall material (1 if brick or stone exterior),
ALUMN	Wall material (1 if aluminum or plastic siding),
SHINGL	Wall material (1 if shingled exterior),
HARDWD	Floor material (1 if hardwood floor),
FIREPL	Number of fireplaces,
BATH	Number of full bathrooms $+ 0.5 \cdot$ Number of half bathrooms,
GAREA	Area of garage (1000 sq.ft.),
LOTSIZ	Lot size (1000 sq.ft.),
SCHD(i)	Indicator for school district i (in Waltham and Brockton),
VILL(i)	Indicator for village i (in Barnstable),
SCHOOL	Median number of years of school completed in Census tract,
MOVERS	Percent of persons in same house in 1965 and 1970 in Census tract.

(3) Addition Dummies

ADDMAJ	Addition dummy (1 if major additions),
ADDBK	Addition dummy (1 if bathroom or kitchen renovation),
ADDGAR	Addition dummy (1 if new garage),
ADDMIN	Addition dummy (1 if minor addition),
ADDLOT	Addition dummy (1 if land purchase, -1 if land sale),
ADDPOL	Addition dummy (1 if new pool),

(4) Controls

BASIC MODEL	Excludes housing and neighborhood controls, Equation (5.1),
FULL MODEL	Includes housing and neighborhood controls, Equation (5.3).

(5) Instruments

SMALL SET	Nominal tax rate m_S, town price index I_{Re}/I_S, powers, interactions,
FULL SET	Small set plus all available housing and neighborhood attributes.

(6) Estimation Procedures

OLS	Ordinary least squares, Equation 5.6 with $f(X, \alpha) = X'\alpha$ and $W = I$,
2SLS	Standard two-stage least squares, Equation 5.6 with $f(X, \alpha) = X'\alpha$,
NLLS	Nonlinear least squares, Equation (5.6) with $W = I$,
NL2SLS	Nonlinear two stage least squares, Equation (5.6).

Table 6-4
Anticipation of Property Tax Changes
(in percent)

Functional Form	Nonlinear					Linear				
Controls	Full Model		Basic Model			Full Model		Basic Model		
Estimation	NL2SLS	NLLS	NL2SLS		NLLS	2SLS	OLS	2SLS		OLS
Instruments	Full	None	Full	Small	None	Full	None	Full	Small	None
Column	(N1)	(N2)	(N3)	(N4)	(N5)	(L1)	(L2)	(L3)	(L4)	(L5)
Waltham	.85*	.92*	.90*	.90*	.93*	.81*	.87*	.86*	.89*	.92*
	.47	.67*	.30	.13	.65*	.41	.57*	.22	.07	.55*
Brockton	-.44	-.04	-.33	-.24	.15	-.44	-.08	-.34	-.23	.10
	1.58*	.68*	-.42	.95*	.89*	1.20*	.67*	-1.10	.94*	.88*
Barnstable	-1.20	-.56	-3.40*	-1.80	-.66	-.66	-.72	-3.60*	-1.10	-1.00
	-1.30	-.58	-3.50	-1.90	-.74	-.66	-.75	-3.70	-1.20	-1.10
Arlington				2.00	.87				2.60	.98
				-7.70*	-.44				-8.20*	-.03
Belmont				.82*	.79*				.82*	.82*
				.63	.65				.49	.59
Brookline				.02	.11				.13	.05
				.91	.89				.91	.91
Wellesley				.87	.45				.87	.51
				.00	.40				.00	.41

Notes: The upper entries refer to the degree of anticipation when new assessed values are announced but before the actual new tax bills are sent out. The lower entries refer to the degree of anticipation in the year before announcement of new assessed values. All entries are calculated as the coefficient of DA0 or DA1 divided by the estimated β. An asterisk denotes significance at the 1 percent level.

(5-1) and (5-3). According to Equation (3-25), the capitalization equations with these variables are

$$\frac{\Delta V^*}{V_F^*} = -\frac{\beta \cdot \Delta t^* - \delta_0 \cdot DA0 \cdot t_F^* - \delta_1 \cdot DA1 \cdot t_F^*}{r^* + \beta \cdot t_S^*} \tag{1}$$

for the basic model and

$$\frac{\Delta V^*}{V_F^*} = (1 + Z_2(S - F)\theta)$$
$$\cdot \frac{r^* + \beta \cdot t_F^* - \delta_0 \cdot DA0 \cdot t_F^* - \delta_1 \cdot DA1 \cdot t_F^*}{r^* + \beta \cdot t_S^*} - 1 \tag{2}$$

for the full model. As explained in Chapter 3, after Equation (3-27), δ_i/β can be interpreted as the degree of anticipated capitalization.

Table 6-4 presents our anticipation results, expressed as percentages. We find that the degree of anticipation is very small, although it is statistically significant in several communities. In Waltham and Belmont, less than one percent of the tax change is anticipated in the time between announcement and actual enactment of the revaluation. In Brockton, about one percent of the tax change is anticipated in the year before the revaluation was announced, and in Waltham some additional anticipation can be observed during that period. In all other instances, anticipation is insignificant or, as in Arlington, appears to have a perverse direction.

Given the fairly low tax capitalization rates measured in Table 6-1, these results are not too surprising. If only 20% of tax changes are ever capitalized, one would expect an even smaller degree of capitalization for tax changes that are possible or expected but not yet enacted. Remember that these results do reflect significant coefficients; the anticipation rates in Waltham, Brockton, and Belmont are small but precisely measured.

4. HOUSING AND NEIGHBORHOOD CHARACTERISTICS

The housing and neighborhood characteristics employed as control variables are defined in Table 6-3, and their coefficients are displayed in Tables 6-5 to 6-7. These variables can be divided into three groups: (1) addition variables that measure changes to the physical characteristics of a house that took place between the first and second sale, (2) attributes of the house and its lot, and (3) characteristics of the neighborhood in which the house is located.

In Chapter 3, we showed that the inclusion of housing and neighborhood characteristics in the capitalization equation is necessary only if a house or its neighborhood changed characteristics between first and second sale or if the market value of those characteristics changed during that time.

Housing and neighborhood characteristics per se cancel out because the capitalization equation is written in change form, and neighborhood changes that affect an entire community are eliminated by our price index. Therefore, our housing and neighborhood variables measure second-order effects as opposed to the first-order effects found in the literature, such as the seminal analysis by Oates (1969).

As noted in Chapter 4, we did not collect housing and neighborhood variables for all seven communities. We collected neighborhood indicators only in the communities of Waltham, Brockton, and Barnstable, and only at the time of second sale. We collected data on housing characteristics at the time of second sale in Waltham and Brockton, and data on additions to the house between first and second sale in Waltham.

Perhaps the most important neighborhood attribute is school quality. We account for school quality in Waltham and Brockton with a series of school district dummy variables. In the township of Barnstable, we employ a series of village dummy variables, which serve as an approximation for school quality and other neighborhood characteristics. Finally, we use two additional neighborhood variables in Waltham and Brockton, namely the median education (years of schooling of adults) and the stability (percentage of the population in the same house for five years) in the Census tract in which the house is located.

Table 6-2, which summarizes the goodness of fit for our various models, reveals the importance of including housing and neighborhood variables in the capitalization equation. Compared to the basic model in column (N1), in which the coefficients of all housing and neighborhood attributes are restricted to be zero, the full model in column (N1) has a significantly higher R-squared: .394 versus .301 in Waltham and .386 versus .234 in Brockton. Even with the scant neighborhood data in Barnstable, the full model improves overall fit from .234 to .373.[3]

We now turn to the individual coefficients. Our interpretation is based on the three terms on the right-side of Equation (5-10). The first two terms capture changes in the market value of each individual housing and neighborhood attribute, and the third term captures physical changes to the house. Because of the lack of intertemporal data on housing and neighborhood characteristics, we cannot measure directly the changes in market values of individual attributes. Instead, we account for such changes by interacting each characteristic with the time elapsed between first and second sale. In Waltham, physical changes to a house are measured by dummy variables for various types of additions to the house.

The addition variables (Table 6-5) turn out to be important and to perform as expected. Major additions, such as adding a bath, a kitchen, or a

Table 6-5
Addition Variables
(estimated coefficients; asymptotic *t*-statistics in parentheses)

Waltham Functional Form	Nonlinear				Linear			
Estimator	NL2SLS		NLLS		2SLS		OLS	
Column	(N1)		(N2)		(L1)		(L2)	
ADDMAJ	.2705	(6.86)	.2655	(7.24)	.2694	(6.95)	.2584	(6.93)
ADDBK	.0893	(1.97)	.0653	(1.59)	.0937	(2.05)	.0773	(1.76)
ADDGAR	.1615	(3.53)	.1394	(3.36)	.1615	(3.53)	.1411	(3.22)
ADDMIN	−.0070	(−.16)	.0120	(.31)	−.0125	(−.30)	−.0049	(−.12)
ADDLOT	.0678	(1.08)	.0317	(.54)	.0465	(.75)	.0202	(.33)
ADDPOL	.1281	(2.89)	.1327	(3.14)	.1142	(2.67)	.1180	(2.87)

Note: These variables are defined in Table 6-3.

Table 6-6

Housing Characteristics

(estimated coefficients; asymptotic t-statistics in parentheses)

Functional Form	Nonlinear		Linear	
Estimator	NL2SLS	NLLS	2SLS	OLS
Column	(N1)	(N2)	(L1)	(L2)
Waltham:				
AGE	.0059 (1.20)	.0128 (2.85)	.0072 (1.48)	.0117 (2.58)
HAREA	-.0027 (1.17)	.0002 (.08)	-.0020 (.89)	-.0003 (.12)
ROOMS	-.0106 (2.26)	-.0123 (2.83)	-.0101 (2.19)	-.0112 (2.51)
STUCCO	.0003 (.59)	.0002 (.34)	.0003 (.59)	.0002 (.37)
BRICKS	.0003 (1.35)	.0003 (1.16)	.0003 (1.40)	.0003 (1.21)
ALUMN	.0002 (.69)	.0005 (2.16)	.0002 (1.04)	.0005 (2.15)
SHINGL	.0024 (3.85)	.0022 (3.69)	.0024 (3.79)	.0022 (3.67)
HARDWD	-.0013 (.56)	-.0005 (.24)	-.0009 (-.39)	-.0001 (.04)
FIREPL	-.0002 (.13)	.0006 (.54)	.0000 (-.02)	.0005 (.44)
BATH	.0067 (3.37)	.0065 (3.43)	.0067 (3.43)	.0063 (3.37)
GAREA	-.0143 (3.32)	-.0124 (3.08)	-.0131 (3.10)	-.0113 (2.80)
LOTSIZ	.0018 (1.25)	.0030 (2.20)	.0017 (1.21)	.0021 (1.58)
Brockton:				
AGE	.0211 (2.49)	.0268 (3.09)	.0209 (2.47)	.0242 (2.93)
HAREA	-.0001 (.01)	.0007 (.25)	-.0005 (.18)	.0018 (.72)
ROOMS	-.0237 (.76)	-.0313 (1.01)	-.0232 (.73)	-.0303 (.99)
STUCCO	.0001 (.11)	.0002 (.24)	.0001 (.08)	.0002 (.30)
BRICKS	-.0011 (2.12)	-.0004 (.83)	-.0011 (2.12)	-.0004 (.72)
ALUMN	-.0012 (1.40)	-.0011 (1.38)	-.0012 (1.41)	-.0011 (1.49)
SHINGL	.0015 (.43)	.0046 (2.00)	.0018 (.54)	.0040 (2.04)
HARDWD	-.0011 (.22)	-.0006 (.14)	-.0002 (.03)	-.0020 (.47)
FIREPL	-.0035 (1.79)	-.0034 (1.58)	-.0032 (1.69)	-.0020 (1.07)
BATH	-.0055 (.95)	-.0050 (.91)	-.0048 (.80)	-.0072 (1.35)
GAREA	.0008 (.08)	-.0028 (.29)	.0019 (.18)	-.0038 (.40)
LOTSIZ	-.0088 (2.33)	-.0093 (2.90)	-.0090 (2.19)	-.0101 (3.10)

new garage, add significantly to the value of a house, whereas minor additions or the rare cases of extending lot size are insignificant.

Tables 6-6 and 6-7 display the coefficients of the housing and neighborhood characteristics at the time of second sale, multiplied by the time elapsed between first and second sale (see Equation (3-30)). The attributes whose market values changed are different in Waltham and Brockton. Number of rooms, exterior finish, number of baths, and garage area are significant in Waltham; age of the house, exterior finish, and lot size are significant in Brockton. Some of the school districts (individual villages in Barnstable) also experienced significant changes in their market values. Because these are second-order effects and because they are subject to multicollinearity, we attach little significance to an interpretation of the individual coefficients.[4]

5. RESTRICTIONS ON THE COMPONENTS OF PROPERTY TAX RATE CHANGES

The results in Table 6-1 are based on a single, comprehensive tax capitalization rate, denoted by β in Equations (5-1) and (5-3). However, the intrajurisdictional change in the property tax between first and second sale includes four components:

$$\Delta t^* = t_S^* - t_F^* = (t_S - \bar{t}_S) - (t_F - \bar{t}_F). \qquad (3)$$

If we attach separate capitalization coefficients to each component in Equation (3), the main regression equations become

$$\frac{\Delta V^*}{V_F^*} = \frac{(\beta_1 t_F - \beta_2 \bar{t}_F) - (\beta_3 t_S - \beta_4 \bar{t}_S)}{r + (\beta_3 t_S - \beta_4 \bar{t}_S)} \qquad (4)$$

in the basic model, and

$$\frac{\Delta V^*}{V_F^*} = (1 + Z_2(S - F)\theta) \cdot \left(\frac{r^* + (\beta_1 t_F - \beta_2 \bar{t}_F)}{r^*(\beta_3 t_S - \beta_4 \bar{t}_S)} \right) - 1 \qquad (5)$$

in the full model.

So far, we have implicitly assumed that all four values of β are the same. Reference to the factors that influence β suggests that this assumption may not be correct. The value of β depends on the quality of house seekers' information about relative tax rates. Because of the publicity surrounding revaluation, people may have more information after revaluation than before.[5] If so, β will be higher, all else equal, after revaluation; that is β_3 and β_4 will be greater than β_1 and β_2. Moreover, people may have better information about their own effective tax rate, which they can directly observe, than about the community-wide average tax rate. At both first and second sale,

Table 6-7

Neighborhood Characteristics

(estimated coefficients; asymptotic t-statistics in parentheses)

Functional Form	Nonlinear		Linear	
Estimator	NL2SLS	NLLS	2SLS	OLS
Column	(N1)	(N2)	(L1)	(L2)
Waltham:				
SCHD (1)	.0002 (.99)	−.0003 (1.56)	−.0001 (.34)	−.0005 (1.98)
SCHD (2)	.0000 (.03)	−.0003 (1.39)	−.0004 (1.23)	−.0006 (2.32)
SCHD (3)	.0008 (1.83)	−.0001 (.19)	.0004 (.82)	−.0002 (.40)
SCHD (4)	−.0001 (.39)	−.0005 (2.46)	−.0004 (1.60)	−.0008 (3.05)
SCHD (5)	−.0006 (1.83)	−.0009 (3.03)	−.0009 (2.75)	−.0011 (3.63)
SCHD (6)	−.0002 (.98)	−.0006 (3.00)	−.0006 (2.16)	−.0008 (3.43)
SCHD (7)	−.0002 (.86)	−.0006 (2.74)	−.0005 (2.08)	−.0008 (3.37)
SCHD (8)	−.0002 (.86)	−.0007 (2.88)	−.0006 (2.10)	−.0010 (3.46)
SCHD (9)	.0002 (.74)	−.0007 (2.60)	−.0001 (.35)	−.0007 (2.35)
SCHD (10)	.0000 (.05)	−.0005 (1.80)	−.0003 (.99)	−.0007 (2.12)
SCHOOL	.0293 (2.40)	.0206 (1.81)	.0321 (2.67)	.0274 (2.37)
MOVERS	−.0114 (1.54)	−.0074 (1.08)	−.0130 (1.78)	−.0106 (1.50)

Brockton:

SCHD (1)	.0002	(6.27)	.0002	(.74)	.0005	(1.33)	−.0017	(3.68)
SCHD (2)	−.0002	(.34)	−.0006	(.81)	.0001	(.08)	−.0029	(3.45)
SCHD (3)	−.0007	(.87)	−.0008	(.99)	−.0003	(.34)	−.0033	(3.71)
SCHD (4)	−.0027	(3.76)	−.0024	(3.18)	−.0024	(2.68)	−.0048	(5.55)
SCHD (5)	−.0008	(1.30)	−.0005	(.64)	−.0005	(.65)	−.0026	(3.22)
SCHD (6)	−.0009	(1.19)	−.0008	(1.01)	−.0007	(.77)	−.0031	(3.42)
SCHD (7)	−.0004	(.52)	.0000	(.02)	−.0001	(.17)	−.0023	(2.81)
SCHD (8)	−.0008	(1.14)	−.0005	(.72)	−.0005	(.61)	−.0030	(3.55)
SCHD (9)	−.0015	(1.87)	−.0014	(1.67)	−.0012	(1.38)	−.0037	(4.01)
SCHD (10)	−.0023	(1.75)	−.0021	(2.14)	−.0020	(1.33)	−.0050	(4.50)
SCHOOL	−.0249	(1.22)	−.0213	(1.14)	−.0245	(1.17)	−.0224	(1.20)
MOVERS	.0353	(2.74)	.0311	(2.43)	.0337	(2.54)	.0391	(3.03)

Barnstable:

VILL (1)	.0059	(3.36)	.0066	(3.82)	.0048	(2.66)	.0048	(2.65)
VILL (2)	.0004	(.88)	.0003	(.71)	−.0006	(.70)	−.0005	(.68)
VILL (3)	.0132	(3.80)	.0132	(3.86)	.0117	(3.34)	.0118	(3.35)
VILL (4)	−.0001	(.27)	−.0002	(−.54)	−.0011	(1.53)	−.0011	(1.51)
VILL (5)	.0009	(.93)	.0016	(1.73)	.0016	(1.25)	.0015	(1.32)
VILL (6)	.0001	(.17)	−.0001	(−.07)	−.0010	(.99)	−.0009	(.97)
VILL (7)	−.0019	(.71)	−.0014	(−.51)	−.0023	(.94)	−.0023	(.97)

Note: These variables are defined in Table 6-3.

therefore, the value of β that applies to the house's effective tax rate may be higher than the value that applies to the average rate; that is β_1 and β_3 may be greater than β_2 and β_4. If revaluation is expected to be an ongoing process, as required by law, then the expected persistence of tax differences, and hence the value of β (according to Equation (3-15)), will be smaller after revaluation. In other words, β_3 and β_4 will be smaller than β_1 and β_2.[6]

To determine whether any of these factors are at work, we estimate three versions of our preferred models:

1. Full Restrictions. In these regressions, the coefficients of all four tax rate variables are restricted to be the same.

2. Inter-Period Restrictions. In these regressions, the coefficients of t_S and of t_F are restricted to be the same, and the coefficients of $\bar{t}_S$ and of $\bar{t}_F$ are restricted to be the same.

3. Intra-Period Restrictions. In these regressions, the coefficients of t_S and of $\bar{t}_S$ are restricted to be the same, and the coefficients of t_F and of $\bar{t}_F$ are restricted to be the same.

These restrictions can be tested by comparing the optimal values of the objective function, WSSR(α) in Equation (5-6), which represent the weighted sum of squared residuals (see Amemiya (1983)). Let WSSR$_F$ denote the minimal weighted sum of squared residuals that is achieved when the full set of restrictions is applied, and WSSR$_P$, when only partial restrictions are applied. For a sample of T observations, the test statistic

$$T \cdot \frac{\text{WSSR}_F - \text{WSSR}_P}{\text{WSSR}_P} \tag{6}$$

is asymptotically distributed chi-square with one degree of freedom.

Table 6-8 presents the tax capitalization rates for the full linear (L1) and nonlinear model (N1) in the three communities for which full data were available. To evaluate the significance of the restrictions, Table 6-8 also presents the minimal weighted sum of squared residuals, WSSR, with the values of the test-statistic, Equation (6), following in parentheses.

A significant test-statistic indicates that a model has significantly more explanatory power than the fully restricted model. In Waltham, for example, the large test statistic for the model with intra-period restrictions signifies that there is a significant gain in explanatory power when the inter-period restrictions are removed but the intra-period restrictions are retained.

Table 6-8
Test of Restrictions on Tax Rate Components
(estimated coefficients, objective values, and test statistics)

	Fully Restricted		Intra-Period Restriction[a]		Inter-Period Restriction[a]	
Waltham:						
Full Nonlinear Model (N1)						
ETAXS (*t*-Stat)	.2113	(4.98)	.4927	(5.75)	.2247	(4.94)
ETAXF	.2113		.2169	(5.62)	.2247	
ETBARS	.2113		.4927		.2112	(4.90)
ETBARF	.2113		.2169		.2112	
WSSR (χ²)	.4100		.3070	(118.)[b]	.4020	(7.02)[b]
Full Linear Model (L1)						
ETAXS (*t*-Stat)	.2227	(5.56)	.5118	(5.58)	.2230	(5.43)
ETAXF	.2227		.2245	(5.88)	.2230	
ETBARS	.2227		.5118		.2226	(5.49)
ETBARF	.2227		.2245		.2226	
WSSR (χ²)	.3320		.2290	(158.)[b]	.3320	(.00)[c]
Brockton:						
Full Nonlinear Model (N1)						
ETAXS (*t*-Stat)	.1582	(9.61)	.0805	(.63)	.1555	(7.11)
ETAXF	.1582		.1650	(8.03)	.1555	
ETBARS	.1582		.0805		.1606	(7.76)
ETBARF	.1582		.1650		.1606	
WSSR (χ²)	.2750		.2720	(2.16)[c]	.2750	(.00)[c]
Full Linear Model (L1)						
ETAXS (*t*-Stat)	.1544	(8.23)	−.0993	(−.69)	.1544	(8.22)
ETAXF	.1544		.1653	(7.15)	.1544	
ETBARS	.1544		−.0993		−.0447	(−.35)
ETBARF	.1544		.1653		−.0447	
WSSR (χ²)	.2930		.2580	(26.6)[b]	.2730	(14.4)[b]
Barnstable:						
Full Nonlinear Model (N1)						
ETAXS (*t*-Stat)	.3310	(2.92)	.3655	(1.73)	.5746	(3.05)
ETAXF	.3310		.3216	(2.60)	.5746	
ETBARS	.3310		.3655		.1131	(.64)
ETBARF	.3310		.3216		.1131	
WSSR (χ²)	.5140		.5130	(.19)[c]	.3930	(30.2)[b]
Full Linear Model (L1)						
ETAXS (*t*-Stat)	.4387	(3.56)	.5238	(2.57)	.5201	(3.91)
ETAXF	.4387		.4166	(3.16)	.5201	
ETBARS	.4387		.5238		.1926	(1.01)
ETBARF	.4387		.4166		.1926	
WSSR (χ²)	.4180		.4120	(1.43)[c]	.3560	(17.1)[b]

[a] The fully restricted model estimates one coefficient for all tax rate components in $\Delta t^* = (t_S - \bar{t}_S) - (t_F - \bar{t}_F)$. The intra-period restriction estimates separate coefficients for $(t_S - \bar{t}_S)$ and $(t_F - \bar{t}_F)$, the inter-period restriction for $(t_S - t_F)$ and $(\bar{t}_F - \bar{t}_S)$.

[b] The difference between this partially restricted model and the fully restricted model is significant at the 1% level.

[c] Not significant at the 1% level. The critical value for χ² is 6.635.

The results in Table 6-8 reveal that different factors are at work in different communities. The proposition that there exists a single, comprehensive tax capitalization rate can be rejected in all models except for the nonlinear model in Brockton. In Waltham and Brockton the degree of capitalization appears to be the same within a time period but to differ across time periods.[7] However, the degree of capitalization is larger after revaluation in Waltham and before revaluation in Brockton. These results suggest that revaluation greatly improved the quality of information about relative tax rates in Waltham, thereby boosting the degree of capitalization. In Brockton, on the other hand, revaluation appears to have lowered the expected persistence of tax differences. Indeed, the estimated degree of capitalization after revaluation is not significantly different from zero, which implies that existing tax differences are not expected to persist for any length of time. In Barnstable, the degree of capitalization appears to be the same across time periods but to be higher for the house's effective tax rate than for the town average tax rate. This result suggests that people have better information about their own rate than about the town average. This interpretation is particularly plausible for Barnstable, where the effective tax rate differs by village. People may have a good idea about the effective tax rate in their village but be unaware of the tax rate in other districts and therefore in the town as a whole.

We also attempted to estimate a completely unrestricted model in the three communities with control variables and partially restricted models in the communities without controls. These models are not or are nearly not identified, however, with the consequence that the nonlinear procedure often failed to converge and both procedures produced estimates with low t-statistics. In essence, there is little variation in the average tax rate in each community at the time of the first sale and almost no variation in the average tax rate after revaluation, so the coefficients of these variables cannot be reliably estimated. Because of their near singularity, we do not present the results for these models.

Although either the inter-period or the intra-period restrictions must be rejected in every case, we focus for the most part on the results from the fully restricted model. In Waltham and Brockton, the coefficients of the first-sale tax variables are virtually the same in the preferred model, with only intra-period restrictions, as in the fully restricted model. In other words, the estimated β from the fully restricted model should be interpreted as a measure of capitalization before revaluation. In Barnstable, removing the intra-period restrictions adds to the explanatory power of the model, but also complicates an interpretation of the results, because they no longer directly apply to relative tax rates. We focus on the fully restricted model in Barnstable for ease of interpretation.

6. CONCLUSIONS

Our preferred estimates of the property tax capitalization rate are 21.1% in Waltham and 15.8% in Brockton. These rates are measured consistently and precisely. In these two Massachusetts communities, we find positive but incomplete capitalization of property tax changes into the sales prices of single-family houses. The two-standard-deviation confidence intervals are 12.7 to 29.5% in Waltham and 12.5 to 19.1% in Brockton. We obtain a similar result in Barnstable with less complete data. The estimated degree of capitalization in Barnstable is 33.1%, with a two-standard-deviation confidence interval of 21.7 to 44.5%.

The two other studies of revaluation, Wicks, Little and Beck (1968) and Smith (1970), find somewhat higher degrees of capitalization, 50% and 44%, respectively, assuming a 3% discount rate. Recall that the method used by Wicks et al. biases upward the estimate of capitalization. In addition, the two studies of tax changes associated with Proposition 13 in California, Gabriel (1981) and Rosen (1982), find estimates very close to ours, namely 36% and 22%. Moreover, our estimates bracket Richardson and Thalheimer's (1981) estimate, which is 15% with a 3% discount rate, in their study of intermingled jurisdictions with different tax rates. Nevertheless, except in Belmont, our estimates are substantially lower than those in the widely cited study by Oates (1973), in the similar aggregate study by Rosen and Fullerton (1977) for the same sample of communities, and in Moody's study (1974) of the financing of a transit station. All of these estimates are about 60%, assuming a 3% discount rate. Several other studies, of both inter- and intrajurisdictional capitalization, also obtain estimates in the 50–70% range. Our results therefore reinforce the conclusion that the degree of capitalization is not the same in every case. We return to this issue in Chapter 7, where we consider the reasons why our estimates differ from 100%.

Our results are obtained by (1) using the correct nonlinear functional form, (2) correcting for the simultaneity bias created by the endogeneity of the after revaluation tax rate, and (3) holding constant not only housing and neighborhood characteristics per se, but also changes in them and in their market values. The latter two features of our methodology appear to be essential for obtaining precise and consistent estimation results.

Ignoring the endogeneity bias of the post-revaluation tax rate produces estimates that grossly overstate the true extent of tax capitalization. To make matters worse, these estimates appear to be precise with large estimated t-ratios. This pattern holds in any functional specification, be it linear or nonlinear, and with or without holding housing and neighborhood characteristics constant.

Ignoring the correlation between tax rate changes and housing and neighborhood characteristics, that is, not holding the changes in these attributes constant, yields underestimates of the rate of property tax capitalization. Inclusion of these attributes also produces more precisely measured capitalization rates. It is also important to use interactions between the nominal tax rate and housing and neighborhood characteristics as instruments. If they are neither part of the main regression nor of the instruments, the downward bias is largest.

Ignoring the correct nonlinear form tends to produce in less precise results and a slight overestimate of the tax capitalization rate. Although the differences between linear and nonlinear results are small, which indicates that revaluation largely succeeded in equalizing effective tax rates, in most cases we find a gain in efficiency by employing nonlinear methods.

In four communities, we could not obtain any control variables for housing and neighborhood characteristics. The impact of such controls on estimated capitalization in Waltham, Brockton, and Barnstable implies that this lack of data prevents reliable estimation of the rate of property tax capitalization in these other communities. Using the Waltham, Brockton, and Barnstable results to estimate and correct for the magnitude of the bias in the other four communities, we conclude that Arlington and Wellesley have low capitalization rates, 9% and 12%, whereas Brookline has an intermediate rate, 46%, and Belmont has a high rate, 79%.

NOTES

[1] Remember that housing and neighborhood characteristics appear in different interactions as regressors and instruments.

[2] This argument also suggests that the lack of addition variables may bias downward the estimate of capitalization in Brockton. In fact, omitting the addition variables from the full linear simultaneous model for Waltham does lower the estimate of capitalization, but by less than one percentage point. Leaving out these variables does not appear to be the source of a large bias in Brockton.

[3] More precisely, we can convert the differences in the objective functions WSSR(α) in Equation (5-6) into chi-square distributed test statistics. Let $WSSR_F$ denote the minimal weighted sum of squared residuals of the full model, and $WSSR_B$ of the basic model. For a sample of T observations, the test statistic $T \cdot (WSSR_B - WSSR_F)/WSSR_F$ is asymptotically distributed as χ_k^2 where the degrees of freedom k is the number of housing and neighborhood characteristics included in the full model. Note however that this test requires the same list of instruments in the full and basic model, which is not the case in the estimations reported in Appendix C.

[4] Even with first-order effects, problems of interpretation can be severe. See, for example, Brown and Rosen (1982), Bartik (1987), and Epple (1987).

[5] It is theoretically possible that people have worse information about actual tax rate differences after revaluation because no such differences are supposed to exist. We do not believe this possibility is very likely, however.

[6] It is theoretically possible, but in our judgement unlikely, that people could expect tax differences to persist longer after revaluation. Once a revaluation has been carried out, one might argue, another one will not be necessary for a long time. In Massachusetts, however, all cities are required to revalue every three years. This requirement existed at the time of the revaluations we study and must have influenced house buyers' expectations.

[7] This result is not totally unambiguous. In Waltham, the test statistic for the nonlinear model with inter-period restrictions is just significant, but the two estimated tax coefficients are virtually the same. In Brockton, the test statistic for the linear model with inter-period restrictions is significant, but we focus on the more compelling nonlinear model.

7

Property Tax Capitalization and Public Policy

Many types of public policy alter relative property tax burdens. Assessment reform, for example, redistributes property tax burdens among the households within a jurisdiction. State intergovernmental grants induce cities to spend more on public services, but to some degree they also allow cities to cut their property tax rates.[1] Moreover, some state aid programs are directed toward cities with low property tax bases and therefore allow those cities to cut their property taxes more than other cities.

With capitalization, these changes in relative property taxes lead to changes in house values, that is, to capital gains and losses for current homeowners. These potential capital gains and losses reveal the importance of capitalization for an evaluation of policies that affect property taxes. Without capitalization, and hence without capital gains and losses, these policies only affect future residents; households are affected by the property-tax changes only if they stay in or move to the jurisdiction. But with complete capitalization, residents at the time the policy is implemented bear the full burden of any change in the future stream of property taxes on their houses in the form of a capital gain or loss, regardless of whether they stay in the jurisdiction or move out of it.

In this chapter, we consider various aspects of capitalization and public policy. We begin by providing a detailed interpretation of our results and by exploring why capitalization is less than 100% and why it varies across communities. We then turn to specific public policy issues. We examine the problem capitalization poses for an assessor immediately after a revaluation and we measure the distribution of capital gains and losses caused by revaluation. We analyze the consequences of capitalization for economic efficiency and the fairness of the property tax, as measured by its horizontal and vertical equity. Our discussion is limited to the case of owner-occupied housing; we do not consider, for example, the implications of capitalization for the incidence of the property tax on rental housing or on commercial property.

1. INTERPRETATION OF CAPITALIZATION ESTIMATES

Our main result is that about 15 to 30% of the change in property taxes caused by community-wide revaluation is capitalized into house values.

As summarized in Table 7-1, the estimated degree of capitalization varies by community. In Waltham, for which we have the best data, our estimate is 21%. In Brockton, with good data, the estimate is 16%, and in Barnstable, with neighborhood controls only, the estimate is 33%. All of these estimates are significantly larger than zero and significantly smaller than 100% at a high level of confidence.

The remaining four communities do not have adequate control variables, but by adding the average effect of controls in Waltham, Brockton, and Barnstable, we obtain "corrected" estimates of the degree of capitalization in these communities. These estimates are 9% in Arlington, 12% in Wellesley, 46% in Brookline, and 79% in Belmont.

1.1 Why Is the Degree of Capitalization Less than 100%?

The first question to ask in interpreting these results is: why is the degree of capitalization less than 100%? In our judgement, the main reason appears to be that households do not expect pre-revaluation tax differences to persist — even before revaluation is announced. We have no direct evidence to support this conclusion; so far as we know, no one has conducted a survey of homeowner expectations about revaluation. Nevertheless, the case histories of revaluation in Waltham and Brockton, which were presented in Chapter 4, make it clear that revaluation was discussed — and indeed debated vigorously — for several years before it was actually implemented. People in those communities knew that revaluation was likely to occur in the not-too-distant future. Moreover, in three of the seven communities, including the two with the best data, anticipated tax changes had a significant effect on house values in the period just before revaluation.[2] In Waltham, we find an anticipation effect in both the year before revaluation is announced and during the period between announcement and enactment of revaluation. We also find an anticipation effect in Belmont during the period between announcement and enactment and in Brockton in the year before announcement.[3]

As explained in Chapter 3, the expectation that revaluation will occur in the near future can lead to a degree of capitalization well below 100%. Using Equation (3-15), we show that if current tax differences are expected to persist for only 10 years, the degree of capitalization for those tax differences will be only 26%. This exercise suggests that the degree of capitalization may vary across communities because expectations about the likely persistence of tax differentials varies. In communities with active assessors and a political climate that favors revaluation, house buyers may expect revaluation to take place in just a few years, whereas in communities with a history of inflexible assessments and hostility to revaluation, house buyers may expect revaluation to be postponed indefinitely.

Let us assume for the moment that expectations are the only source of variation in tax capitalization rates. On the basis of this assumption, we can use Equation (3-15) to calculate what our estimated capitalization rates imply about house buyers' expectations for the persistence of tax differentials.[4] The results of this exercise for our seven sample communities are reported in Table 7-1. The range in the implied expected persistence of tax differentials is from 3 years in Arlington to 54 years in Belmont. Belmont is an outlier, however, as the other six communities fall between 3 and 21 years. The actual average time between an observed first sale and revaluation was about 2¼ years in Barnstable and Brockton (where we have no data before 1969) and between 3 and 5 years in the other five communities. Given this actual timing and the active debate over revaluation in most communities, these expectations strike us as plausible, but we cannot directly test the extent to which expectations are at work.[5]

Several authors, including Goodman (1983), have argued that if tax differences are not expected to persist, then one should use a high discount rate in calculating the degree of tax capitalization. This argument is formally correct, but it changes the meaning of capitalization. Our approach focuses on the capitalization of current tax differences; this alternative approach focuses on the capitalization of the expected future stream of taxes. Without imperfect information or high search costs, the statement that current taxes are not fully capitalized because they are not expected to persist is equivalent to the statement that the expected future stream of taxes is fully capitalized. If one estimates the degree to which current taxes are capitalized but wants to calculate the degree to which the expected future stream is capitalized, then

Table 7-1
Estimated Capitalization and Implied Expectations

Community	Estimated Degree of Capitalization (in percent)	Implied Expected Persistence of Tax Differences (in years)[a]
With Complete Data		
Waltham	21	8
Brockton	16	6
With Neighborhood Controls Only		
Barnstable	33	14
Without Housing and Neighborhood Controls[b]		
Arlington	9	3
Belmont	79	54
Brookline	46	21
Wellesley	12	4

[a] Calculated with the formula in footnote 4.
[b] Estimates of capitalization equal the nonlinear two-stage least squares estimates in Table 6-1 corrected for the average effect of controls, as observed in Waltham, Brockton, and Barnstable.

one should use a real discount rate adjusted, in the manner described by Equation (3-4), for the expected persistence of tax differences.[6]

Although this translation between the two meanings of capitalization is always possible, all the research on capitalization, including our study, focuses on the capitalization of current tax differences, which can be observed, instead of on the capitalization of differences in expected tax streams, which cannot. Nevertheless, the important issue for some policy questions is whether the expected stream of taxes is fully capitalized, not whether current taxes are fully capitalized. We believe it is important, therefore, to keep in mind the distinction between these two meanings of capitalization.

Although the implied expectations in Table 7-1 are plausible, they do not constitute a formal test of the hypothesis that expectations cause incomplete capitalization of current tax differences, and they do not rule out the possibility that imperfect information and high search costs are also at work. Indeed, one would expect these other effects to appear in Massachusetts, where effective property tax rates varied widely before revaluation largely because of assessment errors. Within a community, a tax difference cannot be fully capitalized unless house seekers know the town average tax rate as well as the rate on the houses for which they are bidding. Assessment errors make it more difficult to infer the town-wide effective tax rate from the observed tax payments on the few houses that are for sale at a given time and make it more expensive for a house seeker to find a comparable house with a lower tax rate. By undercutting the quality of available information and raising search costs, these errors could lead to incomplete property tax capitalization.[7]

Some of our results in Chapter 6 support this conclusion. In Waltham, for example, we find that the rate of tax capitalization is significantly higher after revaluation than before revaluation, which is consistent with the hypothesis that all the publicity surrounding revaluation improved the quality of the information available to house seekers. Information appears to play a different role in Barnstable, where the degree of capitalization is higher for a house's actual effective tax rate than for the town average effective tax rate. Barnstable contains several villages with different tax rates, so this result is consistent with the view that house seekers are aware of the rate in their village but have imperfect information about the average rate in the town as a whole.

1.2 Why Does the Degree of Capitalization Vary Across Communities?

To further understand the sources of variation in the degree of capitalization across communities, we examined the correlation between the degree of capitalization and various community characteristics. Expectations are likely to be related to the pre-revaluation tax situation. Imperfect information and high search costs are likely to be related to community characteristics that affect the housing market. We find that the degree of capitalization is significantly related to a community's pre-revaluation effective property tax rate, population density, percentage of old housing, and median household income. In particular, the degree of capitalization is significantly higher in communities with a lower pre-revaluation tax rate, a lower population density, more new housing, and a lower median household income.[8]

Our interpretation of these results is as follows: A high property tax rate makes people more aware of property tax differences and increases the pressure for assessment reform.[9] All else equal, therefore, people in communities with high tax rates expect revaluation to occur sooner than people in communities with low tax rates. In addition, factors that add to the complexity of the housing market make it more difficult for house seekers to gather accurate information about the relative value of different houses. If no two houses are alike, for example, a house buyer will have a hard time determining whether the tax payment on one house is higher or lower, relative to its market value, than the tax payment on another house. Communities with very high incomes have more types and styles of housing to choose from. A high population density, which is associated with locations near urban centers, signals that owner-occupied housing is located in a variety of different settings, some next to commerical areas and some mixed with high-rise apartments, that are difficult for house seekers to evaluate. Finally, a high concentration of new housing indicates a changing housing market, in which it is difficult to collect accurate and up-to-date information. House buyers may be uncertain, for example, about future building in a newer neighborhood, and hence about future neighborhood quality. In addition, before revaluation new houses tend to be taxed at a higher effective rate than old houses and builders may not be able to make a profit at a price that fully capitalizes this relatively high tax rate. Because of high search costs, buyers may be willing to pay what builders ask.[10] Thus, high population density, high median income, and extensive new housing measure aspects of housing market complexity.

Most of our sample communities had pre-revaluation effective tax rates near 2.8%; however, Barnstable and Belmont had tax rates about one percentage point lower and Brockton had a rate almost twice this high. In addition, the housing market appears to be relatively complex in Arlington, Barnstable, and Wellesley, and relatively simple in Belmont and Brockton. The sources of housing market complexity vary across communities, however. In Arlington, the complexity is due to an extremely high population density. Wellesley and Barnstable, on the other hand, have relatively low population densities, but nevertheless have complex housing markets, Barnstable because of its high percentage of new housing units and Wellesley because of its very high income. The housing market is simple in Belmont because of a relatively old housing stock, and in Brockton because of a relatively low household income.[11]

According to our interpretation, both a high pre-revaluation tax rate and a complex housing market will be associated with a low degree of capitalization. Thus, Belmont has a high degree of capitalization because it has both a low pre-revaluation tax rate and a simple housing market. Arlington and Wellesley have low capitalization because they have complex housing markets combined with an average pre-revaluation tax rate. Brookline and Waltham have average capitalization because they have average housing-market complexity and average tax rates. Offsetting forces are at work in Barnstable and Brockton. Barnstable has a complex housing market, which drives the degree of capitalization down, but the lowest pre-revaluation tax rate rate, which keeps capitalization high. Brockton has a simple housing market, which keeps capitalization high, and the highest pre-revaluation tax rate, which drives capitalization down. In both cases, the tax-rate effect is somewhat stronger, so the degree of capitalization is somewhat below average in Brockton and somewhat above average in Barnstable.

Overall, we present evidence from a variety of sources to support the conclusion that household expectations about the persistence of tax differences, imperfect information about relative tax rates, and high housing search costs all influence the degree of tax capitalization. We discover that tax changes are anticipated in the period just before revaluation. We observe that our estimates of capitalization have reasonable implications for households' expectations about the persistence of tax differentials, and indeed that these implied expectations are consistent with the actual timing of revaluation in most communities. We find that the degree of capitalization is different before and after revaluation in Waltham and Brockton and higher for the actual than for the town-average effective tax rate in Barnstable, and show how these differences could arise from changes in expectations or imperfect information. Finally, we discover that the degree of capitalization is correlated with one likely source of household expectations, the pre-revaluation effective tax rate, and with community characteristics that are likely to influence the quality of information about relative tax rates and the magnitude of housing search costs.

Taken individually, these results are not convincing. The regressions to explain the degree of capitalization, for example, are based on only 7 observations. But taken as a package, we believe that this evidence provides strong support for the position that capitalization varies from one set of circumstances to another. Unfortunately, we cannot definitively separate the role of expectations from the role of information and search costs. This separation will prove to be important for the policy issues discussed in the rest of this chapter. Our tentative conclusion, based on all this evidence, is that in our sample capitalization is far below 100% primarily because households do not expect current tax differences to persist, but the precise degree of capitalization varies from one community to another because household expectations, information quality, and search costs all are influenced by community characteristics.

1.3   Modeling the Degree of Property Tax Capitalization

Most of the empirical literature on property tax capitalization has attempted to estimate "the" degree of capitalization, assumed to be the same under all circumstances. We believe this assumption is inappropriate. Even in our study, which examines the capitalization of tax changes from a common source in relatively similar communities, variation in household expectations, information, and search costs appears to influence the degree to which current taxes are capitalized into house values. We hope that the focus of future research will be to determine how the degree of capitalization varies from one set of circumstances to another by carefully modeling the sources of variation or change in property taxes, the formation of households' expectations, and the role of housing market characteristics.

Proposition 13 in California, for example, provides an excellent contrast to the situation in Massachusetts. Under the rules of this Proposition, a house's assessed value equals its market values at the time of sale, but then increases only 2% per year until the next sale.[12] This clear legal rule defines households' expectations. Everyone knows that their effective property tax rate will decline over time, so that current taxes will not be fully capitalized into house values. The only variable factor is how long a household expects to stay in the house it wants to buy; the longer the household expects to stay, the longer the decline in effective tax rate will persist, and the lower the degree to which current taxes will be capitalized.[13] With accurate assessments at the point of sale, imperfect information and high search costs should not matter; buyers know that the property tax situation is the same for any house they buy. As a result, one should be able to estimate the degree of intrajurisdictional tax capitalization in California as a function of a household's expected mobility (or of household characteristics associated with mobility).

The importance of circumstances also suggests that interjurisdictional and intrajurisdictional differences in property taxes may be capitalized at different rates. Taxes vary across jurisdictions because of systematic differences in tax bases and spending levels. Because the sources of this variation are systematic, households can obtain information about it more easily than about assessment errors. It follows that imperfect information is not likely to have a large effect on the degree of interjurisdictional property tax capitalization. Furthermore, except under special circumstances, such as an announced intention to change spending or the likelihood of extensive growth in industrial property in a community, current taxes are the best forecast of future taxes in a community, so expectations are unlikely to lower the degree to which current differences in taxes across communities are capitalized into house values.

The role of search costs could work the other way. To be specific, certain types of housing may be clustered in one or two communities. In this case, households may be willing to buy housing in a high-tax jurisdiction without a break in the market price because it would be costly for them to find comparable housing in a low-tax jurisdiction. Hence, a high correlation between community and housing type could lead to a lower degree of capitalization for tax differences across communities than for tax differences within communities. Further research is needed to determine which of these factors has the strongest impact on the degree of interjurisdictional property tax capitalization.

2. THE ASSESSOR'S PROBLEM

We now turn to questions of public policy. The first question is a very practical one: how should an assessor determine assessed values in the period immediately after a revaluation? In the following sections, we examine the implications of tax capitalization for the equity and efficiency of the property tax.

Given a large change in relative tax rates, as with revaluation, the assessor faces a difficult short-run problem. His job is to estimate the market prices of all the houses in his community on the basis of a sample of houses that actually sold. At the time of revaluation, he has observed sales prices from the pre-revaluation regime, but must assess, that is estimate sales prices, for the post-revaluation regime. To carry out this step, he must know a house's pre- and post-revaluation effective property tax rates and then use the analysis described earlier in this book, as summarized by Equation (5-1), to calculate the real percentage change in the house's value.

An exact calculation is difficult because it requires knowledge about the second-sale effective tax rate, which depends on the second-sale house value that the assessor is trying to predict. If revaluation is reasonably accurate, however, the second-sale tax rate will be approximately the same for all houses in the community and it will drop out of the calculation, and the assessor can use a much simpler approach, which is described by Equation (5-9). This equation indicates that the real percentage increase in a house's value equals the difference between the house's pre-revaluation effective tax rate and the town-wide average effective tax rate (on single-family houses) multiplied by the degree of capitalization and divided by the real interest rate.[14]

Suppose, for example, that the real interest rate is 3% and that current taxes are capitalized at a rate of 20%. Then if the pre-revaluation effective tax rate is 2 percentage points above the average, the real change in house value will be $(0.2)(.02)/(.03) = .133$; in other words, the house in this example will experience a 13% real capital gain because of revaluation.[15]

3. CAPITALIZATION AND THE ECONOMIC EFFICIENCY OF THE PROPERTY TAX

Many scholars, including Oates (1972), have argued that the property tax distorts the housing market. As long as assessments are related to market values, the property tax alters the gross price (i.e., the market price plus the tax) a household must pay to buy a house. The logic is analogous to the standard case of a sales tax; because households respond to the price of housing including the property tax, the property tax introduces a wedge between the price to which the households respond and the resource cost of housing. Because of this tax wedge, households consume less than the efficient amount of housing.

The argument becomes more complicated in a second-best world with taxes on other commodities. Following the usual rule, the tax rate on housing should be higher than the tax rate on other goods only to the extent that the price elasticity of demand for housing is lower (in absolute value) than the price elasticity of other goods.[16] In fact, however, the property tax, unlike most other taxes, is levied against an asset instead of against an annual flow. A t percent property tax applied to house value is equivalent to a t/r percent tax applied to the annual value of housing services, where r is the real discount rate. With a real discount rate of 3% for example, a 2% property tax rate is equivalent to a 67% tax on housing services. It follows that property taxes are likely to be far higher than called for by any second-best tax rule.[17]

3.1   The Efficiency Consequences of Assessment Errors

The existence of capitalization fundamentally alters these arguments because the market price of housing reflects the property tax. Consider first the case of assessment errors. These errors lead to inefficiency if they alter housing consumption decisions at the margin. Consider two houses that are identical except that, because of an assessment error, one of them has a higher tax payment. If the market price of each house fully reflects the present value of its relative tax payment, then they will be equally attractive to a household. Even though one house has a higher tax payment, in other words, full capitalization insures that the asset price plus the present value of the tax payment is the same for both houses.[18] With full capitalization, therefore, assessment errors do not influence housing consumption and therefore do not cause any inefficiency.

This argument applies to the capitalization of the expected stream of tax differences, not to the capitalization of current tax differences. If tax differences last only 10 years, then the present value of the stream of tax differences equals only 26% of the present value of current tax differences strung out forever.[19] In this case, full capitalization of current tax differences would overcompensate people who buy houses with high tax rates and distort their housing choices. Consider, for example, two identical households shopping for housing. Suppose only one of these households buys a house with a favorable assessment error. With full capitalization of this error, this household will pay less than the other household for housing and property taxes, and will therefore consume more housing.

A similar distortion arises if poor information or high search costs leads to incomplete capitalization. In this case, a household that purchases a house with an unfavorable assessment error will pay more for housing and taxes than an otherwise identical household that purchases a house with a favorable assessment error. Thus, the first household will consume less housing.

With incomplete tax capitalization, therefore, the extent of inefficiency in the housing market caused by assessment errors depends on the source of the incomplete capitalization. If the source is the expectation that current tax differences will not persist, then assessment errors cause no inefficiency. If, on the other hand, the source is imperfect information or high search costs, then assessment errors do distort housing consumption decisions to some degree. On the basis of our conclusion that expectations are the principal source of incomplete capitalization, we conclude that assessment errors did not cause serious distortion of the housing market in Massachusetts.

3.2   The Efficiency Consequences of Interjurisdictional Tax Rate Differences

Capitalization also alters the efficiency consequences of interjurisdictional property tax rate differences.[20] To examine these consequences, let us assume for convenience that current tax rate differences are expected to persist for a long time.[21] The annual gross price of housing equals the annual market price of housing plus the annual property tax payment per unit of housing services. Capitalization implies, however, that the market price of housing reflects the property tax payment. With full capitalization, a \$1 increase in the present value of property tax payments per unit of housing leads to a \$1 decrease in the market price per unit of housing, so the gross price of housing is the same regardless of the property tax rate. With no capitalization, on the other hand, the gross price varies with the property tax payment; people with higher payments face higher gross prices and consume less housing.

This argument is incomplete, however, because it ignores the fact that only relative differences in tax rates are capitalized. The conceptual framework developed in Chapter 3 indicates that houses with above-average tax-rate increases due to revaluation will experience declines in value relative to the average house in the jurisdiction. Applying the same logic to interjurisdictional tax differences leads to the conclusion that, all else equal, the higher the tax rate in a town the lower the average property value in the town. This framework says nothing about the overall level of housing prices. Strictly speaking, therefore, we have established that complete capitalization eliminates the housing-market inefficiency caused by variation in property taxes, but we have not established that complete capitalization eliminates inefficiency caused by the overall level of property taxes in a metropolitan area.

An analysis of the link between the level of property taxes and housing-market inefficiency is provided by Yinger (1985). This analysis combines two approaches to housing-price determination. According to the standard model of urban structure, the housing market expands outward in an urban area until its price equals the opportunity cost of taking the required resources out of some other activity, say agriculture. According to the standard asset-pricing model, however, the price of a house also must equal the rental value of housing adjusted for property taxes, or, according to Equation (3-4), the before-tax annual rental value of housing divided by the sum of the discount rate and the effective property tax rate. In combination, these two approaches imply that in a community at the outer edge of the metropolitan area, the opportunity cost of housing must equal the before-tax rental value of housing divided by the sum of the discount rate and the property tax rate. Equivalently, the before-tax rental value of housing must equal the opportunity cost of housing multiplied by the sum of the discount and tax rates. Although this analysis applies to one "reference" jurisdiction at the outer edge of the urban area, a competitive housing market insures that the before-tax rental value of housing will be the same in all other jurisdictions. In other words, the before-tax rental value of housing throughout the urban area reflects the effective property tax rate in the reference jurisdiction. The higher this reference tax rate, the higher the gross price of housing, and the greater the distortion in the housing market.

In short, full capitalization of the expected stream of tax differences eliminates all distortion from variation in the property tax rate across houses within a jurisdiction or across jurisdictions. But it does not eliminate distortion from the property tax altogether. Even with full capitalization, the property tax rate in the reference jurisdiction affects the "before-tax" price of housing services and therefore introduces a tax wedge into the housing market. With less-than-complete capitalization, some additional distortion arises from variation in the property tax rate.

Differences in public service quality may also be capitalized. Although full capitalization eliminates distortion from variation in the property tax, it does not eliminate distortion from variation in public service quality. With complete capitalization of public services, the before-tax price of housing reflects service quality, not just the resource cost of providing housing and the reference property tax rate. Household decisions do not satisfy the relevant efficiency conditions because the price of housing is too high in jurisdictions with relatively high service quality and too low in jurisdictions with relatively low service quality. For a detailed discussion of this issue, see Yinger (1985).

4. CAPITALIZATION AND THE HORIZONTAL EQUITY OF THE PROPERTY TAX

Several authors, including Hamilton (1976a), have argued that capitalization guarantees horizontal equity—the equal treatment of people in the same circumstances—for the property tax. With full capitalization, all variation in taxes is reflected in prices, so nobody gains from purchasing a house with low taxes. For a house with given structural and neighborhood characteristics, in other words, everyone pays the same gross price. Tax equity depends on the final burden of a tax, not on the tax actually paid to the government. With capitalization, the burden of the tax, as measured by the gross price, is the same for all house purchasers. Note that the relevant concept here is the capitalization of expected tax streams, not of current taxes; horizontal equity is achieved if people are fully compensated, in the form of lower house values, for the present value of the property taxes they expect to pay.[22]

4.1   The Horizontal Equity of Tax Rate Changes

As Aaron (1975) and Feldstein (1976) make clear, however, this argument does not apply to changes in effective property tax rates. According to Feldstein, "tax changes are a source of horizontal inequity because individuals make commitments based on the existing tax law. . . . Commitments involving property may easily be reversed but the sale of assets will involve a capital loss. . . . Individuals who were equally well off before the tax change are not equally well off after the change" (p. 95–96).

  Thus, capitalization insures that all new buyers are on the same footing, but it also insures that current owners bear the full burden of any unanticipated changes in future property taxes. When assessment quality deteriorates, for example, or when past assessment errors are corrected, some owners receive property tax cuts and others receive property tax increases. As long as these tax changes were not anticipated, each current owner experiences a capital gain or loss equal to the present value of the change in her stream of property taxes. This outcome violates the principle of horizontal equity.

  With complete capitalization, unanticipated property tax changes have the same impact on a homeowner regardless of whether she sells her house, and thereby realizes the capital gain or loss on it, or stays in her house, and thereby pays the new property tax stream. In other words, capitalization eliminates the option of moving to avoid paying an unanticipated property increase and opens the option of moving to cash in on an unanticipated property tax cut. The magnitude of the capital gains and losses, and hence the extent of the horizontal inequity, depends on the degree to which current property tax differences are capitalized into house values. The higher the degree of capitalization, the greater the horizontal inequity from any unanticipated property tax change.

In short, complete property tax capitalization insures that once it has become established any set of effective property tax rates is horizontally equitable whereas any change in these rates is not. Without capitalization, variation in effective tax rates is a source of horizontal inequity, whereas changes in effective tax rates are not, because they do not lead to capital gains and losses.

4.2   The Case for Assessment Reform

The existence of capitalization therefore provides a strong argument for keeping assessments up to date. To promote horizontal equity, local assessors should avoid the arbitrary changes in effective tax rates caused by assessment errors or by holding assessments constant while market values diverge. Any such changes lead to capital gains and losses and therefore violate the principle of horizontal equity. Furthermore, a well-publicized policy of regular revaluation will lead house buyers' to expect that current tax differences will not persist. This expectation will lower the extent to which current tax differences are capitalized into house values and therefore will lower the gains and losses associated with changes in tax rates brought on by assessment errors or market trends.[23]

Aaron's and Feldstein's analyses also reveal, however, that capitalization complicates the case for assessment reform. Once assessment errors have been introduced into the system and home buyers have adjusted to them, revaluation causes changes in effective tax rates, which result in capital gains and losses for current owners and therefore violate the principle of horizontal equity. A compensation scheme could eliminate this problem but, as Feldstein points out, "such compensation would not be technically feasible for many important tax reforms, and may always be politically impossible" (p. 98).

In the case of revaluation, compensation would involve a payment to homeowners who received relative tax increases and hence capital losses and a windfall tax on homeowners who received relative tax decreases and hence capital gains. Strictly speaking, this compensation policy should recognize anticipation and the length of homeownership. People who bought their house a long time ago may already have experienced capital gains or losses as their effective tax rate diverged from the average. If so, the capital losses or gains from revaluation simply offset the gains or losses from the introduction of assessment errors. And if revaluation is anticipated, then recent purchasers will not experience a capital gain or loss from revaluation, regardless of the change in their effective tax rate. Needless to say, these complexities make it unlikely than an acceptable compensation scheme could be devised.

Whenever large assessment errors exist, therefore, town policy makers must decide whether the benefits of revaluation, in the form of greater economic efficiency, greater long-term horizontal equity, and perhaps greater resident satisfaction with the property tax, offset the short-term horizontal inequity of the resulting capital gains and losses. In our view, the benefits are likely to outweigh the costs, particularly if revaluation is an ongoing process, not a one-time correction. If revaluation is carried out once but arbitrary assessment errors are then allowed to reappear, the gains and losses from revaluation are followed by gains and losses that appear even more capricious. If, however, revaluation is combined with an updated assessment system that prevents the reappearance of large assessment errors, then economic efficiency and horizontal equity will be well served in the long run. Furthermore, the belief that assessments will be updated holds down the degree to which current tax differences are capitalized into house values and therefore minimizes the capital gains and losses that arise from any assessment errors that do occur, either through inaccurate revaluation or through between-revaluation changes in market values. These long-term gains clearly justify some horizontal inequity in the short run.[24]

Feldstein also points out that the gains and losses from tax reform can be minimized by postponement, that is, by a pause between the announcement and implementation of the reform.[25] Postponing implementation lowers the present value of the tax cuts or tax increases from revaluation, and therefore lowers the associated capital gains and losses. Moreover, the pause between announcement and implementation allows people to prepare for the reform and eliminates the possibility that people will experience a large gain or loss immediately after purchasing a house. As reported in Chapter 6, we find evidence that this announcement effect is indeed at work in the case of revaluation; in several of our sample communities, house values change in anticipation of an announced, but as yet unimplemented, revaluation.

A lag between announcement and implementation is not necessary if revaluation takes place regularly, but appears to be a common practice when revaluation has not occurred for many years, precisely because a long-postponed revaluation causes painful losses for some taxpayers. In Boston, for example, revaluation was resisted for many years, despite the State Supreme Court ruling requiring it, because assessment errors there were huge and some taxpayers would suffer severe losses from revaluation. Indeed, it was nine years between the major court decision and the first major revaluation in Boston. During this period, the inevitability of revaluation became clear and taxpayers had plenty of time to prepare for it.[26]

If imperfect information and high search costs lead to incomplete capitalization, that is, if the expected stream of future tax differences is incompletely capitalized, then horizontal equity does not exist, even for buyers, unless the effective tax rate is the same for everyone. Before assessment reform, people who stumble onto houses with low effective rates bear a smaller tax burden than people who stumble onto houses with high effective rates. This unequal treatment of people in the same circumstance violates the principle of horizontal equity. Incomplete capitalization of the stream of expected tax differences does lessen the unfairness of arbitrary changes in effective tax rates or of revaluation by lowering the capital gains and losses that such changes cause. In other words, compared to complete capitalization of expected tax differences, incomplete capitalization leads to more horizontal inequity from having assessment errors and to less horizontal inequity from introducing or correcting those errors. This incomplete capitalization therefore strengthens the case for assessment reform. Regardless of the degree of capitalization, the only way to maintain horizontal equity after revaluation is to keep all effective tax rates in a jurisdiction the same through regular, accurate assessment.

Taxpayers with relatively high effective tax rates have been known to sue assessors, not just to correct their assessments but also to obtain compensation for their relatively high tax payments in the past. Our analysis sheds some light on these suits. With complete capitalization, people who buy houses with relatively high effective tax rates pay relatively low housing prices and are no worse off than other buyers. Unless these people experience unanticipated tax rate increases after they buy their houses, they have not been treated unfairly and, in our judgement, do not deserve compensation. With incomplete capitalization of expected tax streams, people who buy houses with relatively high tax rates are not fully compensated by lower housing prices and some compensation may be appropriate. We conclude, therefore, that people who have paid relatively high effective property tax rates deserve compensation only to the extent that the capitalization of future tax streams is incomplete or to the extent that those relatively high rates reflect unanticipated tax increases that occurred after they bought their houses.[27]

5. THE DISTRIBUTION OF GAINS AND LOSSES FROM REVALUATION IN WALTHAM

In Massachusetts, a long history of inflexible assessment procedures produced wide disparities in effective tax rates within a community. Because current effective tax rates are capitalized into house values to a significant degree, this inflexibility insured that the owners of houses with relatively rapid value growth would receive arbitrary capital gains and owners of houses with relatively slow value growth would receive arbitrary capital losses. Moreover, to the extent that incomplete capitalization of current taxes is caused by imperfect information and high search costs, the variation in effective tax rates caused horizontal inequity among house buyers. To prevent future arbitrary gains and losses and to insure horizontal equity for house buyers, reform, in the form of community-wide revaluations, was needed. Nevertheless, revaluation often was resisted, at least in part because of the capital gains and losses that it would impose on homeowners.[28]

To shed light on this issue, we now report on the distribution of gains and losses from revaluation in Waltham. We do not face the assessor's dilemma in calculating these gains and losses because we are able to observe post-revaluation sales prices and tax rates. As a result, we can calculate capital gains and losses directly with Equation (5-1). The left side of this equation is the real change in house value due solely to revaluation.

Our results are summarized in Figure 7-1. The distribution of gains and losses in Waltham is remarkably compact. The average house in the

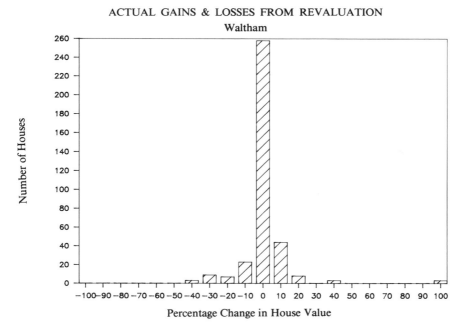

FIGURE 7-1

sample experienced a 0.1% gain, and the standard deviation of the gain is less than 10 percentage points.[29] Indeed, 311 (or 88%) of the 353 houses in the sample experienced a change in house value between −10 and +10%, and 94% of the houses experienced value changes between −20 and +20%. One house, for which revaluation lowered the effective tax rate by over 14 percentage points, experienced a gain of almost 100%, and another house, for which revaluation raised the effective tax rate by over 6 percentage points, experienced a loss greater than 40%. But most houses experienced more modest gains or losses.

Overall, therefore, the capital gains and losses from revaluation in Massachusetts were not very dramatic and certainly did not offset, even in the short run, the advantages of assessment reform. Only a handful of taxpayers, namely those with extremely high or extremely low effective tax rates before revaluation, experienced changes in house values that either threatened the equity in their homes or that gave them an unacceptable windfall. Moreover, some of the people with gains (losses) from revaluation previously experienced capital losses (gains) because of pre-revaluation tax changes; that is, the gains and losses from revaluation to some degree offset previous losses and gains. This point should not be pushed too far, however, because the link between previous losses and revaluation gains (or previous gains and revaluation losses) only exists for owners who experienced unanticipated effective tax rate changes before revaluation.[30]

One might ask how the distribution of gains and losses changes as the degree of capitalization changes. What if, for example, the degree of capitalization in Waltham were as high as it appears to be in Belmont? This situation could have arisen in Waltham if revaluation were imposed on the city without warning, so that, at the time of revaluation, the expected persistence of existing tax differences was 50 years instead of 8 years. This type of hypothetical question is answered in Figure 7-2, which plots the distribution of capital gains and losses for four capitalization rates: 21%, 50%, 75%, and 100%. Even with complete capitalization of current tax differences, the distribution of gains and losses is still tightly clustered around zero. With 21% capitalization, 96% of the houses have value changes between −25 and +25%; with 100% capitalization, 73% of the value changes fall within this range and 86% fall between −50 and +50%. Raising the capitalization rate pushes the extreme cases much farther from zero, however. With 100% capitalization, one house has a capital gain of 453%, one has a loss of −212%, and 4.5% of the houses have gains or losses that exceed 100%.

These calculations reveal the horizontal inequity that can arise from an unexpected revaluation imposed after a long history of inaccurate assessments. If revaluation is not expected, that is, if current tax differences are expected to persist, the degree of capitalization is likely to be high, so that

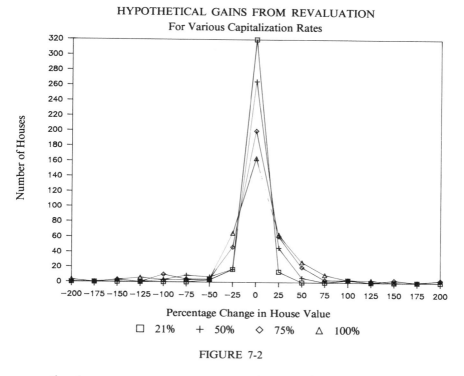

HYPOTHETICAL GAINS FROM REVALUATION
For Various Capitalization Rates

□ 21% + 50% ◇ 75% △ 100%

FIGURE 7-2

correcting large assessment errors causes large capital gains and losses, at least for some taxpayers. This situation and the associated inequity can be avoided, however, by moving gradually to the first revaluation after a long period of inaccurate assessment, and by maintaining accurate assessments after an initial revaluation.

Because it promotes efficiency and long-term horizontal equity, assessment reform constitutes sound public policy. Despite the attention they sometimes receive, short-term capital gains and losses should not be a barrier to implementing this reform.

6. CAPITALIZATION AND THE VERTICAL EQUITY OF THE PROPERTY TAX

Policy makers may also care about the relative treatment of different income classes of households, that is, about vertical equity. In this section we examine the implications of tax capitalization for the vertical equity of the property tax.

Without accurate assessments, effective property tax rates in a community may be systematically linked to income. In fact, one would expect effective tax rates to be lower for relatively expensive houses, which are more likely to be purchased by high-income people. The effective tax rate is proportional to the assessed value divided by the market value. With assessments held constant, changes in the effective tax rate are determined by changes in market value. Market value often grows more rapidly for houses that begin with high values; in addition, market value will be particularly high if it has grown rapidly in recent years. Over time, therefore, the effective property tax rate on high-valued property tends to fall below the rate on low-valued property, even if the two rates start out the same.[31]

Although the effective tax rate may vary with house value, capitalization insures that the real burden of the property tax does not. Everyone, regardless of his or her income, is willing to pay $1 to avoid $1 of property taxes. If this willingness to pay shows up in house values, that is, if the capitalization of the expected tax stream is complete, then the burden of the property tax is the same for all house buyers, regardless of their income, even if effective tax rates are systematically linked to income. In other words, full capitalization of the expected tax stream insures that property taxes impose the same burden per unit of housing, regardless of income or of willingness to spend on housing. From the perspective of new buyers, therefore, capitalization enforces proportionality; the burden of the property tax is a constant fraction of house value. With capitalization, the property tax cannot be either progressive or regressive with respect to house value.

This argument must be qualified in two ways. First, the capital gains and losses associated with unanticipated changes in property tax rates may not be distributed proportionally. Indeed, if relative effective tax rates on relatively expensive houses systematically decline over time, then the high-income people who own those houses will systematically receive capital gains while the owners of relatively inexpensive houses will receive capital losses. The only way to avoid this regressive outcome is to keep assessments equal to market values.

Second, house values may not be proportional to income, so it is possible to have a progressive or regressive outcome with respect to income even when one has a proportional outcome with respect to house value. Most studies find that spending on housing increases less then proportionally with income.[32] With full capitalization, therefore, the property tax will be regressive with respect to income even from the perspective of new buyers. This link to income is an important one; most discussions of vertical equity focus on taxes as a fraction of income, not of property value.

If imperfect information and high search costs cause incomplete capitalization, only a portion of expected future tax differences is offset by differences in housing prices. If expensive houses face relatively low effective tax rates, these lower taxes are not fully reflected in higher house values. Some share of the regressivity or progressivity in the assessment system (with respect to house value) remains in final tax burdens. On the other hand, this incomplete capitalization lowers the gains and losses that accompany unanticipated changes in effective tax rates and thereby lessens the vertical inequity that may be associated with such changes.

7. CONCLUSIONS

We find strong evidence to support the hypothesis that differences in effective property tax rates are, to some extent, capitalized into the price of housing. In the communities with the best data, Waltham, Brockton, and Barnstable, we find that the degree of tax capitalization is 21%, 16%, and 33%, respectively.

The degree of capitalization reflects households' expectations about future tax changes. In the Massachusetts case, variation in effective tax rates is caused by assessment errors and, because of much public debate about revaluation, households know that these errors will eventually be corrected. This type of expectation appears to be largely responsible for the incomplete capitalization of current tax differences. The estimated rate in Waltham, for example, could be caused simply by the expectation that current tax differences will persist for only 8 years. If household expectations are the only factor at work, then the incomplete capitalization of current tax differences is equivalent to complete capitalization of the expected future tax stream. To some extent, however, the rate of tax capitalization also appears to be affected by imperfect information and high housing search costs.

The degree of capitalization can vary from one set of circumstances to another. We study the capitalization of intrajurisdictional tax changes caused by revaluation. Studies of other situations, such as tax rate differences caused by Proposition 13 in California or interjurisdictional tax rate differences, are likely to find different degrees of capitalization. Furthermore, the degree of capitalization appears to reflect characteristics of the local housing market that influence the quality of information about tax differences and the magnitude of housing search costs.

Property tax capitalization has important implications for public policies, such as assessment reform and intergovernmental aid, that alter the relative property tax rates of owner-occupied houses; in the presence of capitalization, all such policies impose capital gains and losses on current property owners.

Some of the policy implications of capitalization are very practical; for example, a knowledge of capitalization can help an assessor calculate accurate assessments in the period right after revaluation. Other policy implications are more abstract. We show, for example, that complete capitalization eliminates the housing-market distortions associated with variation in property tax rates across communities but does not alter the housing-market distortion caused by the average property tax rate in a metropolitan area. Even with complete capitalization, the property tax causes underconsumption of housing.

Capitalization greatly alters an analysis of the horizontal equity of the property tax. On the one hand, complete capitalization of the expected tax stream insures that the real burden of the property tax is the same for all house buyers in a metropolitan area, regardless of the effective tax rate on the house they buy. On the other hand, complete capitalization also insures that any change in relative property tax rates will be accompanied by capital gains and losses for current owners, which violates the principle of horizontal equity. Ironically, this lack of horizontal equity arises both for the arbitrary changes in effective tax rates that arise over time when assessments are not updated and for the changes in tax rates caused by revaluation, which are designed to correct these assessment errors.

Despite the short-run horizontal inequity of revaluation, we believe that moving to regular, accurate assessments is good public policy because it promotes horizontal equity in the long run by eliminating the arbitrary changes in effective property tax rates, and accompanying capital gains and losses, that arise as assessed values and market values diverge. Incomplete capitalization, as in Massachusetts, strengthens the case for assessment reform because it lessens the short-term horizontal inequity of revaluation; indeed, we show that the gains and losses from revaluation in Waltham are small.

Finally, capitalization insures that the burden of the property tax on owner-occupied housing is proportional with respect to property value, even if the effective tax rate declines as house value increases. Even with complete capitalization of expected tax streams, however, the property tax on owner-occupied housing remains regressive with respect to income, because higher-income households tend to spend a smaller fraction of their income on housing. Moreover, capitalization insures that inflexible assessments will lead to capital gains for homeowners whose house values grow relatively rapidly, typically high-income people, and to capital losses for homeowners whose house values grow relatively slowly. This regressive distribution of gains and losses strengthens the case for assessment reform.

NOTES

[1] For a review of the literature on the behavioral effects of state grants, see Rubinfeld (1985).

[2] Smith (1970) also found that anticipated tax changes from revaluation are capitalized in the period after revaluation has been announced but before it is implemented.

[3] These announcement effects are small in magnitude. This finding suggests either that property tax changes were anticipated and capitalized well before revaluation was announced, or that anticipation has a small effect on house values. With no way to choose between these opposite conclusions, we do not place much weight on the magnitude of the anticipation coefficients.

[4] Equation (3-15) gives the degree of capitalization as a function of the expected persistence of tax differentials, so all it takes is a little algebra to solve for the (implied) expected persistence of tax differentials as a function of the (estimated) degree of capitalization. The answer is that N', the expected persistence of tax differentials, equals $-\ln(1 - \beta)/\ln(1 + r)$, where ln stands for a natural logarithm, β is the estimated degree of capitalization, and r is the real interest rate, which in our case is 3%. This formula is used to calculate the entries in Table 7-1.

[5] Differences in the expected persistence of tax differences also could explain why Smith (1970) obtains a higher estimate of capitalization than we do in most of our communities. The revaluation he studies was required by a state law and may not have been actively debated at the city level, so that until shortly before the law was passed, house buyers may have expected tax differentials to persist for a long time. Using the formula in Footnote 4 and Smith's estimate that capitalization is 44% (with a 3% discount rate), we find that the implied expected persistence of tax differentials in his case is 20 years.

[6] Although this point has been recognized at an intuitive level, to our knowledge, it has never been stated precisely. According to Equation (3-15), the coefficient of the tax difference variable is β', the degree of capitalization based on imperfect information and high search costs, multiplied by the ratio r/r', where r' is the real discount rate with an infinite horizon that is equivalent to the real discount rate r with horizon defined by the persistence of tax differences. The degree of capitalization for current tax differences is $\beta'r/r'$, whereas the degree of capitalization for the expected stream of tax differences is simply β'. The capitalization ratio, which many studies estimate, is the coefficient of the tax difference variable divided by r, which reduces to β'/r'. To find $\beta'r/r'$, therefore, one must multiply the estimated tax coefficient by r; whereas to obtain β' alone, one must multiply it by r'.

[7] This argument is also made by Ihlanfeldt and Jackson (1982). They make the conceptual argument that systematic assessment errors are easier to identify and less likely to be corrected and are therefore more likely to be capitalized than random assessment errors. Their results suggest the opposite; the degree of capitalization is larger, although less significant, for random assessment errors. As explained in Chapter 2, however, their methodology is seriously flawed. Furthermore, as pointed out in a comment by Gerking and Dickie (1985), their definition of "random" assessment error is quite narrow, namely "the portion of assessment error that is not correlated with house value."

[8] These conclusions come from a regression of the degree of capitalization on community characteristics. The coefficient (t-statistic) is -15.8 (-4.0) for the pre-revaluation effective tax rate, -0.07 (-3.6) for population density, 0.025 (5.09) for percentage old housing, and -0.03 (-3.85) for median income. The r-squared for this regression is 0.95. None of these explanatory variables is statistically significant in a bivariate regression to explain the degree of capitalization.

[9] The simple correlation between the pre-revaluation effective tax rate and city popula-

tion is about 0.9. Moreover, by substituting for the effective tax rate in the regression in footnote 8, we find that population has a significant effect on the degree of capitalization. An alternative interpretation of this result, therefore, is that it takes house seekers longer to gather comparative tax information in larger communities than in smaller ones.

[10] This explanation is not the same as the supply-side explanation offered by Edel and Sclar (1974), Noto (1976) and Hamilton (1976b). In their argument, builders respond to situations in which taxes are low, and hence prices are high, by building more housing, thereby driving down the price and eliminating capitalization. Because of assessment practices in Massachusetts, however, new housing was taxed at a relatively high rate, which, when capitalized, resulted in a lower price for new housing than for existing housing. This lower price cannot induce a supply response. Noto tested and rejected this alternative hypothesis by interacting her tax rate variable with the rate of growth in community population. See the discussion of her study in Chapter 2. In our sample, the simple correlation between the percentage of old housing and the rate of change in community population between 1970 and 1980 is about −0.8, but the percentage change in population, unlike the percentage of old housing, is not significantly related to the degree of capitalization.

[11] In fact, the housing stock in Belmont is very homogeneous, and housing seekers may be able to inspect several similar houses. In this case, random assessment errors are revealed in comparisons of the tax payments of these houses, and bids on housing do reflect relative tax rates. These observations come from one of the authors, who lived in Belmont for ten years and had a strong professional and personal interest in the prices of the three types of colonial houses that comprise most of the housing stock in the town.

[12] To be precise, assessed value increases at 2% or at the same rate as house value, whichever is smaller. Given the rapid recent appreciation in house values in California, however, we doubt that anyone expects assessments to increase by less than 2%. It should also be pointed out that for owners at the time the proposition passed, assessed values were rolled back to 1975 levels. For some evidence on the intrajurisdictional variation in effective tax rates caused by Proposition 13, see Wiseman (1986). Two studies discussed in Chapter 2, Gabriel (1981) and Rosen (1982), examine interjurisdictional tax differences caused by Proposition 13. Because these interjurisdictional differences are likely to be long-lived, it may seem surprising that these studies obtain estimates of capitalization that are similar to ours, namely 36% and 22%. However, general uncertainty about the effects of the Proposition on taxes and services may have kept capitalization low in the year immediately after it passed.

[13] The expected growth rate is slower for tax payments than for house values, so the real discount rate is higher for tax payments than for house values. This case is analogous to Equation (3-15), therefore, in which the degree to which current taxes are capitalized reflects the relatively high discount rate for taxes. Strictly speaking, one should also consider households' beliefs about the expectations of people to whom they are likely to sell their house; the expectations of those future buyers also may have a small effect on current house values.

[14] This argument applies to the sample of houses that sold before revaluation. To predict the post-revaluation value of houses that did not sell before revaluation, the assessor also must have an accurate estimate of their value in the pre-revaluation regime. To obtain such an estimate, he must account for their pre-revaluation relative effective tax rate. Note also that with a guess about the expected persistence of tax differences, an assessor can read from right to left in Table 7-1, or use Equation (3-15), to obtain a rough estimate of the degree of tax capitalization.

[15] In principle, the same logic can help an assessor account for interjurisdictional tax capitalization. Suppose the assessor knows that the town's effective tax rate is going to change relative to other towns. This relative change will cause a real change in the value of all houses in the town. This problem is much more difficult to solve, however, because the assessor must know what is going to happen to the tax rates in other towns and he cannot use the shortcut in

the text because the second-sale tax rate may not be equal to the area-wide average. (Actually, the average rate is not quite right. See Yinger, 1985.) This problem can be solved if the assessor knows how much money the property tax must raise, but the algebra is very complicated and is not presented here. Note that this interjurisdictional problem does not raise a fairness issue. A change in the town's average tax rate will have the same percentage impact on all houses in the town and will therefore have the same impact on the effective tax rate of every house in the town — even if the assessor does not account for it. This problem also disappears in the long run as the assessor observes house sales after the relative tax change.

[16] For a discusion of this rule, see Atkinson and Stiglitz (1981).

[17] The price elasticity of demand for housing appears to be about −0.5. For a recent review of the literature, see Mayo (1981). This elasticity is not close enough to zero to justify an extremely high second-best tax rate on housing.

[18] The text asks whether assessment errors distort housing choices made at the time of purchase. One could also ask whether these errors distort decisions to upgrade or renovate housing. Aaron (1975) argues that they do. There exists no mechanism to capitalize property taxes into the price of these housing changes, so Aaron argues that households with higher effective tax rates will undertake less rehabilitation. This argument does not apply in Massachusetts, however, because assessors ignore minor rehabilitation and value all major additions or renovations at some fraction of their cost, regardless of the household's effective property tax rate. In other words, the marginal property tax rate, which influences decisions to upgrade, does not vary across households, despite assessment errors that exist before upgrading.

[19] Strictly speaking, a distortion can arise if expectations about the persistence of tax differences differ from the actual persistence of tax differences. Because the implied expectations are close to correct in most of the communities we study, we believe that this type of distortion is inconsequential.

[20] Two technical points: First, we limit our analysis to existing housing and do not consider the consequences of capitalization for the efficiency of housing construction. By raising the price of land in low-tax towns, capitalization might cause an inefficient shift away from land and toward capital in the construction of housing in those towns. Second, Hamilton (1983) provides an alternative approach to the analysis of capitalization and the efficiency of the property tax. He argues that if the price of housing reflects both the benefits of public services and the property tax, then the property tax must be serving as a price for public services. By drawing an analogy to the operation of a price in a private market, Hamilton concludes that the property tax does not distort the housing market. However, his argument is based on the incorrect assumption, which was discussed in Chapter 2, that $1 of public spending yields $1 of benefits. In fact, the demand curve for public spending, like the demand curve for anything else, is downward sloping, not horizontal as this assumption implies, and varies from one household to another. Moreover, even with this assumption, Hamilton only shows that the average benefit equals the average cost — not, as efficiency requires, that the marginal benefit equals the marginal cost.

[21] The discussion could be extended to consider tax differences that were not expected to persist. As in the case of assessment errors, this extension shifts the focus from the capitalization of current tax differences to the capitalization of the expected stream of tax differences.

[22] As in the efficiency discussion in Section 3, the difference between expectations and realizations might matter. A wide divergence between the expected and actual persistence of tax differences, which does not appear to exist in Massachusetts, could lead to some horizontal inequity in the long run, even with complete capitalization of expected tax streams.

[23] Announcing the switch from a policy of fixed assessments to a policy of regular revaluation will, by itself, cause capital gains and losses (as will any event that changes households' expectations about the persistence of tax differences). The inequity of these one-time

gains and losses is more than offset, however, by equity gains from minimizing capital gains and losses in the future.

[24] Aaron (1975) states the same tradeoff for assessors, but he assumes that the capitalization of current tax differences is likely to be complete in many cases and therefore, in our judgement, overstates the disadvantages of assessment reform.

[25] Zodrow (1980) points out that postponement may not be a good policy if it extends the time period in which large efficiency losses occur. As explained in Section 3, however, assessment errors do not cause inefficiency as long as the expected stream of tax differences is fully capitalized, which appears to be approximately true in Massachusetts. Thus, the efficiency losses from postponing revaluation are likely to be very small.

[26] For some of the history of revaluation in Boston, see Paul (1975) and Avault et al. (1979).

[27] One important application of these arguments is to the so-called Tregor payments made by the City of Boston. For many years, commercial property in Boston paid a higher effective rate than residential property. Several owners of commercial property sued the city for compensation and won. The City was required to pay tens of millions of dollars to these property owners. In our judgement, this compensation was not appropriate. Although we have no direct evidence on the point, we believe that the capitalization mechanism is likely to work very well for commerical property: people who buy such property have good information and full knowledge of the implications of different property tax payments. Thus, people who buy business property with a relatively high effective tax rate are compensated in the form of a lower market price for that property. The real burden of the property tax, in other words, is no higher on them than on the owners of business property with a low effective rate. Thus, it is not fair to compensate the owners of high-tax property again in the form of a payment from the City. Some compensation would be called for if relative taxes on commercial property increased after these people bought it and if this increase were not anticipated by them. This does not appear to have been the case; commercial property was overassessed for many years prior to the Tregor suits. We also cannot prove that the capitalization of expected tax streams was complete. But even if it was only 50%, the awards to these property owners should have been cut in half. So far as we know, the existence of capitalization was not considered by the courts in these cases; as a result, we believe that equitable treatment of taxpayers was not achieved. We must add a footnote to this footnote. The incidence of the property tax on commercial property, unlike on owner-occupied houses, might be affected by backward shifting to factors of production or forward shifting to consumers. We believe that such shifting is not important in evaluating the Tregor payments. For more on the Tregor payments and their impact on Boston's finances, see Bradbury and Yinger (1984). For a discussion of revaluation and classification in Boston, see Avault et al. (1979).

[28] The high rates on commercial property in Boston caused a similar transition problem. Moving to the same effective tax rate for all kinds of property not only eliminates unfair treatment within a property type, it also eliminates the relatively high tax rate on commercial property. As a result, the tax rate on residential property would go up. With full capitalization, this rate increase would lead to a capital loss for the average homeowner. This outcome was not politically acceptable in Boston and was a key obstacle to assessment reform. This obstacle was eliminated by allowing property tax classification, which involves different nominal tax rates and hence different effective tax rates even with accurate assessment, for different types of property. The combination of revaluation and tax classification allowed Boston to eliminate variation in effective tax rates within classes of property but to retain the relatively high effective rate on commercial property. See Avault et al. (1979).

[29] These capital gains and losses are primarily caused, of course, by the changes in relative effective property tax rates that occur because of revaluation. The mean and standard

deviation of the distribution of these tax rate changes are zero and 1.45 percentage points, respectively.

[30] In principle, a compensation scheme for these people could be devised, along with a windfall tax on people with capital gains. As pointed out earlier, however, such a scheme would be complicated and probably not politically feasible.

[31] A negative link between effective tax rate and house value has been found by several studies. See, for example, Chun and Linneman (1985).

[32] For a recent review of this literature, see Mayo (1981).

Appendix A
Data Sources

In this appendix, we describe our data sources and methods of data collection. We discuss the sources for three categories of data: sales and assessment information, housing characteristics (for Brockton and Waltham), and nominal tax rates.

1. SALES AND ASSESSMENT DATA

1.1 Description of Major Data Sources

As discussed in the text, we relied on five sources for sales and assessment data. The first three, Massachusetts Department of Revenue, Metropolitan Mortgage Bureau, and the Rothenberg tape, were our primary sources. The final two, Real Estate Transfer Directory, and the files of local assessors, were used to fill in missing information.

Massachusetts Department of Revenue (formerly called the Massachusetts Department of Corporations and Taxation)

As part of its biennial property tax equalization study, the Department of Revenue, DOR, collects information from local assessors on all real property transactions. Local assessors submit monthly typed reports with sales price,

151

assessed valuation, date of sale, type of property, and mortgage information on forms provided by the DOR. Forms on file at DOR date back to 1969 or 1970 for all communities in our sample. Although the layout of the form was modified twice, the information collected remained the same throughout the period 1969–1977.

The quality of the data appears to be quite high especially for the period after the 1974 Sudbury court case that gave the DOR (then the Department of Corporations and Taxation) responsibility for enforcing full value assessment throughout the state. A relatively sophisticated equalization estimating procedure was introduced at that time. Although the method of estimating equalized valuation was less accurate before 1974, the assessors' reports for this early period, in general, appear to be reasonably accurate and comprehensive. This conclusion is based on our examination of the forms, discussions with DOR officials, and cross checking with sales and assessed value data from other sources. Where problems arose with this data, we relied on other sources whenever possible. The nature of these problems and our solutions to them are discussed in Section 1.2 of Appendix A in the context of each community in our sample.

For each sale of a single-family house, we copied on cards the address and date of sale, sales price, and assessed valuation. Identical last names of buyers and sellers plus notations by assessors or the DOR helped us rule out non-arms-length transactions. Our cards were arranged by street address to facilitate the identification of double sales, as obtained from the DOR, and in preparation for the next stage of the data gathering effort at the Metropolitan Mortgage Bureau.

The Metropolitan Mortgage Bureau

The Metropolitan Mortgage Bureau, MMB, collects for use by its member banks the date of sale, sales value, assessed value and mortgage data for real property transactions in forty-five Boston area communities. These data are available by town on microfilm from 1946 through 1972 and microfiche thereafter. Since the MMB is a private company, academic researchers are not generally granted access to its data. By working with the State Banking Commissioner's Office, however, we were able to gain access to this data at a reduced rate during a four-week period in September and October 1978.

Both the microfilm and the microfiche contain index card images of property transactions grouped by address for each town, an organizational format particularly useful for locating double sales. Because of the shift to microfiche in 1973, however, finding double sales that straddle the shift requires simultaneous examination of the fiche and the film. On the basis of a preliminary investigation of this data during the spring of 1978, staff researchers from the State Banking Commissioner's Office determined that simultaneous examination would be too time consuming and expensive given the restrictions imposed by the MMB on the number of researchers who could be at the Bureau at any one time. The time aspect was of particular concern since the MMB wanted to keep to a minimum the number of days researchers would be in its office. More importantly, we learned from John Avault of the Boston Redevelopment Authority that the quality of the MMB data declined significantly after 1972 because of insufficient staff to do the necessary data checks. Thus, both quality and cost considerations induced us to rely on the MMB primarily for data on the microfilm. To conserve time spent at the MMB, we further limited our data collection efforts there for some of our sample communities.

MMB microfilm data (for 1946–1972 transactions) are complete with one significant exception. Assessed values are not available for communities in Middlesex County. This influenced our selection of sample communities. Other minor problems with the data will be noted below in connection with the details of our data gathering effort. Briefly, these include an occasional one-month delay in reporting sales and an occasional failure to update the assessment after a change in assessed value.

The Rothenberg Tape

This tape, whose existence was made known to us by Dr. Katharine Bradbury, was obtained from Professor Jerome Rothenberg of the Massachusetts Institute of Technology (MIT). It includes information on all double sales from 1946–1970 for forty-five communities in the Boston Metropolitan Area. The data were collected directly from the Metropolitan Mortgage Borad by researchers at MIT during the early 1970's. At that time, MMB kept its records on index cards rather than microfilm, but it is the images of these index cards that appear on the microfilm. Thus the information on the tape is an exact subset of information currently available at MMB.

For our purposes the tape has both advantages and disadvantages. The data on the tape are well suited for the construction of our price indices and our basic analysis: No single sales are included and all double sales include the year of sale, sales price, and assessed value information for each sale. The availability of the tape thus saved us a significant amount of time and money, compared with gathering data at MMB. On the other hand, absence of address information means that we are unable to find out the characteristics of the properties involved in these double sales, thereby limiting our ability to control for confounding changes in these characteristics. In addition, but of limited importance, the date of sales is reported only by year.

This fact rules out the use of quarterly or monthly housing price indexes as a way to increase the precision of our estimates.

Real Estate Transfer Directory

Auto Data Systems, a private company in Natick, Massachusetts, maintains listings of all real estate transfers by community since 1971. This Real Estate Transfer Directory, RETD, reports the names of the buyer and seller, address of property, date of sale, sales price, amount of mortgage, and name of mortgagee. The entries are arranged by street address. When relying on this data source, we followed the same procedure used for the DOR data. First, we copied all single sales. Second, we matched these with other single sales in other years arranged by street address to locate double sales.

Because aassessed values are not reported, sales data from this source must be supplemented with assessed value data from the files of local assessors for all double sales that straddle the revaluation year. Fortunately, the RETD provides sufficient information to locate the properties in the assessor's files. Also missing from this source is information on structure type. By using this source in conjunction with other sources, however, sales of non-single-family houses were eliminated.

Local Assessors Files

Local assessors' files contain copies of the monthly reports sent to the DOR, annual records of assessed valuations by owner's name, and books from which plot numbers can be converted to street addresses. The earliest year of such records varies by community in our sample. We used this data source only as a supplement to the other more readily available data sources. It should be noted, however, that all our assessed value data is local assessors' data, even though we copied it from other sources.

1.2   Data Collection by Community

Arlington, Belmont, and Waltham

Our data-gathering strategy in Arlington, Belmont, and Waltham involved using the DOR data for all transactions after 1971, MMB data for double sales that straddled 1970, and the Rothenberg tape for double sales between 1960 and 1970. This strategy assured that all double sales were collected, that the overall quality of our sample was maximized, and that minimal time was spent at the MMB so as not to unduly increase the overall time and cost of the data-gathering effort.

First, we copied information on all sales of single-family houses from the DOR records starting in 1971 and continuing through 1974 for Arlington, 1973 for Belmont, and 1976 for Waltham. In each case, the final year is the fifth year after revaluation. Filing the sales by street address enabled us to find double or multiple sales beginning and ending during the period for which we gathered data at the DOR. All other single sales plus all first sales of such double sale pairs were then treated as potential second sales and taken to the MMB to be matched, if possible, with a first sale during the period 1960–1970. If a property sold more than once during these years, the latest sale was recorded as the relevant first sale to the second sale found at the DOR. The earlier double sale was not copied because it is included on the Rothenberg tape.

We performed an extensive check on most of the data and pursued all possible sources to assure its completeness. Based on an initial check of a random sample of data from the MMB, we decided to check every double sale straddling revaluation. We hired a research assistant not involved in the initial data collection for this task. Second, where assessed values were not available at the MMB or the DOR, we used the names of buyers and sellers to track down assessed value information from local assessors' files. Third, we made every possible effort to check the data sources against each other wherever they overlapped. In particular, 1971 and 1972 data collected from the DOR were checked at the MMB. With the exception of a one-month timing discrepancy relating to the date of sale and a few other easily resolved problems, the data were found to be comparable. The timing discrepancy was decided in favor of the DOR source in all cases because officials at the MMB explained that the MMB date of sale reflects the date at which the transaction was recorded at the MMB. Finally, we went over the data in detail to make sure that all transactions were arm's-length sales of single-family houses without any peculiar characteristics.

Upon completion of this data checking process, the double sales for which both sales occurred after 1970 (exclusively from DOR data), the double sales that straddled 1970 (with second sale from the DOR and first sale from the MMB), and the double sales for which both sales occurred between 1960 and 1970 (from the Rothenberg tape) were merged to form our final data sets for Arlington, Belmont, and Waltham. Specifics of the data collection effort for each town are summarized below.

Arlington (1969 Revaluation)

The only variation in the basic procedure involved obtaining sales and assessed value information directly from the local assessor for the period July to December 1973 because the information was not available at the DOR.

These data appeared to be complete and were recorded on the regular DOR forms.

For some transactions, plot numbers had to be converted to street addresses at the local assessor's office. A summary of the unsolved problems connected with the single-sale data collected at the DOR follows:

			Jan/June	July/Dec	
	1971	1972		1973	1974
Problem					
No. Street Address	4	2	12	19	16
Miscellaneous	2	6	1	3	0
Total	6	8	13	22	16

The single sales collected from the Department of Revenue were then matched with each other and with sales before 1971 at the MMB, yielding a total of 447 double sales (not including those on the Rothenberg tape). Our checking procedures turned up the following problems:

Assessed value needed	43
One-month date discrepancy between the MMB and the DOR	106
Miscellaneous	17
	166

Of these 166 problems, all but five were resolved. In the case of missing assessed values, buyers' or sellers' names were used to determine the assessed values from the local assessor for the appropriate year. This procedure was straightforward except for new houses with no assessment listed as of the beginning of the year. For these properties, we used the buyer's name to determine the assessed value the following year, a reasonable procedure because assessed values rarely change except during an across-the-board revaluation. As noted earlier, the timing discrepancy problem was resolved in favor of the DOR in all cases.

Five unresolved problems left 442 potentially usable double sales. Subsequent checking of the data from printouts reduced this number to 434. These plus the 49 double sales from the Rothenberg tape make a total of 483 double sales for Arlington.

Belmont (1968 Revaluation)

Three problems remained unsolved because of missing street numbers in connection with the single-sale data collected from the DOR. The single sales were then matched with each other and with sales before 1971 at the MMB yielding a total of 166 double sales (not including those on the Rothenberg tape). Our checking procedures uncovered the following problems:

Assessed value needed	3
One-month date discrepancy between the MMB and the DOR	12
Other MMB and DOR conflicts	10
Miscellaneous	5
	30

Of these 30 problems, all but four were resolved using methods similar to those described for Arlington. This left 162 potentially usable double sales, 3 of which were later eliminated as part of a final data check. These plus the 40 double sales on the Rothenberg tape make a total of 199 double sales.

Waltham (1971 Revaluation)

Missing forms at the DOR for the periods November–December 1972 and September–December 1973 forced reliance on the RETD for sales values and on local assessors for assessed values during those periods. With this exception, the procedures followed were identical to those for Arlington and Belmont.

The following unsolved problems remained in connection with the single-sale data collected from the DOR and the RETD.

	1971–1976
Not single-family	15
Sale not found at MMB	15
Data conflict with other sources	3
Total	33

The single sales collected from the DOR and the RETD were then matched with each other and with sales before 1971 at the MMB, yielding a total of 617 double sales (not including those on the Rothenberg tape). Our checking procedures uncovered the following problems:

Assessed value needed	108
One-month date discrepancy between the MMB and the DOR	67
Other conflicts between the MMB and the DOR	59
Miscellaneous	44
	278

Of these 278 problems, all but 37 were resolved using methods similar to those described for Arlington, leaving 580 potentially usable double sales. These plus the 42 double sales on the Rothenberg tape made a total of 622 potentially usable double sales. Examination of the data printout resulted in the elimination of 3, thereby giving a total of 599 double sales.

Brookline and Wellesley

For the towns of Brookline and Wellesley, we modified our data-gathering strategy to rely primarily on the MMB data and the Rothenberg tape with no use of the DOR data. This modification made sense for Wellesley because we needed double sales only through 1972 (five years after the 1967 revaluation), the final year covered by the MMB microfilm. We determined that copying double sales only from the MMB would be significantly cheaper than copying all *single* sales for 1971 and 1972 from the DOR forms and then matching them with sales before 1971 at the MMB. Brookline's 1968 revaluation required sales data through 1973. Our initial attempt to gather the 1973 data from the DOR proved unsuccessful because of poor reporting. Hence, we used the MMB microfiche for 1973 sales and the microfilm for 1971 and 1972 sales and for sales straddling 1970.

Our data checking and augmenting procedures for these towns were essentially the same as those for Arlington, Belmont, and Waltham. Again, all double sales straddling revaluation were checked by a research assistant not involved in the initial data gathering effort, missing assessed value data were obtained where possible from the local assessors, and every effort was made to assure that all transactions were arm's-length sales of single-family homes without any peculiar characteristics.

Brookline (1968 Revaluation)

Because no single sales were copied for Brookline, all potential problems relate to double sales gathered at the MMB. Of the 223 double sales found (not including those on the Rothenberg tape), 12 were missing assessed values and 24 had miscellaneous problems. Of these 36 problems, all but 10 were solved by methods described for Arlington, leaving 223 potentially usable double sales. These sales plus the 44 double sales on the Rothenberg tape made a total of 267 double sales. With additional data checking, we discovered that at least 15 of the post-revaluation assessed values recorded by the MMB were incorrect. This problem apparently reflects the MMB's failure to update assessments for some houses selling during the first few years after revaluation. For most of these houses we obtained correct assessments from the local assessors' published records. Our final sample size is 265.

Wellesley (1967 Revaluation)

As for Brookline, all potential problems relate to double sales because no single-sale information was collected. Of the 484 double sales found at the MMB (not including those on the Rothenberg tape), 74 were missing assessed values and 21 had miscellaneous problems. We were unable to solve many of these problems because the necessary assessed-value data for the years involved were no longer available from the local assessor. As a result, 86 problems remained unsolved, leaving 398 usable double sales. These sales plus the 39 double sales from the Rothenberg tape made a total of 437 potentially usable double sales. After data consistency checks, 10 more were eliminated leaving a total of 427 double sales.

Brockton (1974 Revaluation)

Brockton falls into a separate category because it is included neither on the Rothenberg tape nor in the MMB files. Fortunately, Brockton's 1974 revaluation is sufficiently recent to allow us to rely primarily on the DOR and local assessor's files. The following documentation of our data-gathering efforts is organized by year.

1969

Approximately 240 single-family arm's-length sales were collected from the DOR. Because most of these sales were recorded by plot number, we had to convert to street address using conversion books available at the local assessor's office. In 19 cases, we were unable to determine street numbers.

1970

1970 sales data were not available from any source. We checked the DOR, RETD, and the local assessor's office.

1971

Our source for sales data was the RETD for Plymouth County. We copied details of approximately 1100 transfers of all types of property, including buyers' and sellers' names. RETD sales that included complete street information were matched with sales of single-family houses from other years to locate usable double sales. Assessed values for these double sales were then obtained from the local assessor. For those RETD sales identified by plot number rather than street address, we sought street address and assessed values from the 1971 Brockton assessment books. We used the seller's name to obtain this information because the assessors keep records by the owner's name as of January 1 of each year. Those properties that we could not locate by the seller's name were assumed to be new homes in 1971. Such sales were then traced through the 1972 assessment books using the 1971 buyer's name. 110 problems remained unsolved, 100 because of missing street numbers.

1972

We copied details of approximately 350 single-family sales from DOR records. As in the case of 1969 sales, these sales were recorded by plot number rather than street address, thereby requiring conversion using the conversion books at the Brockton assessor's office. In 34 cases, we were unable to determine the street number.

1973

We copied details of single-family house sales from DOR records. The data through May appeared to be in good order with the only problem being the absence of some street addresses. These addresses were traced through the conversion books at the assessor's office. Starting in June, the records are less satisfactory, with frequent missing data, crossed-out information, and other deviations from normal reporting procedures. As evidenced by the time lag between the date of property sales and the date forms were submitted to the DOR, much of the record keeping for the latter part of 1973 occurred early in 1974, the year Brockton revalued all property. The confusion surrounding revaluation probably accounts for the below-standard record keeping for this period. We were unable to obtain the missing assessed values for new houses sold in 1973 at the assessor's office because the assessor records property ownership only as of January 1 each year, nor was this information available in the 1974 records because of the revaluation. 62 unsolved problems remained, 27 because of missing street numbers and 31 because of missing assessed values.

1974–1977

We copied details of single-family house sales from DOR records. When street addresses were missing, we used the conversion book at the assessor's office to convert plot numbers to street addresses. 44 unsolved problems remained because of missing street numbers.

After all data checks, we have a total of 559 double sales.

Barnstable

Our approach to collecting sales and assessment information for Barnstable was similar to that for Brockton. Again we relied primarily on DOR data supplemented by information from the RETD and local assessors. Our data-gathering effort was complicated by the division of Barnstable into seven separate villages.

Basic sales and assessed value data for single sales were collected for the years 1969–1977 (other than April–December 1973) from DOR records. Two problems arose with these data. The village name was missing for most of the 1974 sales information and street numbers were frequently missing in all years. To deal with the 1974 problem, we first had to link street names to villages. Where duplication of street names across villages prevented village identification, we looked up the sales by date of sale in the RETD. We successfully identified villages for most 1974 sales.

The absence of street-number information was a more serious problem. Using counter books at the town engineer's office, we tried to convert lot numbers, when we had them, to street numbers and street numbers to lot numbers, hoping to match sales either by lot number and street name or by street number and name. In addition, names of buyers and sellers were used as supplemental information to match sales. This task of obtaining the additional information necessary to match sales was time consuming because it involved a large number of single sales and was subject to error because of duplication of lot numbers. In addition, incomplete information in the counter books meant that a substantial number of single sales could not be used.

The DOR records for April–December 1973 were incomplete. Hence we turned to the RETD to obtain sales information for these months. For 1973 sales matching sales in other years, we collected assessment information from the local assessor. Again, missing street numbers presented a major obstacle to the matching process.

Because Barnstable is a resort community, its housing market differs from those of our other communities. In addition, the town experienced rapid growth and a housing boom during the early part of our sample period. These facts complicated our task of determining which sales were valid arm's-length transactions of single-family houses without any peculiar characteristics. Examination of the data showed that 72 of the 290 double sales we had coded and keypunched as potentially usable were unacceptable. Some of these double sales occurred in the same or sequential months and were characterized by dramatic price increases that probably reflect the behavior of housing market speculators. Others with very low recorded prices at the time of first sale may represent vacant lots that were subsequently sold with houses on them. Other double sales were discarded on the grounds that there was a high probability that the two sales had been incorrectly matched. Our final data set consists of 208 double sales.

2. HOUSING AND NEIGHBORHOOD CHARACTERISTICS

Housing and neighborhood characteristics played a peripheral role in our initial conception of this study. While we recognized the possibility that the exclusion of structural and neighborhood characteristics might bias our tax capitalization estimates, we believed that the bias would be minimal. To check our methodology, however, we gathered housing characteristics data for Waltham and Brockton, the two communities with the largest sample sizes. We collected this data from local sources and the 1970 Census of Population for all double sales in Waltham and all double sales straddling revaluation in Brockton.

2.1 Waltham

The Waltham Board of Assessors was very cooperative in connection with our data-gathering effort. The Board's staff readily answered questions and permitted our research assistants direct access to the relevant assessment cards. For each house in our sample (other than the 40 from the Rothenberg tape for which we had no addresses) we collected two types of information from the assessing records: structural characteristics and the type and timing of renovations. Part A of Table A-1 lists the structural characteristics we collected. An asterisk indicates that the characteristic was used in the final specification of the model.

   As shown in Part B of Table A-1, renovations fall into six major types. Renovation dummy variables were used in the price index equations and the capitalization model whenever housing characteristics were included.

   In addition, we linked each house to 1 of 11 census tracts and 1 of 10 school districts by overlaying tract and district maps on a Waltham street map. When a street crossed a tract or district boundary, the election district registry was used to divide the street by house number. Part C of Table A-1 lists the 1970 Census tract information used as neighborhood variables in the analysis. We were unable to obtain information such as test scores and teacher-pupil ratios by school district. Hence, school district variation was captured by a series of dummy variables.

2.2 Brockton

The Brockton assessors initially turned down our request for housing characteristics. Unlike in Waltham, where our research assistants were allowed

Table A-1
Housing and Neighborhood Characteristics for Waltham and Brockton

Part A. Housing Characteristics
  1. Year of construction
    *age (= 1979 – year of construction)
  2. Area
    *assessors weighted area
  3. Attic and basement
    extent and type
  4. Number of rooms
    *total[a]
    type or by floor
  5. Construction materials
    *wall
    roof
    floor
  6. Bathrooms
    *number of regular bathrooms[b]
    number of half bathrooms
  7. Other internal
    *number of fireplaces
    presence of central air conditioning
  8. External
    *lot size
    number and area of non-garage detached buildings
    presence of detached garage
    *area of garage
    quality of neighborhood (not available in Brockton)
    **condition, desirability and usefulness of the building (not available in Waltham).

Part B. Renovations (not available in Brockton)
  1. Major additions
  2. Renovations—bathroom or kitchen
  3. New garage
  4. Minor additions and renovations
  5. Land purchase or sale
  6. New pool

Part C. Neighborhood characteristics
  1. Census tracts
    percent of persons in same house in 1965 and 1970
    median years of school completed
  2. School districts

* Housing characteristic variable used in both Brockton and Waltham models.
** Housing characteristic variable used in Brockton model only.
[a] In Brockton, two variables are used: bedrooms and all other rooms.
[b] The variable used in the analysis is defined as the number of full bathrooms plus .5 times the number of half bathrooms.

direct access to the files, the Brockton assessors' office required that its own staff members pull the cards from the files. The assessors claimed that they could not make available the staff time necessary to pull the 631 cards we initially requested. We reached agreement by reducing our request to the 216 properties whose sales unambiguously straddle the 1974 revaluation. As requested by the assessors, we then provided a list of the 216 addresses ordered by map and route numbers. While the vast majority of the cards were correctly pulled, wrong cards were pulled for some addresses. This problem reduced our sample of properties with housing characteristics to 206.

As shown in Table A-1, the housing characteristics data collected for Brockton are essentially the same as the data for Waltham. With one exception, only minor definitional differences distinguish the two sets of housing characteristics variables used in the analysis. The exception is the addition in Brockton of the assessor's subjective rating of the condition, desirability, and usefulness of the building. Because of our lack of direct access to the files, we were unable to collect renovation data for Brockton.

Following the procedure used in Waltham, houses were linked to 1 of 20 elementary school districts and to 1 of 17 census tracts. When a street ran through more than one census tract, school district information was used to determine in which tract a particular house was located. Information from the 1970 census on median years of schooling and percentage of the 1970 residents living in the tract in 1965 was merged with the sales, assessment, and housing characteristics data by address. To assure a minimum number of observations from each district, we consolidated the 20 school districts into 11. With the advice of the Brockton School Department, we grouped together districts with similar socio-economic characteristics that feed to the same junior high school.

3. NOMINAL TAX RATES

We obtained nominal tax rates for six of the seven communities from the Massachusetts Taxpayers' Foundation. Before 1974, the tax rates apply to calendar years. Starting with fiscal year 1975, they apply to the period July 1 to June 30. We doubled the six-month tax rate of the transition period January to June 1974 to obtain the appropriate 12-month tax rate for sales during that period. These tax rates are presented in Table A-2.

The existence of five separate fire districts complicates slightly the determination of the appropriate tax rates in Barnstable. Properties throughout the town are subject both to the town-wide tax rate available to us from the Massachusetts Taxpayers' Foundation and to the rate levied by the relevant fire districts. These latter rates, which vary both across districts and across years, were obtained from the Barnstable tax assessor. Four of the five districts are coterminous with villages. Hence, the village identification allows us to attribute to each double sale the appropriate nominal tax rate, calculated as the sum of the town and fire rates. The nominal tax rates in Barnstable are listed in Table A-3.

Table A-2
Nominal Tax Rates for All Communities Except Barnstable[a]

Year	Arlington	Belmont	Brockton	Brookline	Waltham	Wellesley
1960	70.20	53.00		54.00	55.40	58.60
1961	82.60	53.00		52.50	57.80	60.00
1962	85.00	53.00		48.50	61.20	64.00
1963	84.60	53.00		51.00	64.20	68.00
1964	92.60	60.00		56.00	67.20	72.60
1965	97.60	63.00		56.50	77.00	74.40
1966	97.60	66.00		56.00	77.00	78.40
1967	106.00	70.00		65.00	79.80	29.00
1968	124.00	23.00		41.50	86.80	32.00
1969	41.00	29.50	130.60	49.00	95.20	36.50
1970	48.20	37.00	154.60	59.00	110.70	45.00
1971	51.80	39.50	179.00	63.50	42.50	48.20
1972	56.80	45.75	185.00	71.50	48.30	50.00
1973	56.80	49.00	180.00	73.00	44.80	
1974 (6 mo.)	56.40	49.00	48.00	73.00	44.80	
1975 (FY)	67.20		48.00		52.40	
1976 (FY)			54.20		54.80	
1977 (FY)			61.00		58.60	
1978 (FY)			61.90			

[a] Dollars per $1000 of assessed valuation. Through 1973, the rates apply to the calendar year. The 1974 reported 6-month rate was doubled to convert it to a 12-month rate. FY refers to the July 1 – June 30 fiscal year.
SOURCE: Massachusetts Taxpayers Foundation.

Table A-3
Nominal Tax Rates for Barnstable[a]

Year	Town	Fire Districts				
		Barnstable	West Barnstable	Hyannis	Centerville Osterville Marston Mills	Cotuit
1969	64.00	7.00	5.60	5.80	6.80	8.00
1970	76.00	8.00	5.80	6.40	6.40	7.20
1971	82.00	6.40	6.00	7.40	6.20	8.00
1972	84.00	8.00	7.40	8.00	7.00	8.00
1973	14.80	1.50	0.60	1.90	1.40	1.90
1974 (6 mo.)	14.30	1.30	0.60	1.90	1.40	1.90
1975 (FY)	15.30	1.65	1.35	2.05	1.90	1.90
1976 (FY)	18.70	1.80	1.25	2.55	1.75	1.85
1977 (FY)	18.70	2.20	2.05	2.60	2.20	1.55
1978 (FY)	19.25	2.40	1.90	3.10	2.55	1.50

[a] Dollars per $1000 of assessed valuation. Through 1973, the rates apply to the calendar year. The 1974 reported 6-month rate was doubled to convert it to a 12-month rate. FY refers to the July 1–June 30 fiscal year.
SOURCE: Massachusetts Taxpayers Foundation and Barnstable assessor.

Appendix B
Housing Price Indices

We obtained a housing price index for each community by estimating the Bailey, Muth, and Nourse (1963) model for double-sales data. In this appendix, we describe the model and present the regression results.

The model is based on the following relationship

$$R_i = \frac{I_k}{I_j} u_i, \tag{1}$$

where

R_i = the sales price ratio for house i with first sale in period j and second sale in period k,
I_k = the price index for period k,
I_j = the price index for period j, and
u_i = a random error term.

Taking the natural logarithm of Equation (1) yields

$$\log R_i = \log I_k - \log I_j + \log u_i, \tag{2}$$

which, assuming a zero mean and constant variance for $\log u_i$, can be estimated using ordinary least squares. For estimation purposes, we define a set of dummy variables, D_k, for periods k = 1 to K, with k = 0 as our base

Table B-1
Waltham Price Indices[a]

Period	Price Index With Renovations α_k (t-statistic)	Price Index ($=e^{\alpha_k}$)	Price Index Without Renovations α_k (t-statistic)	Price Index ($=e^{\alpha_k}$)
D60	base	1.000	base	1.000
D61	.034 (.069)	1.034	.046 (0.95)	1.048
D62	.089 (2.11)	1.093	.012 (2.44)	1.108
D63	.130 (2.96)	1.138	.143 (3.30)	1.154
D64	.166 (3.84)	1.181	.175 (4.07)	1.192
D65	.145 (3.35)	1.156	.167 (3.90)	1.182
D66	.249 (5.68)	1.283	.266 (6.17)	1.305
D67	.234 (5.84)	1.263	.250 (6.30)	1.284
D68	.318 (7.48)	1.375	.335 (7.94)	1.397
D69	.374 (8.91)	1.454	.399 (9.61)	1.490
D70	.384 (9.12)	1.468	.405 (9.70)	1.500
DWS71	.484 (12.03)	1.622	.505 (12.66)	1.657
DSF71	.506 (13.17)	1.658	.530 (13.99)	1.699
DWS72	.591 (15.04)	1.805	.615 (15.85)	1.849
DSF72	.589 (15.65)	1.803	.620 (16.89)	1.860
DWS73	.607 (15.56)	1.835	.630 (16.35)	1.878
DSF73	.662 (16.62)	1.939	.689 (17.50)	1.992
DWS74	.789 (18.46)	2.200	.808 (18.98)	2.244
DSF74	.743 (16.71)	2.101	.773 (17.58)	2.167
DWS75	.790 (19.79)	2.203	.816 (20.62)	2.262
DSF75	.758 (17.02)	2.133	.783 (17.94)	2.189
DWS76	.753 (15.68)	2.123	.790 (16.78)	2.204
DSF76	.801 (17.44)	2.227	.838 (18.67)	2.311
ADD1	.157 (2.42)			
ADD2	.101 (1.25)			
ADD3	.058 (0.90)			
ADD4	.096 (1.99)			
ADD5	.030 (0.41)			
ADD6	.088 (1.20)			
Sample Size	599		599	
Degrees of Freedom	571		577	
R^2	.84		.84	
SEE	.030		.031	

[a] See text of Appendix B for discussion of model. Each time variable refers to a specific period as follows: Di refers to the ith year as denoted by its last two digits; DWSi refers to winter – spring of the ith year; and DSFi to summer – fall of the ith year. The corresponding values of the price index are attributed to the month of July for the year-long periods and to either April or October for the half-year periods. The renovation variables are dummy variables that take on the value 1 as follows: ADD1, major additions; ADD2, bathroom or kitchen renovation; ADD3, new garage; ADD4, minor additions or renovations; ADD5, land purchase (-1 if land sale); and ADD6, new pool.

Table B-2
Brockton Price Index[a]

Period	α_k (t-statistic)	Price Index ($= e^{\alpha_k}$)
D69	base	1.000
D70	no observations	
DWS71	.218 (7.60)	1.243
DSF71	.290 (10.59)	1.336
DWS72	.246 (8.75)	1.279
DSF72	.263 (9.46)	1.301
DWS73	.351 (12.96)	1.421
DSF73	.383 (15.37)	1.467
DWS74	.468 (18.47)	1.598
DSF74	.477 (18.51)	1.611
DWS75	.516 (18.79)	1.675
DSF75	.502 (19.69)	1.653
DWS76	.572 (22.82)	1.773
DSF76	.551 (22.12)	1.735
DWS77	.598 (23.33)	1.819
Sample Size	545	
Degrees of Freedom	532	
R²	.68	
SEE	.023	

[a] See text of Appendix B for discussion of model. Each variable refers to a specific period as follows: Di refers to the ith year as denoted by its last two digits; DWSi refers to winter–spring of the ith year; and DSFi to summer–fall of the ith year. The corresponding values of the price index are attributed to the month of July for the year-long periods and to either April or October for the half-year periods.

period, such that

$$D_{ki} = \begin{cases} -1 & \text{if the first sale for house i occurred in period k,} \\ 1 & \text{if the second sale for house i occurred in period k, and} \end{cases}$$

Hence, we have the estimating equation

$$\log R_i = \sum_{k=1}^{K} \alpha_k D_{ki} + \log u_i, \tag{3}$$

where α is the natural logarithm of the price index for period k. It follows that $\exp \alpha_k$ equals the price index for period k.

Consider a house that sells first during the base period zero and again during period four. In this case, Equation (3) simplifies to

$$\log R_i = \alpha_4 + \log u_i.$$

Table B-3
Arlington Price Index[a]

Period	α_k (t-statistic)	Price Index ($=e^{\alpha_k}$)
D60	base	1.000
D61	.034 (0.91)	1.034
D62	.016 (0.42)	1.016
D63	.088 (2.48)	1.092
D64	.124 (3.78)	1.133
D65	.162 (4.89)	1.176
D66	.166 (4.67)	1.180
D67	.213 (6.30)	1.238
D68	.299 (8.53)	1.348
D69	.353 (10.67)	1.423
D70	.413 (12.55)	1.511
DWS71	.433 (14.50)	1.541
DSF71	.451 (15.59)	1.570
DWS72	.529 (16.83)	1.698
DSF72	.548 (19.06)	1.730
DWS73	.596 (18.57)	1.815
DSF73	.665 (19.37)	1.944
D74	.685 (23.19)	1.984
Sample Size	483	
Degrees of Freedom	466	
R²	.84	
SEE	.023	

[a] See text of Appendix B for discussion of model. Each variable refers to a specific period as follows: Di refers to the ith year as denoted by its last two digits; DWSi refers to winter–spring of the ith year; and DSFi to summer–fall of the ith year. The corresponding values of the price index are attributed to the month of July for the year-long periods and to either April or October for the half-year periods.

Taking antilogs yields

$$R_i = e^{\alpha_4} u_i, \tag{4}$$

which implies that the price ratio for house i equals the price index for the 4th period multiplied by a random disturbance term. Consider a second example in which house i sells in periods 2 and 4. Then we obtain

$$\log R_i = \alpha_4 - \alpha_2 + \log u_i$$

or

$$R_i = \frac{e^{\alpha_4}}{e^{\alpha_2}} u_i, \tag{5}$$

Table B-4
Wellesley Price Index[a]

Period	α_k (t-statistic)	Price Index ($= e^{\alpha_k}$)
D60	base	1.000
D61	.029 (0.68)	1.030
D62	.079 (2.15)	1.083
D63	.053 (1.44)	1.055
D64	.089 (2.47)	1.093
D65	.119 (3.40)	1.127
D66	.175 (5.09)	1.191
D67	.235 (6.92)	1.265
D68	.286 (8.93)	1.331
D69	.374 (11.44)	1.453
D70	.392 (11.60)	1.480
D71	.466 (15.70)	1.594
D72	.538 (18.13)	1.713
Sample Size	424	
Degrees of Freedom	412	
R^2	.85	
SEE	.014	

[a] See text of Appendix B for discussion of model. Each variable refers to a specific period as follows: Di refers to the ith year as denoted by its last two digits; DWSi refers to winter–spring of the ith year; and DSFi to summer–fall of the ith year. The corresponding values of the price index are attributed to the month of July for the year-long periods and to either April or October for the half-year periods.

which implies that the price ratio for house i equals the ratio of the price indices for periods 4 and 2 multiplied by an error term.

Thus, from estimates of the coefficients in equation 3, we can readily calculate price indices for each period. The absence of month-of-sale information for sales obtained from the Rothenberg tape makes a year the shortest possible period for the early years in our samples. For the later years, for which we have month-of-sale information, the appropriate period length depends on the distribution of single sales. Whenever the number of observations permits, we use half-year periods. For the year-long periods, we attribute the calculated price index to the month of July. For the half-year periods, we attribute one calculated index to April and the other to October. The resulting price indices are reported in Tables B-1 to B-7. For our capitalization regressions, we deflated house values using monthly price indices, which were derived from the indices in Tables B-1 to B-7 by interpolation based on geometric growth.

Table B-5
Brookline Price Index[a]

Period	α_k (t-statistic)	Price Index ($=e^{\alpha_k}$)
D60	base	1.000
D61	.003 (0.02)	1.003
D62	.043 (0.49)	1.044
D63	.107 (1.17)	1.113
D64	.193 (2.16)	1.213
D65	.236 (2.61)	1.266
D66	.254 (2.55)	1.289
D67	.335 (3.61)	1.389
D68	.353 (4.67)	1.424
D69	.425 (5.25)	1.530
D70	.488 (5.81)	1.629
DWS71	.612 (7.57)	1.844
DSF71	.619 (8.01)	1.857
DWS72	.628 (7.54)	1.874
DSF72	.652 (8.70)	1.920
DWS73	.718 (7.85)	2.051
DSF73	.798 (10.35)	2.221
Sample Size	264	
Degrees of Freedom	248	
R^2	.62	
SEE	.090	

[a] See text of Appendix B for discussion of model. Each variable refers to a specific period as follows: Di refers to the ith year as denoted by its last two digits; DWSi refers to winter–spring of the ith year; and DSFi to summer–fall of the ith year. The corresponding values of the price index are attributed to the month of July for the year-long periods and to either April or October for the half-year periods.

We estimated a single price index for each of our communities, except Waltham for which we estimated two. In each case, we used all double sales, including those straddling and those not straddling revaluation. The samples include double sales with incomplete or invalid assessment information, which are excluded from the capitalization equations.

Our goal was to use all available information to estimate each price index. In Waltham, we also made use of the information on renovations that we had gathered along with housing characteristics data. Thus, one of the Waltham price index equations includes six renovation dummy variables. We used the price index series calculated from this equation in the Waltham capitalization equations. We present both price indexes to reveal the impact of the renovation variables.

Table B-6
Barnstable Price Index[a]

Period	α_k (t-statistic)	Price Index ($=e^{\alpha_k}$)
D69	base	1.000
D70	.199 (4.88)	1.221
D71	.285 (6.70)	1.330
D72	.345 (8.59)	1.412
D73	.507 (10.18)	1.661
D74	.505 (6.93)	1.658
D75	.534 (12.28)	1.707
D76	.560 (11.80)	1.750
D77	.567 (12.97)	1.763
Sample Size	202	
Degrees of Freedom	194	
R^2	.58	
SEE	.052	

[a] See text of Appendix B for discussion of model. Each variable refers to a specific period as follows: Di refers to the ith year as denoted by its last two digits; DWSi refers to winter–spring of the ith year; and DSFi to summer–fall of the ith year. The corresponding values of the price index are attributed to the month of July for the year-long periods and to either April or October for the half-year periods.

Table B-7
Belmont Price Index[a]

Period	α_k (t-statistic)	Price Index ($=e^{\alpha_k}$)
D60	base	.977[b]
D61	base	1.023
D62	.068 (1.28)	1.071
D63	.116 (2.38)	1.123
D64	.151 (2.64)	1.163
D65	.189 (3.85)	1.208
D66	.220 (4.06)	1.246
D67	.176 (3.60)	1.192
D68	.291 (5.19)	1.338
D69	.420 (8.19)	1.522
D70	.527 (9.37)	1.693
D71	.456 (12.84)	1.578
D72	.539 (13.82)	1.714
D73	.640 (15.74)	1.896
Sample Size	192	
Degrees of Freedom	180	
R^2	.76	
SEE	.034	

[a] See text of Appendix B for discussion of model. Each variable refers to a specific period as follows: Di refers to the ith year as denoted by its last two digits; DWSi refers to winter–spring of the ith year; and DSFi to summer–fall of the ith year. The corresponding values of the price index are attributed to the month of July for the year-long periods and to either April or October for the half-year periods.
[b] January 1961 = 1.00.

Appendix C
Complete Estimation Results

In this appendix, we present our estimation results for all communities and all models. The results are organized by community, in alphabetical order. Each regression is identified by a heading of the following form:

Taxcap Estimation Results
Town: 6, Model: 1, Linear: 1, Restrictions: 5

WSSR = 6.935, SSR = 6.935, R − SQ = .307, NOBS = 353

In this heading, "Town" is coded as follows:

1 = Arlington (313 observations),
2 = Barnstable (98 observations),
3 = Belmont (111 observations),
4 = Brookline (140 observations),
5 = Brockton (282 observations, 196 with housing characteristics),
6 = Waltham (353 observations),
7 = Wellesley (175 observations).

"Model" indicates whether housing characteristic were included and what estimation procedure was used. The terms "basic model" and "full model" are defined in the text.

1 = Basic model, ordinary least squares,
2 = Basic model, two-stage least squares (instruments are the nominal tax rate, a housing price index, and powers and combinations of them)

175

3 = Basic model, two-stage least squares (instruments are the nominal tax rate, a housing price index, and housing and neighborhood characteristics)

4 = Full model, ordinary least squares,

5 = Full model, two-stage least squares (instruments are the nominal tax rate, a housing price index, and housing and neighborhood characteristics)

"Linear" identifies the regression technique:

$$0 = \text{Nonlinear}$$
$$1 = \text{Linear}$$

"Restrictions" indicates which restrictions are imposed on the coefficients of the tax rates. Full restrictions, i.e. Restrictions = 5, are always employed for models 1 to 4.

3 = 2 within-period restrictions: coefficients of the first- and second-sale average effective tax rates set equal, coefficients of the first- and second-sale deviations from the average tax rate set equal;

4 = 2 across-period restrictions: coefficients of the two first-sale tax rates set equal; coefficients of the two second-sale tax rates set equal.

5 = 3 restrictions: coefficient of all four tax variables set equal.

The first summary statistic is WSSR, the properly weighted sum of squared residuals, which is the objective function to be minimized. All chi-square statistics must be based on this value. SSR is the unweighted sum of squared residuals. For ordinary least squares, WSSR equals SSR. In other cases, SSR is not a very meaningful statistic. The R-squared, $R - SQ$, is calculated as the squared correlation between $\Delta V/V$ and its predicted value. This definition coincides with the standard definition in the ordinary least squares case and can be generalized to the two-stage least squares case. It is not the R-squared of the second-stage regression, which makes little sense. Finally, NOBS is the number of dwellings in the sample.

This heading is followed by the parameter estimates and t-statistics. The principal variable names are as follows:

CONST	Constant term
ETAXS	Second-sale relative effective tax rate
ETAXF	First-sale relative effective tax rate
ETBARS	Second-sale average effective tax rate
ETBARF	First-sale average effective tax rate
DA0	Anticipation variable (see Chapter 3)
DA1	Anticipation variable (see Chapter 3).

Names of the other variables correspond to the housing and neighborhood characteristics listed in Table 6-3.

The final entry in each table, which appears only if the regression was estimated with a simultaneous equations procedure, is a list of the instruments from the "first-stage" regression. The term first-stage is in quotations because, as explained in Chapter 5, nonlinear two-stage least squares must be estimated in a single stage. These instruments, which are identified by number, are listed at the end of this appendix.

---

1. Results for Arlington

Taxcap Estimation Results
Town: 1, Model: 1, Linear: 1, Restrictions: 5

WSSR = 7.510, SSR = 7.510, R − SQ = .144, NOBS = 313

Parameter Estimates with Asymptotic t-Statistics:

ETAXS:	.1922	9.3880
ETAXF:	.1922	.0000
ETBARS:	.1922	.0000
ETBARF:	.1922	.0000
DA0:	−.0019	−1.3075
DA1:	.0012	1.3037
CONST:	.0175	2.8057

Taxcap Estimation Results
Town: 1, Model: 1, Linear: 0, Restrictions: 5

WSSR = 7.557, SSR = 7.557, R − SQ = .148, NOBS = 313

Parameter Estimates with Asymptotic t-Statistics:

ETAXS:	.2056	9.4267
ETAXF:	.2056	.0000
ETBARS:	.2056	.0000
ETBARF:	.2056	.0000
DA0:	−.0018	−1.2908
DA1:	.0009	.9305

Taxcap Estimation Results
Town: 1, Model: 2, Linear: 1, Restrictions: 5

WSSR = .083, SSR = 8.202, R − SQ = .079, NOBS = 313

Parameter Estimates with Asymptotic t-Statistics:

ETAXS:	.0377	1.3751
ETAXF:	.0377	.0000
ETBARS:	.0377	.0000
ETBARF:	.0377	.0000

DA0:	−.0010	−.6620
DA1:	.0031	3.0709
CONST:	.0180	2.7568

List of Instruments:
1 2 3 4 5 6 7 8 9 10 11 12

Taxcap Estimation Results
Town: 1, Model: 2, Linear: 0, Restrictions: 5

WSSR = .184, SSR = 8.288, R − SQ = .081, NOBS = 313

Parameter Estimates with Asymptotic t-Statistics:

ETAXS:	.0392	1.3996
ETAXF:	.0392	.0000
ETBARS:	.0392	.0000
ETBARF:	.0392	.0000
DA0:	−.0008	−.5246
DA1:	.0030	2.9975

List of Instruments:
1 2 3 4 5 6 7 8 9 10 11 12

---

2. Results for Barnstable

Taxcap Estimation Results
Town: 2, Model: 1, Linear: 1, Restrictions: 5

WSSR = 4.352, SSR = 4.352, R − SQ = .297, NOBS = 98

Parameter Estimates with Asymptotic t-Statistics:

ETAXS:	.3574	7.0007
ETAXF:	.3574	.0000
ETBARS:	.3574	.0000
ETBARF:	.3574	.0000
DA0:	.0036	2.3202
DA1:	.0041	1.9422
CONST:	.0364	2.3529

Taxcap Estimation Results
Town: 2, Model: 1, Linear: 0, Restrictions: 5

WSSR = 4.553, SSR = 4.553, R − SQ = .280, NOBS = 98

Parameter Estimates with Asymptotic t-Statistics:

ETAXS:	.4725	5.4601
ETAXF:	.4725	.0000
ETBARS:	.4725	.0000
ETBARF:	.4725	.0000
DA0:	.0031	1.7950
DA1:	.0035	1.6060

Taxcap Estimation Results
Town: 2, Model: 2, Linear: 1, Restrictions: 5

WSSR = .370, SSR = 4.355, R − SQ = .297, NOBS = 98

Parameter Estimates with Asymptotic *t*-Statistics:

ETAXS:	.3407	2.5505
ETAXF:	.3407	.0000
ETBARS:	.3407	.0000
ETBARF:	.3407	.0000
DA0:	.0038	1.9963
DA1:	.0042	1.8398
CONST:	.0360	2.2801

List of Instruments:
1   2   3   4   5   6   7   8   9   10   11   12

Taxcap Estimation Results
Town: 2, Model: 2, Linear: 0, Restrictions: 5

WSSR = .493, SSR = 4.709, R − SQ = .265, NOBS = 98

Parameter Estimates with Asymptotic *t*-Statistics:

ETAXS:	.2595	2.0738
ETAXF:	.2595	.0000
ETBARS:	.2595	.0000
ETBARF:	.2595	.0000
DA0:	.0047	2.5311
DA1:	.0051	2.2272

List of Instruments:
1   2   3   4   5   6   7   8   9   10   11   12

Taxcap Estimation Results
Town: 2, Model: 3, Linear: 1, Restrictions: 5

WSSR = .750, SSR = 4.733, R − SQ = .249, NOBS = 98

Parameter Estimates with Asymptotic *t*-Statistics:

ETAXS:	.1504	1.2742
ETAXF:	.1504	.0000
ETBARS:	.1504	.0000
ETBARF:	.1504	.0000
DA0:	.0054	2.8985
DA1:	.0055	2.4049
CONST:	.0312	1.9088

List of Instruments:
7   8   9   10   11   12   13   14   15   16   17   18   19   20

Taxcap Estimation Results
Town: 2, Model: 3, Linear: 0, Restrictions: 5

WSSR = .831, SSR = 4.900, R − SQ = .234, NOBS = 98

Parameter Estimates with Asymptotic *t*-Statistics:

ETAXS:	.1644	1.1547
ETAXF:	.1644	.0000
ETBARS:	.1644	.0000
ETBARF:	.1644	.0000
DA0:	.0055	2.7905
DA1:	.0058	2.4271

List of Instruments:
7 8 9 10 11 12 13 14 15 16 17 18 19 20

Taxcap Estimation Results
Town: 2, Model: 4, Linear: 1, Restrictions: 5

WSSR = 3.658, SSR = 3.658, R − SQ = .409, NOBS = 98

Parameter Estimates with Asymptotic *t*-Statistics:

ETAXS:	.4156	7.8441
ETAXF:	.4156	.0000
ETBARS:	.4156	.0000
ETBARF:	.4156	.0000
DA0:	.0030	1.9605
DA1:	.0031	1.5049
VILL(1):	.0048	2.6548
VILL(2):	−.0005	−.6812
VILL(3):	.0118	3.3591
VILL(4):	−.0011	−1.5189
VILL(5):	.0015	1.3279
VILL(6):	−.0009	−.9795
VILL(7):	−.0023	−.9731
CONST:	.0634	1.5674

Taxcap Estimation Results
Town: 2, Model: 4, Linear: 0, Restrictions: 5

WSSR = 3.818, SSR = 3.818, R − SQ = .385, NOBS = 98

Parameter Estimates with Asymptotic *t*-Statistics:

ETAXS:	.5031	6.0371
ETAXF:	.5031	.0000
ETBARS:	.5031	.0000
ETBARF:	.5031	.0000
DA0:	.0028	1.6063
DA1:	.0029	1.4084
VILL(1):	.0066	3.8261
VILL(2):	.0003	.7118
VILL(3):	.0132	3.8630

VILL(4):	−.0002	−.5439
VILL(5):	.0016	1.7364
VILL(6):	−.0001	−.0798
VILL(7):	−.0014	−.5129

Taxcap Estimation Results
Town: 2, Model: 5, Linear: 1, Restrictions: 5

WSSR = .418, SSR = 3.662, R − SQ = .409, NOBS = 98

Parameter Estimates with Asymptotic t-Statistics:

ETAXS:	.4387	3.5637
ETAXF:	.4387	.0000
ETBARS:	.4387	.0000
ETBARF:	.4387	.0000
DA0:	.0029	1.6106
DA1:	.0029	1.2755
VILL(1):	.0048	2.6613
VILL(2):	−.0006	−.7016
VILL(3):	.0117	3.3464
VILL(4):	−.0011	−1.5317
VILL(5):	.0016	1.2596
VILL(6):	−.0010	−.9978
VILL(7):	−.0023	−.9427
CONST:	.0646	1.5802

List of Instruments:
1 2 3 4 5 6 7 8 9 10 11 12 34 35 36 37 38 39 40

Taxcap Estimation Results
Town: 2, Model: 5, Linear: 0, Restrictions: 5

WSSR = .514, SSR = 3.929, R − SQ = .373, NOBS = 98

Parameter Estimates with Asymptotic t-Statistics:

ETAXS:	.3310	2.9195
ETAXF:	.3310	.0000
ETBARS:	.3310	.0000
ETBARF:	.3310	.0000
DA0:	.0039	2.1402
DA1:	.0043	1.9820
VILL(1):	.0059	3.3677
VILL(2):	.0004	.8822
VILL(3):	.0132	3.8085
VILL(4):	−.0001	−.2721
VILL(5):	.0009	.9316
VILL(6):	.0001	.1708
VILL(7):	−.0019	−.7108

List of Instruments:
1 2 3 4 5 6 7 8 9 10 11 12 34 35 36 37 38 39 40

Taxcap Estimation Results
Town: 2, Model: 5, Linear: 1, Restrictions: 4

WSSR = .412, SSR = 3.729, R − SQ = .404, NOBS = 98

Parameter Estimates with Asymptotic t-Statistics:

ETAXS:	.5238	2.5708
ETAXF:	.4166	3.1623
ETBARS:	.5238	.0000
ETBARF:	.4166	.0000
DA0:	.0032	1.6694
DA1:	.0032	1.3576
VILL(1):	.0048	2.6241
VILL(2):	−.0006	−.7607
VILL(3):	.0116	3.2712
VILL(4):	−.0011	−1.4925
VILL(5):	.0022	1.2816
VILL(6):	−.0011	−1.0632
VILL(7):	−.0020	−.7887

List of Instruments:
1 2 3 4 5 6 7 8 9 10 11 12 34 35 36 37 38 39 40

Taxcap Estimation Results
Town: 2, Model: 5, Linear: 0, Restrictions: 4

WSSR = .513, SSR = 3.891, R − SQ = .379, NOBS = 98

Parameter Estimates with Asymptotic t-Statistics:

ETAXS:	.3655	1.7324
ETAXF:	.3216	2.6070
ETBARS:	.3655	.0000
ETBARF:	.3216	.0000
DA0:	.0041	1.9322
DA1:	.0045	1.8885
VILL(1):	.0059	3.3635
VILL(2):	.0004	.7806
VILL(3):	.0132	3.7830
VILL(4):	−.0001	−.2723
VILL(5):	.0010	.9538
VILL(6):	.0001	.1160
VILL(7):	−.0018	−.6540

List of Instruments:
1 2 3 4 5 6 7 8 9 10 11 12 34 35 36 37 38 39 40

Taxcap Estimation Results
Town: 2, Model: 5, Linear: 1, Restrictions: 3

WSSR = .356, SSR = 3.668, R − SQ = .413, NOBS = 98

Parameter Estimates with Asymptotic *t*-Statistics:

ETAXS:	.5201	3.9175
ETAXF:	.5201	.0000
ETBARS:	.1926	1.0134
ETBARF:	.1926	.0000
DA0:	.0022	1.2246
DA1:	.0021	.8883
VILL(1):	.0056	2.9846
VILL(2):	.0006	.5802
VILL(3):	.0135	3.6714
VILL(4):	−.0002	−.2146
VILL(5):	.0031	1.9976
VILL(6):	−.0001	−.1104
VILL(7):	−.0011	−.4532
CONST:	.0102	.1963

List of Instruments:

1 2 3 4 5 6 7 8 9 10 11 12 34 35 36 37 38 39 40

Taxcap Estimation Results
Town: 2, Model: 5, Linear: 0, Restrictions: 3

WSSR = .393, SSR = 3.712, R − SQ = .406, NOBS = 98

Parameter Estimates with Asymptotic *t*-Statistics:

ETAXS:	.5746	3.0569
ETAXF:	.5746	.0000
ETBARS:	.1131	.6448
ETBARF:	.1131	.0000
DA0:	.0040	1.7574
DA1:	.0035	1.3288
VILL(1):	.0056	3.3172
VILL(2):	.0008	1.6187
VILL(3):	.0141	4.0385
VILL(4):	.0000	−.0912
VILL(5):	.0010	1.0569
VILL(6):	.0002	.2158
VILL(7):	−.0016	−.5796

List of Instruments:

1 2 3 4 5 6 7 8 9 10 11 12 34 35 36 37 38 39 40

3. Results for Belmont

Taxcap Estimation Results
Town: 3, Model: 1, Linear: 1, Restrictions: 5

WSSR = 2.320, SSR = 2.320, R − SQ = .431, NOBS = 111

Parameter Estimates with Asymptotic *t*-Statistics:

ETAXS:	.6950	12.6920

ETAXF:	.6950	.0000
ETBARS:	.6950	.0000
ETBARF:	.6950	.0000
DA0:	$-.0057$	-8.0047
DA1:	$-.0041$	-1.6198
CONST:	.0013	.1347

Taxcap Estimation Results
Town: 3, Model: 1, Linear: 0, Restrictions: 5

WSSR $= 2.106$, SSR $= 2.106$, R $-$ SQ $= .487$, NOBS $= 111$

Parameter Estimates with Asymptotic t-Statistics:

ETAXS:	.7384	16.7374
ETAXF:	.7384	.0000
ETBARS:	.7384	.0000
ETBARF:	.7384	.0000
DA0:	$-.0058$	-9.0984
DA1:	$-.0048$	-2.0342

Taxcap Estimation Results
Town: 3, Model: 2, Linear: 1, Restrictions: 5

WSSR $= .485$, SSR $= 2.424$, R $-$ SQ $= .431$, NOBS $= 111$

Parameter Estimates with Asymptotic t-Statistics:

ETAXS:	.5256	4.9974
ETAXF:	.5256	.0000
ETBARS:	.5256	.0000
ETBARF:	.5256	.0000
DA0:	$-.0043$	-4.0870
DA1:	$-.0026$	$-.9510$
CONST:	.0022	.2223

List of Instruments:
1 2 3 4 5 6 7 8 9 10 11 12

Taxcap Estimation Results
Town: 3, Model: 2, Linear: 0, Restrictions: 5

WSSR $= .367$, SSR $= 2.107$, R $-$ SQ $= .486$, NOBS $= 111$

Parameter Estimates with Asymptotic t-Statistics:

ETAXS:	.7360	7.4755
ETAXF:	.7360	.0000
ETBARS:	.7360	.0000
ETBARF:	.7360	.0000
DA0:	$-.0060$	-6.3522
DA1:	$-.0046$	-1.8463

List of Instruments:
1 2 3 4 5 6 7 8 9 10 11 12

4. Results for Brookline

Taxcap Estimation Results
Town: 4, Model: 1, Linear: 1, Restrictions: 5

WSSR = 5.104, SSR = 5.104, R − SQ = .316, NOBS = 140

Parameter Estimates with Asymptotic t-Statistics:

ETAXS:	.3705	11.0652
ETAXF:	.3705	.0000
ETBARS:	.3705	.0000
ETBARF:	.3705	.0000
DA0:	−.0002	−.1656
DA1:	−.0034	−1.4159
CONST:	.0139	1.1964

Taxcap Estimation Results
Town: 4, Model: 1, Linear: 0, Restrictions: 5

WSSR = 4.576, SSR = 4.576, R − SQ = .387, NOBS = 140

Parameter Estimates with Asymptotic t-Statistics:

ETAXS:	.4493	14.5895
ETAXF:	.4493	.0000
ETBARS:	.4493	.0000
ETBARF:	.4493	.0000
DA0:	−.0005	−.4445
DA1:	−.0040	−1.8623

Taxcap Estimation Results
Town: 4, Model: 2, Linear: 1, Restrictions: 5

WSSR = .742, SSR = 5.203, R − SQ = .316, NOBS = 140

Parameter Estimates with Asymptotic t-Statistics:

ETAXS:	.4474	4.5162
ETAXF:	.4474	.0000
ETBARS:	.4474	.0000
ETBARF:	.4474	.0000
DA0:	−.0006	−.5121
DA1:	−.0041	−1.5925
CONST:	.0135	1.1512

List of Instruments:
1 2 3 4 5 6 7 8 9 10 11 12

Taxcap Estimation Results
Town: 4, Model: 2, Linear: 0, Restrictions: 5

WSSR = .708, SSR = 4.607, R − SQ = .385, NOBS = 140

Parameter Estimates with Asymptotic t-Statistics:

ETAXS:	.4068	6.2665
ETAXF:	.4068	.0000
ETBARS:	.4068	.0000
ETBARF:	.4068	.0000
DA0:	$-.0001$	$-.0774$
DA1:	$-.0037$	-1.6523

List of Instruments:
1 2 3 4 5 6 7 8 9 10 11 12

5. Results for Brockton

Taxcap Estimation Results
Town: 5, Model: 1, Linear: 1, Restrictions: 5

WSSR = 5.897, SSR = 5.897, R − SQ = .168, NOBS = 282

Parameter Estimates with Asymptotic t-Statistics:

ETAXS:	.1944	10.3051
ETAXF:	.1944	.0000
ETBARS:	.1944	.0000
ETBARF:	.1944	.0000
DA0:	$-.0002$	$-.4013$
DA1:	$-.0017$	-4.6728
CONST:	.0062	1.0034

Taxcap Estimation Results
Town: 5, Model: 1, Linear: 0, Restrictions: 5

WSSR = 5.842, SSR = 5.842, R − SQ = .176, NOBS = 282

Parameter Estimates with Asymptotic t-Statistics:

ETAXS:	.2034	10.9213
ETAXF:	.2034	.0000
ETBARS:	.2034	.0000
ETBARF:	.2034	.0000
DA0:	$-.0003$	$-.5360$
DA1:	$-.0018$	-4.8774

Taxcap Estimation Results
Town: 5, Model: 2, Linear: 1, Restrictions: 5

WSSR = .439, SSR = 6.031, R − SQ = .166, NOBS = 282

Parameter Estimates with Asymptotic t-Statistics:

ETAXS:	.1273	5.4696
ETAXF:	.1273	.0000
ETBARS:	.1273	.0000
ETBARF:	.1273	.0000
DA0:	.0003	.5138

DA1:	$-.0012$	-3.0350
CONST:	.0064	1.0290

List of Instruments:
1 2 3 4 5 6 7 8 9 10 11 12

Taxcap Estimation Results
Town: 5, Model: 2, Linear: 0, Restrictions: 5

WSSR = .452, SSR = 6.017, R − SQ = .171, NOBS = 282

Parameter Estimates with Asymptotic t-Statistics:

ETAXS:	.1263	5.5240
ETAXF:	.1263	.0000
ETBARS:	.1263	.0000
ETBARF:	.1263	.0000
DA0:	.0003	.5289
DA1:	$-.0012$	-3.0257

List of Instruments:
1 2 3 4 5 6 7 8 9 10 11 12

Taxcap Estimation Results
Town: 5, Model: 3, Linear: 1, Restrictions: 5

WSSR = .186, SSR = 3.309, R − SQ = .226, NOBS = 196

Parameter Estimates with Asymptotic t-Statistics:

ETAXS:	.1195	6.8248
ETAXF:	.1195	.0000
ETBARS:	.1195	.0000
ETBARF:	.1195	.0000
DA0:	.0004	.7917
DA1:	.0013	1.0437
CONST:	$-.0026$	$-.5476$

List of Instruments:
7 8 9 10 11 12 13 14 15 16 17 18 19 20 21

Taxcap Estimation Results
Town: 5, Model: 3, Linear: 0, Restrictions: 5

WSSR = .187, SSR = 3.272, R − SQ = .243, NOBS = 196

Parameter Estimates with Asymptotic t-Statistics:

ETAXS:	.1202	7.0425
ETAXF:	.1202	.0000
ETBARS:	.1202	.0000
ETBARF:	.1202	.0000
DA0:	.0004	.8423
DA1:	.0005	.8041

List of Instruments:
7   8   9   10   11   12   13   14   15   16   17   18   19   20   21

Taxcap Estimation Results
Town: 5, Model: 4, Linear: 1, Restrictions: 5

WSSR = 4.731, SSR = 4.731, R − SQ = .332, NOBS = 282

Parameter Estimates with Asymptotic t-Statistics:

ETAXS:	.2400	12.4254
ETAXF:	.2400	.0000
ETBARS:	.2400	.0000
ETBARF:	.2400	.0000
DA0:	.0002	.2602
DA1:	−.0016	−4.4132
AGE:	.0242	2.9396
HAREA:	.0018	.7216
ROOMS:	−.0303	−.9993
STUCCO:	.0002	.3015
BRICKS:	−.0004	−.7260
ALUMN:	−.0011	−1.4967
SHINGL:	.0040	2.0419
HARDWD:	−.0020	−.4728
FIREPL:	−.0020	−1.0768
BATH:	−.0072	−1.3561
GAREA:	−.0038	−.4013
LOTSIZ:	−.0101	−3.1008
SCHD(1):	−.0017	−3.6813
SCHD(2):	−.0029	−3.4535
SCHD(3):	−.0033	−3.7126
SCHD(4):	−.0048	−5.5551
SCHD(5):	−.0026	−3.2285
SCHD(6):	−.0031	−3.4295
SCHD(7):	−.0023	−2.8138
SCHD(8):	−.0030	−3.5518
SCHD(9):	−.0037	−4.0132
SCHD(10):	−.0050	−4.5076
SCHOOL:	−.0224	−1.2016
MOVERS:	.0391	3.0320
CONST:	.0854	5.9657

Taxcap Estimation Results
Town: 5, Model: 4, Linear: 0, Restrictions: 5

WSSR = 4.957, SSR = 4.957, R − SQ = .308, NOBS = 282

Parameter Estimates with Asymptotic t-Statistics:

ETAXS:	.2338	12.3089
ETAXF:	.2338	.0000
ETBARS:	.2338	.0000
ETBARF:	.2338	.0000

DA0:	.0001	.2304
DA1:	−.0016	−4.1592
AGE:	.0268	3.0949
HAREA:	.0007	.2588
ROOMS:	−.0313	−1.0156
STUCCO:	.0002	.2491
BRICKS:	−.0004	−.8391
ALUMN:	−.0011	−1.3826
SHINGL:	.0046	2.0038
HARDWD:	−.0006	−.1465
FIREPL:	−.0034	−1.5856
BATH:	−.0050	−.9126
GAREA:	−.0028	−.2976
LOTSIZ:	−.0093	−2.9018
SCHD(1):	.0002	.7449
SCHD(2):	−.0006	−.8128
SCHD(3):	−.0008	−.9901
SCHD(4):	−.0024	−3.1894
SCHD(5):	−.0005	−.6402
SCHD(6):	−.0008	−1.0160
SCHD(7):	.0000	−.0251
SCHD(8):	−.0005	−.7204
SCHD(9):	−.0014	−1.6773
SCHD(10):	−.0021	−2.1480
SCHOOL:	−.0213	−1.1430
MOVERS:	.0311	2.4316

Taxcap Estimation Results
Town: 5, Model: 5, Linear: 1, Restrictions: 5

WSSR = .293, SSR = 2.681, R − SQ = .364, NOBS = 196

Parameter Estimates with Asymptotic t-Statistics:

ETAXS:	.1544	8.2342
ETAXF:	.1544	.0000
ETBARS:	.1544	.0000
ETBARF:	.1544	.0000
DA0:	.0007	1.3974
DA1:	−.0019	−1.3788
AGE:	.0209	2.4759
HAREA:	−.0005	−.1864
ROOMS:	−.0232	−.7377
STUCCO:	.0001	.0820
BRICKS:	−.0011	−2.1211
ALUMN:	−.0012	−1.4118
SHINGL:	.0018	.5427
HARDWD:	−.0002	−.0377
FIREPL:	−.0032	−1.6926
BATH:	−.0048	−.8034
GAREA:	.0019	.1840

LOTSIZ:	−.0090	−2.1903
SCHD(1):	.0005	1.3340
SCHD(2):	.0001	.0868
SCHD(3):	−.0003	−.3436
SCHD(4):	−.0024	−2.6877
SCHD(5):	−.0005	−.6505
SCHD(6):	−.0007	−.7746
SCHD(7):	−.0001	−.1755
SCHD(8):	−.0005	−.6126
SCHD(9):	−.0012	−1.3853
SCHD(10):	−.0020	−1.3333
SCHOOL:	−.0245	−1.1778
MOVERS:	.0337	2.5450
CONST:	−.0116	−.6283

List of Instruments:
7 8 9 10 11 12 13 14 15 16 17 18 19 20 21 22 23 24 25 26
27 28 29 30 31 32 33 34 35 36 37 38 39 40 41 42 43 44 45

Taxcap Estimation Results
Town: 5, Model: 5, Linear: 0, Restrictions: 5

WSSR = .275, SSR = 2.593, R − SQ = .386, NOBS = 196

Parameter Estimates with Asymptotic t-Statistics:

ETAXS:	.1582	9.6072
ETAXF:	.1582	.0000
ETBARS:	.1582	.0000
ETBARF:	.1582	.0000
DA0:	.0007	1.2648
DA1:	−.0025	−4.8308
AGE:	.0211	2.4956
HAREA:	−.0001	−.0192
ROOMS:	−.0237	−.7693
STUCCO:	.0001	.1180
BRICKS:	−.0011	−2.1203
ALUMN:	−.0012	−1.4067
SHINGL:	.0015	.4306
HARDWD:	−.0011	−.2262
FIREPL:	−.0035	−1.7900
BATH:	−.0055	−.9579
GAREA:	.0008	.0847
LOTSIZ:	−.0088	−2.3324
SCHD(1):	.0002	6.2777
SCHD(2):	−.0002	−.3403
SCHD(3):	−.0007	−.8700
SCHD(4):	−.0027	−3.7686
SCHD(5):	−.0008	−1.3016
SCHD(6):	−.0009	−1.1964
SCHD(7):	−.0004	−.5231
SCHD(8):	−.0008	−1.1404

SCHD(9):	−.0015	−1.8762
SCHD(10):	−.0023	−1.7550
SCHOOL:	−.0249	−1.2268
MOVERS:	.0353	2.7478

List of Instruments:

7 8 9 10 11 12 13 14 15 16 17 18 19 20 21 22 23 24 25 26
27 28 29 30 31 32 33 34 35 36 37 38 39 40 41 42 43 44 45

Taxcap Estimation Results
Town: 5, Model: 5, Linear: 1, Restrictions: 4

WSSR = .258, SSR = 3.762, R − SQ = .123, NOBS = 196

Parameter Estimates with Asymptotic t-Statistics:

ETAXS:	−.0993	−.6889
ETAXF:	.1653	7.1547
ETBARS:	−.0993	.0000
ETBARF:	.1653	.0000
DA0:	.0004	.5604
DA1:	−.0017	−1.0239
AGE:	.0258	2.4791
HAREA:	−.0037	−.9916
ROOMS:	−.0034	−.0879
STUCCO:	−.0001	−.0764
BRICKS:	−.0016	−2.2975
ALUMN:	−.0014	−1.3327
SHINGL:	.0004	.0964
HARDWD:	.0009	.1429
FIREPL:	−.0032	−1.4268
BATH:	−.0087	−1.1708
GAREA:	.0001	.0068
LOTSIZ:	−.0097	−1.9691
SCHD(1):	.0011	1.9742
SCHD(2):	.0008	.7727
SCHD(3):	.0007	.5911
SCHD(4):	−.0017	−1.5547
SCHD(5):	.0000	−.0308
SCHD(6):	.0000	−.0046
SCHD(7):	.0001	.1439
SCHD(8):	.0002	.1988
SCHD(9):	−.0006	−.4990
SCHD(10):	−.0010	−.5433
SCHOOL:	−.0312	−1.2466
MOVERS:	.0392	2.4482
CONST:	−.0353	−1.3757

List of Instruments:

7 8 9 10 11 12 13 14 15 16 17 18 19 20 21 22 23 24 25 26
27 28 29 30 31 32 33 34 35 36 37 38 39 40 41 42 43 44 45

Taxcap Estimation Results
Town: 5, Model: 5, Linear: 0, Restrictions: 4

WSSR = .272, SSR = 2.900, R − SQ = .307, NOBS = 196

Parameter Estimates with Asymptotic t-Statistics:

ETAXS:	.0805	.6315
ETAXF:	.1650	8.0301
ETBARS:	.0805	.0000
ETBARF:	.1650	.0000
DA0:	.0006	.9696
DA1:	−.0031	−2.8574
AGE:	.0223	2.4522
HAREA:	−.0008	−.2697
ROOMS:	−.0178	−.5277
STUCCO:	.0001	.0849
BRICKS:	−.0013	−2.0869
ALUMN:	−.0013	−1.4108
SHINGL:	.0008	.2197
HARDWD:	−.0006	−.1184
FIREPL:	−.0036	−1.7209
BATH:	−.0072	−1.0815
GAREA:	.0012	.1099
LOTSIZ:	−.0096	−2.2895
SCHD(1):	.0003	2.2219
SCHD(2):	−.0001	−.1255
SCHD(3):	−.0005	−.5709
SCHD(4):	−.0026	−3.4988
SCHD(5):	−.0008	−1.2037
SCHD(6):	−.0008	−.9909
SCHD(7):	−.0004	−.5260
SCHD(8):	−.0007	−.9180
SCHD(9):	−.0014	−1.5835
SCHD(10):	−.0023	−1.6006
SCHOOL:	−.0259	−1.2027
MOVERS:	.0373	2.6607

List of Instruments:
7   8   9   10   11   12   13   14   15   16   17   18   19   20   21   22   23   24   25   26
27   28   29   30   31   32   33   34   35   36   37   38   39   40   41   42   43   44   45

Taxcap Estimation Results
Town: 5, Model: 5, Linear: 1, Restrictions: 3

WSSR = .273, SSR = 2.671, R − SQ = .366, NOBS = 196

Parameter Estimates with Asymptotic t-Statistics:

ETAXS:	.1544	8.2210
ETAXF:	.1544	.0000
ETBARS:	−.0447	−.3504
ETBARF:	−.0447	.0000

DA0:	.0007	1.3548
DA1:	.0023	.7561
AGE:	.0207	2.4446
HAREA:	−.0014	−.5016
ROOMS:	−.0190	−.5994
STUCCO:	.0002	.2672
BRICKS:	−.0011	−2.0472
ALUMN:	−.0012	−1.4305
SHINGL:	.0008	.2295
HARDWD:	−.0002	−.0391
FIREPL:	−.0030	−1.6012
BATH:	−.0048	−.8007
GAREA:	−.0027	−.2485
LOTSIZ:	−.0079	−1.8947
SCHD(1):	.0019	1.9572
SCHD(2):	.0013	1.1438
SCHD(3):	.0010	.7988
SCHD(4):	−.0007	−.5359
SCHD(5):	.0008	.7312
SCHD(6):	.0008	.6150
SCHD(7):	.0013	1.0656
SCHD(8):	.0009	.7338
SCHD(9):	.0000	−.0022
SCHD(10):	−.0007	−.4151
SCHOOL:	−.0242	−1.1591
MOVERS:	.0335	2.5258
CONST:	−.1394	−1.6794

List of Instruments:
7 8 9 10 11 12 13 14 15 16 17 18 19 20 21 22 23 24 25 26
27 28 29 30 31 32 33 34 35 36 37 38 39 40 41 42 43 44 45

Taxcap Estimation Results
Town: 5, Model: 5, Linear: 0, Restrictions: 3

WSSR = .275, SSR = 2.592, R − SQ = .387, NOBS = 196

Parameter Estimates with Asymptotic t-Statistics:

ETAXS:	.1555	7.1119
ETAXF:	.1555	.0000
ETBARS:	.1606	7.7572
ETBARF:	.1606	.0000
DA0:	.0007	1.2671
DA1:	−.0023	−2.5377
AGE:	.0212	2.4913
HAREA:	−.0001	−.0298
ROOMS:	−.0239	−.7728
STUCCO:	.0001	.1028
BRICKS:	−.0011	−2.1118
ALUMN:	−.0012	−1.3816
SHINGL:	.0016	.4547

HARDWD:	−.0011	−.2200
FIREPL:	−.0035	−1.7918
BATH:	−.0054	−.9105
GAREA:	.0008	.0763
LOTSIZ:	−.0087	−2.2772
SCHD(1):	.0002	1.4049
SCHD(2):	−.0002	−.2853
SCHD(3):	−.0006	−.7517
SCHD(4):	−.0026	−3.5001
SCHD(5):	−.0008	−1.1761
SCHD(6):	−.0009	−1.1341
SCHD(7):	−.0003	−.4670
SCHD(8):	−.0007	−1.0349
SCHD(9):	−.0015	−1.7926
SCHD(10):	−.0023	−1.6350
SCHOOL:	−.0252	−1.2321
MOVERS:	.0351	2.7137

List of Instruments:
7 8 9 10 11 12 13 14 15 16 17 18 19 20 21 22 23 24 25 26
27 28 29 30 31 32 33 34 35 36 37 38 39 40 41 42 43 44 45

---

6. Results for Waltham

Taxcap Estimation Results
Town: 6, Model: 1, Linear: 1, Restrictions: 5

WSSR = 6.935, SSR = 6.935, R − SQ = .307, NOBS = 353

Parameter Estimates with Asymptotic t-Statistics:

ETAXS:	.3464	17.3502
ETAXF:	.3464	.0000
ETBARS:	.3464	.0000
ETBARF:	.3464	.0000
DA0:	−.0032	−13.6607
DA1:	−.0019	−3.6372
CONST:	.0208	3.9270

Taxcap Estimation Results
Town: 6, Model: 1, Linear: 0, Restrictions: 5

WSSR = 6.973, SSR = 6.973, R − SQ = .311, NOBS = 353

Parameter Estimates with Asymptotic t-Statistics:

ETAXS:	.4181	16.6138
ETAXF:	.4181	.0000
ETBARS:	.4181	.0000
ETBARF:	.4181	.0000
DA0:	−.0039	−13.9571
DA1:	−.0027	−5.0317

Taxcap Estimation Results
Town: 6, Model: 2, Linear: 1, Restrictions: 5

WSSR = .125, SSR = 7.939, R − SQ = .294, NOBS = 353

Parameter Estimates with Asymptotic t-Statistics:

ETAXS:	.1456	3.4710
ETAXF:	.1456	.0000
ETBARS:	.1456	.0000
ETBARF:	.1456	.0000
DA0:	−.0013	−2.8889
DA1:	−.0001	−.1231
CONST:	.0205	3.6157

List of Instruments:
1 2 3 4 5 6 7 8 9 10 11 12

Taxcap Estimation Results
Town: 6, Model: 2, Linear: 0, Restrictions: 5

WSSR = .268, SSR = 8.102, R − SQ = .298, NOBS = 353

Parameter Estimates with Asymptotic t-Statistics:

ETAXS:	.1554	3.3976
ETAXF:	.1554	.0000
ETBARS:	.1554	.0000
ETBARF:	.1554	.0000
DA0:	−.0014	−2.8738
DA1:	−.0002	−.2751

List of Instruments:
1 2 3 4 5 6 7 8 9 10 11 12

Taxcap Estimation Results
Town: 6, Model: 3, Linear: 1, Restrictions: 5

WSSR = .423, SSR = 7.587, R − SQ = .301, NOBS = 353

Parameter Estimates with Asymptotic t-Statistics:

ETAXS:	.1846	5.2827
ETAXF:	.1846	.0000
ETBARS:	.1846	.0000
ETBARF:	.1846	.0000
DA0:	−.0016	−4.4358
DA1:	−.0004	−.7182
CONST:	.0206	3.7108

List of Instruments:
7 8 9 10 11 12 13 14 15 16 17 18 19 20 21

Taxcap Estimation Results
Town: 6, Model: 3, Linear: 0, Restrictions: 5

WSSR = .554, SSR = 7.731, R − SQ = .307, NOBS = 353

Parameter Estimates with Asymptotic *t*-Statistics:

ETAXS:	.2014	5.2487
ETAXF:	.2014	.0000
ETBARS:	.2014	.0000
ETBARF:	.2014	.0000
DA0:	−.0018	−4.4925
DA1:	−.0006	−.9896

List of Instruments:
7   8   9   10   11   12   13   14   15   16   17   18   19   20   21

Taxcap Estimation Results
Town: 6, Model: 4, Linear: 1, Restrictions: 5

WSSR = 5.637, SSR = 5.637, R − SQ = .437, NOBS = 353

Parameter Estimates with Asymptotic *t*-Statistics:

ETAXS:	.3657	17.6732
ETAXF:	.3657	.0000
ETBARS:	.3657	.0000
ETBARF:	.3657	.0000
DA0:	−.0032	−13.1315
DA1:	−.0021	−4.2172
ADDMAJ:	.2584	6.9342
ADDBK:	.0773	1.7635
ADDGAR:	.1411	3.2227
ADDMIN:	−.0049	−.1262
ADDLOT:	.0202	.3399
ADDPOL:	.1180	2.8726
AGE:	.0117	2.5874
HAREA:	−.0003	−.1210
ROOMS:	−.0112	−2.5184
STUCCO:	.0002	.3792
BRICKS:	.0003	1.2135
ALUMN:	.0005	2.1533
SHINGL:	.0022	3.6734
HARDWD:	−.0001	−.0468
FIREPL:	.0005	.4454
BATH:	.0063	3.3745
GAREA:	−.0113	−2.8055
LOTSIZ:	.0021	1.5875
SCHD(1):	−.0005	−1.9880
SCHD(2):	−.0006	−2.3297
SCHD(3):	−.0002	−.4023
SCHD(4):	−.0008	−3.0508
SCHD(5):	−.0011	−3.6346
SCHD(6):	−.0008	−3.4312
SCHD(7):	−.0008	−3.3742

SCHD(8):	−.0010	−3.4676
SCHD(9):	−.0007	−2.3565
SCHD(10):	−.0007	−2.1280
SCHOOL:	.0274	2.3787
MOVERS:	−.0106	−1.5092
CONST:	.0447	3.4758

Taxcap Estimation Results
Town: 6, Model: 4, Linear: 0, Restrictions: 5

WSSR = 5.523, SSR = 5.523, R − SQ = .449, NOBS = 353

Parameter Estimates with Asymptotic t-Statistics:

ETAXS:	.4484	17.2858
ETAXF:	.4484	.0000
ETBARS:	.4484	.0000
ETBARF:	.4484	.0000
DA0:	−.0041	−14.2672
DA1:	−.0030	−6.0833
ADDMAJ:	.2655	7.2460
ADDBK:	.0653	1.5944
ADDGAR:	.1394	3.3628
ADDMIN:	.0120	.3114
ADDLOT:	.0317	.5479
ADDPOL:	.1327	3.1466
AGE:	.0128	2.8527
HAREA:	.0002	.0867
ROOMS:	−.0123	−2.8386
STUCCO:	.0002	.3477
BRICKS:	.0003	1.1675
ALUMN:	.0005	2.1602
SHINGL:	.0022	3.6901
HARDWD:	−.0005	−.2435
FIREPL:	.0006	.5409
BATH:	.0065	3.4386
GAREA:	−.0124	−3.0807
LOTSIZ:	.0030	2.2069
SCHD(1):	−.0003	−1.5666
SCHD(2):	−.0003	−1.3948
SCHD(3):	−.0001	−.1996
SCHD(4):	−.0005	−2.4678
SCHD(5):	−.0009	−3.0305
SCHD(6):	−.0006	−3.0053
SCHD(7):	−.0006	−2.7437
SCHD(8):	−.0007	−2.8881
SCHD(9):	−.0007	−2.6026
SCHD(10):	−.0005	−1.8026
SCHOOL:	.0206	1.8169
MOVERS:	−.0074	−1.0844

Taxcap Estimation Results
Town: 6, Model: 5, Linear: 1, Restrictions: 5

WSSR = .332, SSR = 6.058, R − SQ = .411, NOBS = 353

Parameter Estimates with Asymptotic t-Statistics:

ETAXS:	.2227	5.5592
ETAXF:	.2227	.0000
ETBARS:	.2227	.0000
ETBARF:	.2227	.0000
DA0:	−.0018	−4.5831
DA1:	−.0009	−1.5652
ADDMAJ:	.2694	6.9584
ADDBK:	.0937	2.0539
ADDGAR:	.1615	3.5380
ADDMIN:	−.0125	−.3082
ADDLOT:	.0465	.7513
ADDPOL:	.1142	2.6797
AGE:	.0072	1.4845
HAREA:	−.0020	−.8900
ROOMS:	−.0101	−2.1965
STUCCO:	.0003	.5960
BRICKS:	.0003	1.4015
ALUMN:	.0002	1.0469
SHINGL:	.0024	3.7980
HARDWD:	−.0009	−.3999
FIREPL:	.0000	−.0244
BATH:	.0067	3.4331
GAREA:	−.0131	−3.1091
LOTSIZ:	.0017	1.2115
SCHD(1):	−.0001	−.3484
SCHD(2):	−.0004	−1.2397
SCHD(3):	.0004	.8261
SCHD(4):	−.0004	−1.6098
SCHD(5):	−.0009	−2.7553
SCHD(6):	−.0006	−2.1604
SCHD(7):	−.0005	−2.0822
SCHD(8):	−.0006	−2.1091
SCHD(9):	−.0001	−.3535
SCHD(10):	−.0003	−.9906
SCHOOL:	.0321	2.6727
MOVERS:	−.0130	−1.7869
CONST:	.0385	2.8708

List of Instruments:
7 8 9 10 11 12 13 14 15 16 17 18 19 20 21 22 23 24 25 26
27 28 29 30 31 32 33 34 35 36 37 38 39 40 41 42 43 44 45
48 49 50 51 52 53

Taxcap Estimation Results
Town: 6, Model: 5, Linear: 0, Restrictions: 5

WSSR = .410, SSR = 6.279, R − SQ = .394, NOBS = 353

Parameter Estimates with Asymptotic t-Statistics:

ETAXS:	.2113	4.9779
ETAXF:	.2113	.0000
ETBARS:	.2113	.0000
ETBARF:	.2113	.0000
DA0:	−.0018	−4.2933
DA1:	−.0010	−1.6041
ADDMAJ:	.2705	6.8617
ADDBK:	.0893	1.9739
ADDGAR:	.1615	3.5364
ADDMIN:	−.0070	−.1691
ADDLOT:	.0678	1.0897
ADDPOL:	.1281	2.8982
AGE:	.0059	1.2085
HAREA:	−.0027	−1.1720
ROOMS:	−.0106	−2.2619
STUCCO:	.0003	.5931
BRICKS:	.0003	1.3597
ALUMN:	.0002	.6959
SHINGL:	.0024	3.8547
HARDWD:	−.0013	−.5667
FIREPL:	−.0002	−.1361
BATH:	.0067	3.3719
GAREA:	−.0143	−3.3297
LOTSIZ:	.0018	1.2539
SCHD(1):	.0002	.9937
SCHD(2):	.0000	−.0334
SCHD(3):	.0008	1.8328
SCHD(4):	−.0001	−.3906
SCHD(5):	−.0006	−1.8307
SCHD(6):	−.0002	−.9886
SCHD(7):	−.0002	−.8610
SCHD(8):	−.0002	−.8679
SCHD(9):	.0002	.7401
SCHD(10):	.0000	−.0581
SCHOOL:	.0293	2.4062
MOVERS:	−.0114	−1.5432

List of Instruments:
7   8   9   10   11   12   13   14   15   16   17   18   19   20   21   22   23   24   25   26
27   28   29   30   31   32   33   34   35   36   37   38   39   40   41   42   43   44   45
48   49   50   51   52   53

Taxcap Estimation Results
Town: 6, Model: 5, Linear: 1, Restrictions: 4

WSSR = .229, SSR = 5.480, R − SQ = .460, NOBS = 353

Parameter Estimates with Asymptotic t-Statistics:

ETAXS:	.5118	5.5770
ETAXF:	.2245	5.8829
ETBARS:	.5118	.0000
ETBARF:	.2245	.0000
DA0:	−.0018	−4.7382
DA1:	−.0006	−1.0478
ADDMAJ:	.2497	6.6902
ADDBK:	.0658	1.4889
ADDGAR:	.1415	3.2275
ADDMIN:	.0008	.0196
ADDLOT:	.0121	.2025
ADDPOL:	.1018	2.4996
AGE:	.0103	2.2020
HAREA:	.0035	1.3006
ROOMS:	−.0124	−2.7972
STUCCO:	.0001	.2770
BRICKS:	.0002	.9381
ALUMN:	.0004	1.7325
SHINGL:	.0017	2.6372
HARDWD:	.0004	.1947
FIREPL:	.0006	.5174
BATH:	.0054	2.8595
GAREA:	−.0086	−2.0400
LOTSIZ:	.0034	2.3912
SCHD(1):	−.0003	−1.3000
SCHD(2):	−.0003	−1.2583
SCHD(3):	−.0001	−.1416
SCHD(4):	−.0005	−2.0467
SCHD(5):	−.0009	−2.7569
SCHD(6):	−.0006	−2.3411
SCHD(7):	−.0006	−2.2660
SCHD(8):	−.0007	−2.5678
SCHD(9):	−.0002	−.4468
SCHD(10):	−.0004	−1.1740
SCHOOL:	.0237	2.0269
MOVERS:	−.0154	−2.2047
CONST:	.0369	2.8896

List of Instruments:
7   8   9   10   11   12   13   14   15   16   17   18   19   20   21   22   23   24   25   26
27   28   29   30   31   32   33   34   35   36   37   38   39   40   41   42   43   44   45
48   49   50   51   52   53

Taxcap Estimation Results
Town: 6, Model: 5, Linear: 0, Restrictions: 4

WSSR = .307, SSR = 5.126, R − SQ = .493, NOBS = 353

Parameter Estimates with Asymptotic t-Statistics:

ETAXS:	.4927	5.7489
ETAXF:	.2169	5.6162
ETBARS:	.4927	.0000
ETBARF:	.2169	.0000
DA0:	−.0018	−4.7261
DA1:	−.0007	−1.2114
ADDMAJ:	.2488	6.9163
ADDBK:	.0654	1.6330
ADDGAR:	.1423	3.4525
ADDMIN:	.0117	.3096
ADDLOT:	.0536	.9491
ADDPOL:	.1263	3.1334
AGE:	.0067	1.5348
HAREA:	.0021	.8241
ROOMS:	−.0122	−2.9064
STUCCO:	.0002	.5523
BRICKS:	.0003	1.4321
ALUMN:	.0002	.7497
SHINGL:	.0014	2.2861
HARDWD:	−.0006	−.2796
FIREPL:	.0005	.4428
BATH:	.0059	3.2400
GAREA:	−.0118	−2.9689
LOTSIZ:	.0032	2.4319
SCHD(1):	.0000	.0925
SCHD(2):	.0000	.1817
SCHD(3):	.0003	.7903
SCHD(4):	−.0002	−.6694
SCHD(5):	−.0005	−1.8053
SCHD(6):	−.0003	−1.2172
SCHD(7):	−.0002	−.9615
SCHD(8):	−.0003	−1.0533
SCHD(9):	.0003	1.0397
SCHD(10):	−.0001	−.5003
SCHOOL:	.0217	1.9228
MOVERS:	−.0137	−2.0599

List of Instruments:
7 8 9 10 11 12 13 14 15 16 17 18 19 20 21 22 23 24 25 26
27 28 29 30 31 32 33 34 35 36 37 38 39 40 41 42 43 44 45
48 49 50 51 52 53

Taxcap Estimation Results
Town: 6, Model: 5, Linear: 1, Restrictions: 3

WSSR = .332, SSR = 6.057, R − SQ = .411, NOBS = 353

Parameter Estimates with Asymptotic t-Statistics:

ETAXS:	.2230	5.4303
ETAXF:	.2230	.0000
ETBARS:	.2226	5.4888
ETBARF:	.2226	.0000
DA0:	−.0018	−4.5516
DA1:	−.0009	−1.5613
ADDMAJ:	.2695	6.9409
ADDBK:	.0937	2.0462
ADDGAR:	.1614	3.5316
ADDMIN:	−.0125	−.3070
ADDLOT:	.0465	.7508
ADDPOL:	.1142	2.6760
AGE:	.0072	1.4826
HAREA:	−.0020	−.8787
ROOMS:	−.0101	−2.1906
STUCCO:	.0003	.5955
BRICKS:	.0003	1.3926
ALUMN:	.0002	1.0455
SHINGL:	.0024	3.7920
HARDWD:	−.0009	−.3991
FIREPL:	.0000	−.0230
BATH:	.0067	3.4203
GAREA:	−.0131	−3.1046
LOTSIZ:	.0017	1.2101
SCHD(1):	−.0001	−.3267
SCHD(2):	−.0004	−1.1505
SCHD(3):	.0004	.7923
SCHD(4):	−.0004	−1.4887
SCHD(5):	−.0009	−2.5939
SCHD(6):	−.0006	−1.9743
SCHD(7):	−.0005	−1.9146
SCHD(8):	−.0006	−1.9359
SCHD(9):	−.0001	−.3387
SCHD(10):	−.0003	−.9615
SCHOOL:	.0321	2.6688
MOVERS:	−.0129	−1.7100
CONST:	.0383	2.7070

List of Instruments:
7   8   9   10   11   12   13   14   15   16   17   18   19   20   21   22   23   24   25   26
27   28   29   30   31   32   33   34   35   36   37   38   39   40   41   42   43   44   45
48   49   50   51   52   53

Taxcap Estimation Results
Town: 6, Model: 5, Linear: 0, Restrictions: 3

WSSR = .402, SSR = 6.207, R − SQ = .401, NOBS = 353

Parameter Estimates with Asymptotic t-Statistics:

ETAXS:	.2247	4.9417
ETAXF:	.2247	.0000
ETBARS:	.2112	4.9022
ETBARF:	.2112	.0000
DA0:	−.0019	−4.3289
DA1:	−.0010	−1.6787
ADDMAJ:	.2727	6.9183
ADDBK:	.0876	1.9369
ADDGAR:	.1604	3.5207
ADDMIN:	−.0061	−.1462
ADDLOT:	.0687	1.1060
ADDPOL:	.1281	2.9034
AGE:	.0061	1.2484
HAREA:	−.0024	−1.0442
ROOMS:	−.0108	−2.3160
STUCCO:	.0003	.6206
BRICKS:	.0003	1.3315
ALUMN:	.0002	.7385
SHINGL:	.0024	3.8257
HARDWD:	−.0013	−.5677
FIREPL:	−.0001	−.0917
BATH:	.0067	3.3560
GAREA:	−.0143	−3.3400
LOTSIZ:	.0018	1.2820
SCHD(1):	.0001	.3224
SCHD(2):	−.0002	−.4996
SCHD(3):	.0006	1.3988
SCHD(4):	−.0002	−.8220
SCHD(5):	−.0007	−2.0689
SCHD(6):	−.0004	−1.3523
SCHD(7):	−.0003	−1.2383
SCHD(8):	−.0004	−1.2397
SCHD(9):	.0001	.2171
SCHD(10):	−.0001	−.4029
SCHOOL:	.0296	2.4359
MOVERS:	−.0097	−1.2835

List of Instruments:
7 8 9 10 11 12 13 14 15 16 17 18 19 20 21 22 23 24 25 26
27 28 29 30 31 32 33 34 35 36 37 38 39 40 41 42 43 44 45
48 49 50 51 52 53

7. Results for Wellesley

Taxcap Estimation Results
Town: 7, Model: 1, Linear: 1, Restrictions: 5

WSSR = 2.474, SSR = 2.474, R − SQ = .102, NOBS = 175

Parameter Estimates with Asymptotic *t*-Statistics:

ETAXS:	.1968	6.2129
ETAXF:	.1968	.0000
ETBARS:	.1968	.0000
ETBARF:	.1968	.0000
DA0:	−.0010	−.4878
DA1:	−.0008	−.6740
CONST:	.0038	.5953

Taxcap Estimation Results
Town: 7, Model: 1, Linear: 0, Restrictions: 5

WSSR = 2.470, SSR = 2.470, R − SQ = .104, NOBS = 175

Parameter Estimates with Asymptotic *t*-Statistics:

ETAXS:	.2020	6.3523
ETAXF:	.2020	.0000
ETBARS:	.2020	.0000
ETBARF:	.2020	.0000
DA0:	−.0009	−.4215
DA1:	−.0008	−.7456

Taxcap Estimation Results
Town: 7, Model: 2, Linear: 1, Restrictions: 5

WSSR = .144, SSR = 2.593, R − SQ = .101, NOBS = 175

Parameter Estimates with Asymptotic *t*-Statistics:

ETAXS:	.0687	1.7438
ETAXF:	.0687	.0000
ETBARS:	.0687	.0000
ETBARF:	.0687	.0000
DA0:	−.0006	−.2721
DA1:	.0000	−.0270
CONST:	.0045	.6839

List of Instruments:
1   2   3   4   5   6   7   8   9   10   11   12

Taxcap Estimation Results
Town: 7, Model: 2, Linear: 0, Restrictions: 5

WSSR = .147, SSR = 2.595, R − SQ = .101, NOBS = 175

Parameter Estimates with Asymptotic t-Statistics:

ETAXS:	.0692	1.7691
ETAXF:	.0692	.0000
ETBARS:	.0692	.0000
ETBARF:	.0692	.0000
DA0:	−.0006	−.2919
DA1:	.0000	−.0284

List of Instruments:

1 2 3 4 5 6 7 8 9 10 11 12

Instruments for Simultaneous Equations Procedures

No.	Description	
1	Price index at revaluation over index at second sale = PRIRAT	
2	Second-sale nominal tax rate = NTAXS	
3	PRIRAT · NTAXS = NTAXC	
4	PRIRAT squared	
5	NTAXS squared	
6	NTAXC squared	
7	Constant	
8	First-sale effective tax rate = ETAXF	
9	First-sale average effective tax rate = ETBARF	
10	Second-sale average effective tax rate = ETBARS	
11	First anticipation variable = DA0 · (ETBARF − ETAXF)	
12	Second anticipation variable = DA1 · (ETBARF − ETAXF)	
13	NTAXC (Same as (3))	
14	HAREA · NTAXC	[in Barnstable, VILL(1) · (S − F) · NTAXC]
15	FIRPL · NTAXC	[in Barnstable, VILL(2) · (S − F) · NTAXC]
16	BATH · NTAXC	[in Barnstable, VILL(3) · (S − F) · NTAXC]
17	GAREA · NTAXC	[in Barnstable, VILL(4) · (S − F) · NTAXC]
18	AGE · HAREA · NTAXC	[in Barnstable, VILL(5) · (S − F) · NTAXC]
19	(BATH/HAREA) · NTAXC	[in Barnstable, VILL(6) · (S − F) · NTAXC]
20	LOTSIZ · SCH · NTAXC	[in Barnstable, VILL(7) · (S − F) · NTAXC]
21	LOTSIZ · SHSE · NTAXC	
22	AGE · (S − F)	
23	HAREA · (S − F)	
24	ROOMS · (S − F)	
25	STUCCO · (S − F)	
26	BRICKS · (S − F)	
27	ALUMN · (S − F)	
28	SHINGL · (S − F)	
29	HARDWD · (S − F)	
30	FIRPL · (S − F)	
31	BATH · (S − F)	
32	GAREA · (S − F)	

33	LOTSIZ · (S − F)
34	Dummy for school district 1 = SCHD(1)
	[Dummy for village 1 in Barnstable = VILL(1)]
35	SCHD(2) [in Barnstable, VILL(2)]
36	SCHD(3) [in Barnstable, VILL(3)]
37	SCHD(4) [in Barnstable, VILL(4)]
38	SCHD(5) [in Barnstable, VILL(5)]
39	SCHD(6) [in Barnstable, VILL(6)]
40	SCHD(7) [in Barnstable, VILL(7)]
41	SCHD(8)
42	SCHD(9)
43	SCHD(10)
44	SCHOOL · (S − F) (where SCHOOL is median years of schooling in tract)
45	MOVE · (S − F) (where MOVE is percentage of nonmovers in tract)
48	ADDMAJ
49	ADDBK
50	ADDGAR
51	ADDMIN
52	ADDLOT
53	ADDPOL

Notes: (S − F) is the number of years between house sales. See Appendix A for detailed definitions of housing and additions variables.

References

Aaron, H. J. (1975). *Who Pays the Property Tax?: A New View.* Washington, D.C.: The Brookings Institution.

Amemiya, T. (1974). "The Nonlinear Two-Stage Least-Squares Estimator," *Journal of Econometrics* 2:105–10.

Amemiya, T. (1983). *Advanced Econometrics.* Cambridge, Massachusetts: Harvard University Press.

Atkinson, A. B. and J. E. Stiglitz. (1981). *Lectures on Public Economics.* New York: McGraw-Hill.

Avault, J., A. Ganz, and D. M. Holland. (1979). "Tax Relief and Reform in Massachusetts," *National Tax Journal* 32, Supplement (June): 289–304.

Bailey, M. J., R. F. Muth, and H. O. Nourse. (1963). "A Regression Model for Real Estate Price Index Construction," *Journal of the American Statistical Association* 58:469–82.

Bartik, T. J. (1987). "The Estimation of Demand Parameters in Hedonic Models," *Journal of Political Economy* 95:81–8.

Bloom, H. S. and H. F. Ladd. (1982). "Property Tax Revaluation and Tax Levy Growth," *Journal of Urban Economics* 11:73–84.

Bloom, H. S., H. F. Ladd, and J. Yinger. (1983). "Are Property Taxes Capitalized Into House Values?" In: *Local Provision of Public Services: The Tiebout Model after Twenty-five Years.* G. S. Zodrow, Ed. New York: Academic Press.

Bradbury, K. L. and J. Yinger. (1984). "Making Ends Meet: Boston's Budget in the 1980s," *New England Economic Review* (March/April):18–28.

Brown, J. N. and H. S. Rosen. (1982). "On the Estimation of Structural Hedonic Price Models," *Econometrica* 50:765–8.

Case, C. E. (1978). *Property Taxation: The Need for Reform.* Cambridge, Massachusetts: Ballinger.

Chinloy, P. (1978). "Effective Property Taxes and Tax Capitalization," *Canadian Journal of Economics* **11**:740–50.

Chun, D. H. and P. Linneman. (1985). "An Empirical Analysis of the Determinants of Intra-juridictional Property Tax Payment Inequities," *Journal of Urban Economics* **18**:90–102.

Church, A. M. (1974). "Capitalization of the Effective Property Tax Rate on Single Family Residences," *National Tax Journal* **27**:113–22.

Copeland, T. E. and J. F. Weston. (1983). *Financial Theory and Corporate Policy,* 2nd Edition. Reading, Massachusetts: Addison-Wesley.

Courant, P. N. (1978). "Racial Prejudice in a Search Model of the Urban Housing Market," *Journal of Urban Economics* **5**:329–45.

Dicoff, D. W. (1962). *Capitalization of the Property Tax.* Ph.D. Dissertation, Department of Economics, University of Michigan.

Dusansky, R., M. Ingber, and N. Karatjas. (1981). The Impact of Property Taxation on Housing Values and Rents," *Journal of Urban Economics* **10**:240–55.

Edel, M., and E. Sclar. (1974). "Taxes, Spending and Property Values: Supply Adjustment in a Tiebout-Oates Model," *Journal of Political Economy* **82**:941–54.

Edelstein, R. (1974). "The Determinants of Value in the Philadelphia Housing Market: A Case Study of the Main Line 1967–1969," *The Review of Economics and Statistics* **56**:319–27.

Engle, Robert F. (1975). "De Facto Discrimination in Residential Assessments: Boston," *National Tax Journal* **28**:445–51.

Epple, D. (1987). "Hedonic Prices and Implicit Markets: Estimating Demand and Supply Functions for Differentiated Products," *Journal of Political Economy* **95**:59–80.

Feldstein, M. S. (1976). "On the Theory of Tax Reform," *Journal of Public Economics* **6**:77–104.

Fomby, T. B., R. C. Hill, and S. R. Johnson. (1984). *Advanced Econometric Methods.* New York: Springer-Verlag.

Gabriel, S. A. (1981). 'Interjurisdictional Capitalization Effects of Proposition 13 in the San Francisco Bay Area," *National Tax Association Proceedings,* pp. 263–71.

Gerking, S. and M. Dickie. (1985). "Systematic Assessment Error and Intrajurisdiction Property Tax Capitalization: Comment," *Southern Economic Journal* **52**:886–90.

Goldberger, A. (1964). *Economic Theory.* New York: John Wiley & Sons.

Goldfeld, S. M. and R. E. Quandt. (1972). *Nonlinear Methods in Econometrics.* Amsterdam: North-Holland.

Goldfeld, S. M., R. E. Quandt, and H. F. Trotter. (1966). "Maximization by Quadratic Hill-Climbing," *Econometrica* **34**:541–51.

Goodman, A. C. (1978). "Hedonic Prices, Price Indices and Housing Markets," *Journal of Urban Economics* **5**:471–84.

Goodman, A. C. (1983). "Capitalization of Property Tax Differentials Within and Among Municipalities," *Land Economics* **59**:211–19.

Gramlich, E. M. (1983). "Models of Inflation Expectations Formation: A Comparison of Household and Economic Forecasts," *Journal of Money, Credit, and Banking* **15**155–73.

Gronberg, T. J. (1979). "The Interaction of Markets in Housing and Local Public Goods: A Simultaneous Equations Approach," *Southern Economics Journal* **46**:445–59.

Gustely, D. (1976). "Local Taxes, Expenditures and Urban Housing: A Reassessment of the Evidence," *Southern Economic Journal* **42**:659–65.

Hamilton, B. W. (1976a). "Capitalization of Intrajurisdictional Differences in Local Tax Prices," *American Economic Review* **66**:743–53.

Hamiliton, B. W. (1976b). "The Effects of Property Taxes and Local Public Spending on Property Values: A Theoretical Comment." *Journal of Political Economy* **84** (June):647–50.

Hamilton, B. W. (1979). "Capitalization and the Regressivity of the Property Tax: Empirical Evidence," *National Tax Journal* 32, Supplement (June):169–80.

Hamilton, B. W. (1983). "A Review: Is the Property Tax a Benefit Tax?" In: *Local Provision of Public Services: The Tiebout Model after Twenty-five Years.* G. R. Zodrow, Ed. New York: Academic Press.

Hausman, J. A. (1978). "Specification Tests in Econometrics," *Econometrica* 46:1251–71.

Halvorsen, R. and H. O. Pollakowski. (1981). "Choice of Functional Form for Hedonic Price Equations," *Journal of Urban Economics* 10:37–49.

Heinberg, J. D. and W. E. Oates. (1970). "The Incidence of Differential Property Taxes on Urban Housing: A Comment and Some Further Evidence," *National Tax Journal* 23:92–98.

Hendershott, Patric H. and David C. Ling. (1986). "Likely Impacts of the Administration's Tax Proposals and HR 3838." In: *Tax Reform and Real Estate.* J. R. Follain, Ed. Washington, DC: The Urban Institute.

Hines, M. A. (1981). *Real Estate Appraisal.* New York: Macmillan Publishing Co.

Hyman, D. and E. C. Pasour. (1973). "Property Tax Differentials and Residential Rents in North Carolina," *National Tax Journal* 26:303–7.

Ihlanfeldt, K. R. and J. D. Jackson. (1982). "Systematic Assessment Error and Intrajurisdictional Property Tax Capitalization," *Southern Economic Journal* 49:417–27.

Ihlanfeldt, K. R. and J. D. Jackson. (1986). "Systematic Assessment Error and Intrajurisdictional Property Tax Capitalization: Reply," *Southern Economic Journal* 52:836–42.

Jensen, J. P. (1931). *Property Taxation in the United States.* Chicago: The University of Chicago Press.

King A. T. (1973). *Property Taxes, Amenities, and Residential Land Values.* Cambridge, Massachusetts: Ballinger.

King, A. T. (1977). "Estimating Property Tax Capitalization: A Critical Comment," *Journal of Political Economy* 85:425–31.

Lea, M. J. (1982). "Local Tax and Expenditure Capitalization: Integrating Evidence from the Market and Political Processes," *Public Finance Quarterly* 10:95–117.

Malpezzi, S., L. Ozanne, and T. G. Thibodeau. (1987). "Housing Depreciation," *Land Economics* 63:372–85.

Mayo, S. K. (1981). "Theory and Estimation in the Economics of Housing Demand," *Journal of Urban Economics* 19:95–116.

McDougall, G. S. (1976). "Local Public Goods and Residential Property Values: Some Insights and Extensions," *National Tax Journal* 29:436–47.

Meadows, G. R. (1976). "Taxes, Spending and Property Values: A Comment and Further Results," *Journal of Political Economy* 84:869–80.

Mills, E. S. (1967). "An Aggregative Model of Resource Allocation in a Metropolitan Area," *American Economic Review* 57:197–210.

Mills, E. S. and B. W. Hamilton. (1984). *Urban Economics,* 3rd Edition. Glenview, Illinois: Scott, Foresman & Co.

Moody, J. P. (1974). "Testing Tax Capitalization: An Experiment Afforded by a Local Public Transit Improvement." Unpublished manuscript. Department of Economics, University of California, Berkeley.

Muth, R. F. (1969). *Cities and Housing.* Chicago: University of Chicago Press.

Noto, N. A. (1976). "The Impact of the Local Public Sector on Residential Property Values," *National Tax Association Proceedings,* pp. 192–200.

Oates, W. E. (1969). "The Effects of Property Taxes and Local Public Spending on Property Values: An Empirical Study of Tax Capitalization and the Tiebout Hypothesis," *Journal of Political Economy* 77:957–71.

Oates, W. E. (1973). "The Effects of Property Taxes and Local Spending on Property Values: A Reply and Yet Further Results," *Journal of Political Economy* **81**:1004–8.

Oates, W. E. (1972). *Fiscal Federalism.* New York: Harcourt Brace Jovanovich.

Oldman, O. and H. Aaron. 1965). "Assessment-Sales Ratios Under the Boston Property Tax," *National Tax Journal* **18**:36–49.

Orr, L. L. (1968). "The Incidence of Differential Property Taxes on Urban Housing," *National Tax Journal* **21**:253–62.

Paul, Diane B. (1975). *The Politics of the Property Tax.* Lexington, Massachusetts: Lexington Books.

Pollakowski, H. O. (1973). "The Effects of Property Taxes and Local Public Spending on Property Values: A Comment and Further Results," *Journal of Political Economy* **81**:994–1003.

Polinsky, A. M. and S. Shavell. (1974). "Amenities and Property Values in a Model of an Urban Area," *Journal of Public Economics* **5**:119–29.

Polinsky, A. M. and D. L. Rubinfeld. (1977). "Property Values and the Benefits of Environmental Improvements: Theory and Measurement." In: *Public Economics and the Quality of Life.* L. Wingo and A. Evans, Eds. Baltimore: The Johns Hopkins University Press.

Reinhard, R. M. (1981). "Estimating Property Tax Capitalization: A Further Comment," *Journal of Political Economy* **89**:1251–60.

Richardson, D. H. and R. Thalheimer. (1981). "Measuring the Extent of Property Tax Capitalization for Single Family Residences," *Southern Economic Journal* **48**:674–89.

Rosen, Kenneth T. (1982). "The Impact of Proposition 13 on House Prices in Northern California: A Test of the Interjurisdictional Capitalization Hypothesis," *Journal of Political Economy* **90**:191–200.

Rosen, H. S. and D. J. Fullerton. (1977). "A Note on Local Tax Rates, Public Benefit Levels and Property Values," *Journal of Political Economy* **85**:433–40.

Rubinfeld, D. L. (1985). "The Economics of the Local Public Sector." In: *Handbook of Public Economics.* Amsterdam: North-Holland.

Seligman, E. R. (1932). *The Shifting and Incidence of Taxation,* 5th Edition. New York: Columbia University Press.

Smith, R. S. (1970). "Property Tax Capitalization in San Francisco," *National Tax Journal* **23**:177–93.

Schafer, R. (1977). "A Comparison of Alternative Approaches to Assessing Residential Property," *Assessors Journal* **12**:81–94.

Theil, H. (1971). *Principles of Econometrics.* New York: John Wiley & Sons.

Wales, T. J. and E. G. Weins. (1974). "Capitalization of Residential Property Taxes: An Empirical Study," *Review of Economics and Statistics* **56**:329–33.

Wicks, J. H., R. A. Little, and R. A. Beck. (1968). "A Note on Capitalization of Property Tax Changes," *National Tax Journal* **21**:263–65.

Wiseman, M. (1986). "Proposition 13 and Effective Property Tax Rates." University of California Institute of Business and Economic Research Research Paper No. 86-8 (Revised). Berkeley: University of California.

Wheaton, W. C. (1984). "The Incidence of Inter-Jurisdictional Differences in Commercial Property Taxes," *National Tax Journal* **37**:515–28.

Woodard, F. O. and R. W. Brady. (1965). "Inductive Evidence of Tax Capitalization," *National Tax Journal* **18**:193–201.

Yinger, J. (1976). "Racial Prejudice and Racial Residential Segregation in an Urban Model," *Journal of Urban Economics* **3**:383–96.

Yinger, J. (1982). "Capitalization and the Theory of Local Public Finance," *Journal of Political Economy* **90**:917–43.

Yinger, J. (1985). "Inefficiency and the Median Voter: Property Taxes, Capitalization, Hetero-geneity, and the Theory of the Second Best." In: *Perspectives on Local Public Finance and Public Policy,* Vol. 2, J. M. Quigley, Ed. Greenwich, Connecticut: JAI Press.

Zodrow, George. (1980). "Optimal Tax Reform: The Case of Property Tax Equalization," *National Tax Association Proceedings,* pp. 240–50.

Subject Index

213

Name Index

217

Studies in Urban Economics

Edited by

Edwin S. Mills,

Princeton University

Norman J. Glickman, *Econometric Analysis of Regional Systems: Explorations in Model Building and Policy Analysis*

J. Vernon Henderson, *Economic Theory and the Cities*

Norman J. Glick, *The Growth and Management of the Japanese Urban System*

George S. Tolley, Philip E. Graves, and John L. Gardner, *Urban Growth Policy in a Market Economy*

David Segal, ed., *The Economics of Neighborhood*

R. D. Norton, *City Life-Cycles and American Urban Policy*

John F. McDonald, *Economic Analysis of an Urban Housing Market*

Daniel Feenberg and Edwin S. Mills, *Measuring the Benefits of Water Pollution Abatement*

Michael J. Greenwood, *Migration and Economic Growth in the United States: National, Regional, and Metropolitan Perspectives*

Takahiro Miyao, *Dynamic Analysis of the Urban Economy*

Katharine L. Bradbury, Anthony Downs, and Kenneth A. Small, *Futures for a Declining City: Simulations for the Cleveland Area*

Charles F. Mueller, *The Economics of Labor Migration: A Behavioral Analysis*

Douglas B. Diamond, Jr., and George S. Tolley, eds., *The Economics of Urban Amenities*

Alax Anas, *Residential Location Markets and Urban Transportation: Economic Theory, Econometrics, and Policy Analysis with Discrete Choice Models*

Joseph Friedman and Daniel H. Weinberg, *The Economics of Housing Vouchers*

George R. Zodrow, ed., *Local Provision of Public Services: The Tiebout Model after Twenty-Five Years*

John Yinger, Howard S. Bloom, Axel Börsch-Supan, and Helen F. Ladd, *Property Taxes and House Values: The Theory and Estimation of Intrajurisdictional Property Tax Capitalization*